"We often imagine that when we care for another, we are the 'giver' and the one we care for is the 'receiver.' But in this important, extensive, and deep exploration of the experience of hospice volunteers, Baugher describes givers who feel like receivers—of gratitude, patience, and wisdom drawn from a deep connection to another human being at an ultimate moment. Having lost his mother as an eighteen-year-old, at the hands of a murderer, yet later bonding with fellow hospice volunteers who are themselves imprisoned for murder, Baugher pioneers for us the very outer frontiers of human empathy. A very important frontier, a very important book."—Arlie Hochschild, author of *Strangers in Their Own Land: Anger and Mourning on the American Right*, a finalist for the National Book Award

"An inspiring and compassionate story of how to transform personal suffering into the ground of mutually beneficial service. It is possible to keep our heart open in hell. This book illuminates the way."—Frank Ostaseski, author of *The Five Invitations: Discovering What Death Can Teach Us About Living Fully*

"Our families, hospitals, prisons, and whole society can benefit from the vision of compassion offered by John Baugher. This is truly a book for the heart."—Thupten Jinpa, principal translator to the Dalai Lama and author of *A Fearless Heart: How the Courage to Be Compassionate Can Transform Our Lives*

"A dazzling study of human vulnerability and connection, *Contemplative Caregiving* is wide-ranging in scope, profound in its intimacy. Based on interviews with diverse hospice caregivers—Vietnam veterans, nurses, housewives, Catholic nuns, convicted murderers—Baugher conjures the transformative potential of care in an array of moving and unexpected insights."—Yasmin Gunaratnam, author of *Death and the Migrant* and *Researching Race and Ethnicity*

D0027878

"*Contemplative Caregiving* is an invitation from author John Baugher to discover with him the transformative potential of love. In both living and dying, Baugher guides us exceedingly well."—Sharon Salzberg, author of *Lovingkindness* and *Real Love*

"There's a lot more to the spiritual path than silent meditation, and *Contemplative Caregiving* shows us how transformative end-of-life hospice work (and other types of compassionate care) can be. I was moved by the personal stories, many of them by prison inmate volunteers, who have a lot to teach the rest of us. A book not just to read but to cherish and share."—David Loy, author of *Ecodharma: Buddhist Teachings for the Ecological Crisis*

"*Contemplative Caregiving* provides the medicine of what is needed: an awake heart-mind, receptivity, and community. Through sharing his personal work, rich storytelling, and historical context, John brings us on a journey to our true home—being in intimate relationship with ourselves and others through service."—Sensei Koshin Paley Ellison, cofounder of the New York Zen Center for Contemplative Care, author of *Wholehearted: Slow Down, Help Out, Wake Up*, and editor of *Awake at the Bedside: Contemplative Teachings on Palliative and End-of-Life Care*

"As someone who transformed my own hell through a deep dive into hospice and contemplative caregiving, I am extremely inspired and moved by Baugher's book *Contemplative Caregiving*. Who better to tell the story of so many transformed by giving and receiving compassionate care at the end of life, including prison inmates, than a man who has so deeply transformed his own unspeakable pain by bringing dignity to the suffering of others. This is a book about life and death, courage and compassion, and the transformative power of love."—Fleet Maull, PhD, author of *Radical Responsibility* and *Dharma in Hell*

"A trenchant and groundbreaking book inviting readers to taste the real, profound, unscripted, and liberating effects experienced by someone generating and enacting compassion for another person. This book can speak to all of us, whoever we are, about ourselves, sounding an infinitely bright and uplifting note in the otherwise mounting overture of despair and confusion in our world today."—Patrick Gaffney, editor of *The Tibetan Book of Living and Dying* and *Talent for Humanity*

"*Contemplative Caregiving* is that rare book that deftly combines empirically grounded social science with an unapologetic vision to recognize and celebrate the dying and the people who care for them. Through the lives and experiences of a diverse sample of hospice volunteers—including prisoners—we come to see the truly transformative power of listening to and caring for people at the end of life."—Clare Stacey, PhD, author of *The Caring Self*

"This book gives the reader an insider's view of the ups and downs, the joys and challenges, the promises and perils of end-of-life caregiving. Here is an invitation to a spiritual practice that can be powerfully transformative and life-giving, not only for those who receive the gift of a caregiver's compassionate presence but also for the caregivers themselves. In contemplatively caring for those who are dying, one may find therein the seeds of peace, hope, a quiet joy, and heartfelt gratitude for this gift of being human, in all it entails."—Ruben L. F. Habito, guiding teacher at Maria Kannon Zen Center, Dallas, Texas, and author of *Living Zen, Loving God* and *Healing Breath*

"In this courageous book, John Baugher connects with the timeless wisdom of spiritual traditions both East and West. Picking up the mantle from Dame Cicely Saunders, Thich Nhat Hahn, and other visionaries, *Contemplative Caregiving* weaves together story and teaching with practical exercises to empower us to extend compassion to ourselves and all others without exception. An invitation to hope and healing in these troubled times."—Matthew Lee, PhD, director of empirical research, Human Flourishing Program at Harvard University, and author of *The Heart of Religion*

"In this beautiful and moving book, we learn what it means to see caregiving as a path of redemption and transformation rather than a source of stress and burnout. The journeys described here are messy, rich, painful, and transcendent. *Contemplative Caregiving* is an absorbing read and an indispensable guide to all of us who live in this mortal world."—Leslie J. Blackhall, MD, MTS, section head, palliative care, Tussi and John Kluge Chair, University of Virginia School of Medicine

"A work of courage and deep vulnerability that can inspire leaders in any field in moving beyond models of heroic action toward authentic, relational encounters with self and others. I invite all who pick up this book to see their own life's journey reflected in its pages and to draw on the creative spaces within themselves to further a more compassionate twenty-first century."—Éliane Ubalijoro, PhD, board member, International Leadership Association; professor of practice, McGill University

Contemplative Caregiving

*Finding Healing, Compassion,
and Spiritual Growth through
End-of-Life Care*

JOHN ERIC BAUGHER

Shambhala   Boulder   2019

Shambhala Publications, Inc.
4720 Walnut Street
Boulder, Colorado 80301
www.shambhala.com

Some of the material in the introduction and chapter six is reprinted by permission of Praeger Publishers: Baugher, John Eric. 2017. "Dignity and Companionship at End-of-Life: Two Contemplations on Hope, Fear, and Human Flourishing." pp. 183–201 in D. Maller & K. Langsam (eds.), *The Praeger Handbook of Mental Health and the Aging Community.* Santa Barbara, CA: Praeger Publishers.

Some of the material in chapters three and four is reprinted by permission of Springer Nature: Baugher, John Eric. "Pathways through Grief to Hospice Volunteering." *Qualitative Sociology* 38, no. 3 (2015): 305–26.

9 8 7 6 5 4 3 2 1

First Edition
Printed in the United States of America

♾ This edition is printed on acid-free paper that meets the American National Standards Institute Z39.48 Standard.
♻ This book is printed on 30% postconsumer recycled paper.
For more information please visit www.shambhala.com.
Shambhala Publications is distributed worldwide by Penguin Random House, Inc., and its subsidiaries.

Designed by Greta D. Sibley

Library of Congress Cataloging-in-Publication Data
Names: Baugher, John E., author.
Title: Contemplative caregiving: finding healing, compassion, and spiritual growth through end-of-life care/John Eric Baugher.
Description: First edition. | Boulder: Shambhala, 2019. | Includes bibliographical references and index.
Identifiers: LCCN 2018034204 | ISBN 9781611807042 (pbk.: alk. paper)
Subjects: LCSH: Hospice care. | Caregivers. | Compassion. | Contemplation. | Spiritual life.
Classification: LCC R726.8.B39 2019 | DDC 616.02/9—dc23
LC record available at https://lccn.loc.gov/2018034204

For my parents,

Anita Grace Baugher and David Grayson Baugher

and for Stamatoula Petsacous Tsalis

A truly new and truly original book would be one which made people love old truths.

Luc de Clapiers, marquis de Vauvenargues (1746)

CONTENTS

LIST OF CONTEMPLATIVE ACTIVITIES

ACKNOWLEDGMENTS

THERE IS A BELIEF among Soto Zen Buddhists in Japan that becoming a priest saves family members nine generations back. In the spirit of the bodhisattva ideal, may the contemplative path that has resulted in this book likewise offer healing and rest to all those who have come before and whose suffering and struggle brought me to end-of-life caregiving.

Writing about my own healing and spiritual growth has, by necessity, required that I tell stories involving family members and others who have shaped my becoming. I have used pseudonyms to protect the anonymity of others as much as possible, although I acknowledge at the outset that the stories I tell about my life are told from my particular vantage point, and that my siblings or other members of my family may have their own interpretations and memories of the events I describe. Writing about my life has been integral to my healing, and my hope is that honoring the truth of my own experience in the pages that follow might contribute to the path of healing for others. Short of that, I hope that it in no way detracts from the integrity of another's experience.

I am indebted to many persons—personal connections, professional colleagues, historical figures—who have made this book possible. I offer deepest thanks to Cicely Saunders for her willingness to challenge convention and persevere in times of grief and suffering in service of a compassionate ideal that became the modern hospice movement. Gratitude as well to David Clark, professor of sociology at University of Glasgow, for his work researching and preserving the legacy of Cicely Saunders. And I thank all who have dedicated their lives to contemplative caregiving, keeping alive and expanding an ideal and practice much needed in our world today.

Over the years, so many hospice patients and family members opened to receive my care, allowing me to experience firsthand the reciprocity of care and healing power of contemplative caregiving described in this book. Thanks to Jerome, and all who followed, for enriching my life with such meaning. May the stories I tell of my experiences at the hospice bedside honor the spirit of all who allowed me to journey with them in this most important time of life.

In researching this book, I interviewed many dozens of hospice volunteers in the United States and Germany. My deepest gratitude to this diverse group of individuals who shared so freely with me their life experiences, and to the many hospice administrators and volunteer coordinators who helped facilitate the research. Some volunteers I interviewed indicated that I could use their actual names in the book, but I have chosen to follow standard convention in sociological research by using pseudonyms for all hospice caregivers, patients, and administrators. In some cases, minor details of individuals' lives have been changed to protect their anonymity, yet each story I tell represents the life experience of an actual person, not a composite constructed from the experience of more than one person. In writing this book, I was not able to include the voice of every person I interviewed, although I hope that all who offer care at the end of life will recognize their experience in the pages that follow.

I thank the National Endowment for the Humanities (grant #FT-59796-12), the Maine Community Foundation, and the Faculty Senate Committees at the State University of New York at New Paltz and the University of Southern Maine for providing funding for conducting portions of the research for this book. I also thank the Evangelische Fachhochschule in Freiburg, Germany, for hosting me in the summer of 2003 while I conducted early interviews for this book.

Over the course of conducting research for this book, I taught many seminars on death and dying, hospice care, and grief and transformation. I thank participants in these courses for their willingness to experiment with contemplative approaches to learning such as the practices included in this book, and gratitude to all who found inspiration in exploring the teachings presented in this book. Thanks also to the many students in the US and Germany who helped with transcription or other aspects of the research.

Many friends and colleagues supported the research and writing of this book. Heartfelt thanks to Sharon Kaplan-Cohen for her help in opening doors, to Elaine Yuen and Clare Stacey for their encouraging feedback on early drafts of several of the chapters, to Raeann LeBlanc for our joyful exchanges on the art of contemplative caregiving, and to Dorothe Bach for our work together on contemplative learning. Several people allowed me to read parts of this book to them while in the process of writing, including Janie Downey Maxwell, Sarah Waite, Andrea Quast-Mortello, and Tula Tsalis. Thanks also to the members of the Writers' Accountability Group at the Thomas Memorial Library in Cape Elizabeth, Maine. And deep bows to Jann Jackson, Mary Pat Brygger, Ryūmon Baldoquin, and Anraku Hondorp for practice support as I wrote this book.

Like all transformational processes, writing this book involved moments of grief and moments of joy and everything in between. Two colleagues were supportive beyond measure throughout the many ups and downs in the writing process. Matt Lee was the first to read most of what is written in this book, and he and Éliane Ubalijoro provided helpful comments on the writing, often on multiple drafts of the same section or chapter. Thanks to you both for the many exchanges around ideas and questions related grief, suffering, and compassionate care, and to Matt for being a virtual sangha in the morning sitting practice. Much had to die so that this book could be born, and Éliane and Matt remained present with me as true spiritual friends through it all. My deepest gratitude to you both.

Thanks to Judith Simmer-Brown for encouraging me to consider Shambhala Publications, and deep bows to David O'Neal, the acquisitions editor who brought the project on board. Gratitude to everyone at Shambhala who helped make this book possible, including Kay Campbell for her hospitality and engaging exchange; Oliver Glosband for his patience and attunement to process; my publicist, Katelin Ross, marketing coordinator, Tori Henson, and the entire marketing team at Shambhala and Penguin Random House for their skill and creativity in sharing this book with the widest audience possible; and my developmental editor, Matt Zepelin, assistant editor, Emily Coughlin, and copyeditor, Jill Rogers (Assured Word), for their skill with the editing process. Matt Z., thanks for your graceful way of suggesting changes to the text, for your flexibility in considering possibilities, and for your encouragement and skillful listening throughout the process. My deepest thanks for all you have done for this book. You are truly a gifted editor.

There is perhaps one person who is as joyful about this book being complete as I—my wife, Andrea Quast-Mortello. Thank you, Andrea, for the many conversations over the years on the teachings and practices in this book, for your trust in the integrity of my work, and for supporting our family during the final stages of writing. Humble bows for the opportunity to journey with you, and may all know that you had the vision, long before I did, that this book would be published by Shambhala.

May the good fortune I have experienced now be offered back as a blessing to all who supported this project and all who would read the pages that follow.

PREFACE

A Matter of Life and Death

We can let the circumstances of our lives harden us so that we become increasingly resentful and afraid, or we can let them soften us and make us kinder and more open to what scares us. We always have this choice.

Pema Chödrön, *The Places That Scare You*

I NEVER WOULD HAVE come to write this book if my mother had not been murdered. I got the call from my younger sister around 7:30 a.m.

"John, we're all at the house. Mom was murdered last night."

"I'll be right there," I stammered, as my legs collapsed from underneath me.

It was December 17, 1987. In the early hours of the morning, James Edward Prince entered the house where my mother was babysitting, attempted to rape her, and then brutally murdered her. I turned nineteen the following year as the State of Maryland sought the death penalty.

A ten-year moratorium on executions ended in 1977, and since that time the United States has executed on average one person every ten days, a ghastly figure for a nation that understands itself as the leader of the civilized world. But a public relations godsend came for proponents of capital punishment in 1989 when the death penalty became symbolically reframed in the mass media as a government service to help survivors heal the trauma of their loss. The catchword was *closure*, the fantasy that survivors have "entitle-ments to death penalties" as a means for resolving their grief and achieving "the satisfying feeling that something bad or shocking has finally ended."[1] Members of my family were told to keep quiet as we sat in the courtroom listening to the prosecutor offer our grief and details of the final moments of our mother's life as grounds for execution. The attorney had a penchant for the dramatic, recounting gruesome specifics of what James had done with the knife, how many times he had pulled the trigger, where the bullets had entered my mother's body. In the months before the trial and sentencing, I fantasized about being the one who would kill him.

James was sentenced to life in prison without parole. And for many years it appeared that I too had been sentenced to a lifetime of imprisonment. I was surviving, perhaps in some ways thriving, yet imprisoned nonetheless, bound in darkness to a man who, in a PCP-induced blackout, had cut short my mother's life, and through that act, threatened to do the same to my own life force. Yet as I would discover in time, freedom can be found in the most unlikely places.

Fast-forward to June 26, 2013. It was the second day of a two-day confer-ence on innovative approaches to health-care provisions for inmates living with terminal illness. The location of the conference was a maximum security prison in the United States where prisoners have the option to vol-unteer in a hospice program to care for their fellow inmates at the end of life. Several of the men who volunteered in the program were present. Near the end of the conference, a story was told of how a terminally ill inmate sentenced to life in prison for murder was granted "compassionate release" so that he could die in the care of loved ones, but following pressure from members of the victim's family, the man was sent back to prison where he died two days later.

The story was painful for many of those present. Questions were raised about the meaning of justice, dignity, and "serving one's time," as well as about rising health-care costs resulting from an aging prison population in an era of mass incarceration. At one point in the conversation, I stood and offered that I had lost my own mother to murder twenty-six years earlier and could identify with the grief of this family. But I explained that, having struggled with the grief of her death and the meaning of my own life for more than two and a half decades, I had come to see that my own healing, and my bond with my mother, were not tied up with whether James or any other inmate died in a prison infirmary rather than in the care of his own family. Most importantly, I continued, was that my own experience as a hospice volunteer, caring for so many men and women at the end of life, had shown me that affirming the humanity of others is crucial to my own joy and sense of vibrancy.

Afterward, one of the men—Wayne,[2] a short, stocky man in his midforties—approached me. He had already served over two decades behind bars on a murder conviction, and he had several more years ahead of him. He had spoken earlier in the day about his experiences as a hospice volunteer, and he thanked me for attending the conference and for what I had said. In turn, I thanked him for the care he offered others at the hospice bedside. Wayne held eye contact with me and in a near whisper stated, "We are all human. We are all human." Feeling into the question behind this statement, I affirmed, "Yes, Wayne, we are all human." Wayne embraced me, and as I held him, he began to shake. I held him tighter as he trembled and wept, abiding with him until his body had released into the felt experience of this shared truth: *we are all human.*

Writing this book has been a matter of life and death. I am now forty-eight years old, which means that, for exactly half of my life, I have been journeying with the moral possibilities of contemplative end-of-life care. I began volunteering for hospice in 1993, and it was through attending to the needs of dying people that I first practiced the sacred act of witnessing the suffering of others, without judgment, without pity. It has been through this work that I have also received the precious gift of attending to my own inner life. This spiritual work of bearing witness to dying has helped me mend the suffering I have routinely inflicted upon myself through a black-and-white division in my heart. The belief that there are those who are worthy of love and compassion and those who are not leads inevitably to painful separations both external and internal. How is it possible to transform suffering and rage, even the wish to kill, into an openness to embrace fear, anger, disgust, or whatever other experiences are present? How it it possible to contact a quality of compassion unbound by the weight of the past, the limitations of culture, or the inhospitable circumstances of one's life?

This book draws on interviews I conducted with hospice caregivers in the United States and Germany, including inmate volunteers at a maximum security prison. Conducting these interviews has been a profoundly educational and meaningful process for me and has allowed me to connect with individuals whose stories I could never have foreseen. But the questions the book addresses extend beyond the hospice bedside and the prison infirmary. This book is not about compassionate release or the death penalty or the aging prison population, although in the pages that follow I will raise important questions pertaining to justice, mercy, and the rehabilitation of all who suffer in a culture of violence and individualism. Fundamentally, this book is an invitation for you to join me as I inquire into the causes and conditions through which caring for others can transform ordinary people like you and me, and how the act of caring itself is central to what it means to be human. This book is about living well in whatever our circumstances are and using end-of-life care as a window into the possibility of compassionately releasing ourselves from the prisons of heart and mind that cause so much unnecessary suffering for ourselves and others.

John Eric Baugher

Cape Elizabeth, Maine

May 30, 2017

Contemplative Caregiving

INTRODUCTION

Significant learning is learning that makes a difference in how people live—and the kind of life they are capable of living.
L. Dee Fink, *Creating Significant Learning Experiences*

I WAS TWENTY-FOUR YEARS OLD and in my second year of graduate school at Tulane University when I signed up to become a volunteer caregiver at a hospice in New Orleans. It was spring 1993, ten years before I would conduct my first interviews for this book. At the hospice, I received no formal training, only an interview with the hospice social worker, who inquired about my motivations to volunteer and offered me a brief history of the modern hospice movement. And then I was set loose to care for dying patients in the Crescent City.

When I rang the doorbell that first afternoon, Jerome, a thin gay man in his forties, greeted me in his underwear and nightshirt. Speaking across the threshold of his French Quarter apartment, he asked, "How do we do this?"

"I don't know," I replied. "I've never done this before."

"Me either," he responded. "I've never died before."

And then he invited me in. With that invitation began my journey of accompanying those who are grieving and dying—embracing not knowing with a heart receptive to whatever might arise, including what at times has presented as seemingly unbearable suffering.

Up to that point in my life, I had never been in the presence of someone who was dying, much less offered that person care. And I had never volunteered anywhere, for anything. Yet there I was, a straight man who found himself in the middle of the AIDS crisis in New Orleans, where for two years I cared almost exclusively for gay men whose lives were being ravaged by a myriad of HIV/AIDS-related complications. For so many reasons, it would seem, I was an unlikely candidate for hospice volunteering. Through my research for this book, however, I have come to see that *there are no unlikely candidates* for this kind of care work. Hospice volunteering draws individuals from diverse walks of life, and there are many paths to the threshold of that initial encounter.

Contemplative Caregiving investigates how caring for those who are dying can offer a path for healing and spiritual growth. In telling this story, I integrate my own experiences at the bedside of those who are sick and dying with interviews I conducted with seventy-five hospice volunteers in the United States and Germany between 2003 and 2015. In the course of my research, I spoke with Christians, Buddhists, Jews, atheists, and New Agers, those who had known grief and those who had not, those in good health and those suffering from terminal illness themselves. In the United States alone, about half a million hospice caregivers volunteer each year, and the increasing number and diversity of individuals who are drawn to end-of-life care tells us something profound about the human spirit and the possibilities of the current era. How is it that the suffering of dying can draw us in, enriching our lives with meaning and purpose? And what opportunities for significant learning and compassionate living open when death and grief are not seen as problems to be managed or avoided but skillfully engaged with complete openness and vulnerability?

In the broadest sense, this book explores the inseparable connection between suffering and joy, grief and becoming, absurdity and meaning, impermanence and play. The individual stories contained in these pages are of personal transformation through compassionate engagement at the hospice bedside. Yet the broader narrative pertaining to the human encounter with suffering and mortality has more universal implications that extend beyond the field of end-of-life care and could inspire compassionate shifts in many spheres of society. To introduce you to the transformative possibilities of caregiving and to the wider implications of this book, I begin with a story of someone I met along the way.

Tom's Education at the Bedside

In medieval times, dying people were seen as prophetic souls, voyagers and pilgrims valuable to the community in a number of ways, not least in the opportunity they provided those around them for service and spiritual growth.
    Sandol Stoddard, *The Hospice Movement*

Tom is a man of slight build, witty, caring, and above all, eager to learn. Like many hospice volunteers, Tom experienced caring for those who are dying as transformative, and it provided him with an experiential and contemplative "education" that brought clarity to his life and continued to deepen his capacity for being in the presence of suffering with courage and compassion. Tom had been volunteering for hospice for about six years when he and I met, and he began our interview by relaying how his encounters with the first individual in his care set him on a path of becoming:

> There was a gentleman that had severe liver disease that was dying—he was an independent individual, so being now in his deathbed, if you will, and not being able to do for himself, it was difficult for him. So, I found it difficult for me not ever being in that capacity of being a caregiver for a dying individual, not knowing what I should do and what I shouldn't do. It's like, okay, where are my boundaries associated with his boundaries? Where do we meet? Where do I step over that? Do I need to pull back? And where do I make sure I go far enough too so I can give him the care that he needs? And so, not knowing that zone, I just stepped in to help wherever I could. And I learned so much!

Tom laughed and then continued his story.

Because his control issues in reference to being able to take care of himself got limited right down to him being able to eat, feed himself, and then, you know, satisfy his thirst, take a drink. And, so, he would try to drink with a straw in his cup, he was lying in bed and he would bring his hand up with the cup and he'd get it almost like an inch from the tip of the straw to his mouth and he'd lose strength and bring his hand back down. And then he'd wait for a second and go again and get like half an inch and lose strength and go back down. It was difficult for me to sit there, and just watch that again and again and again. And finally, he would just look at me, and he was nonverbal, he would look at me, and those eyes would say, "Well? A little help here!" And at that point, I just reached up and helped guide his hand up and then he sipped away, and got the drink he wanted and that was it, and I'd say, "You all set?" And he'd say, "Yep," and I'd take the cup out of his hand and *that* was the spot. That was where he ended and I needed to begin. . . . And once I understood that, and got in line behind him, then we worked as a team.

Listening to Tom speak across our several conversations, I heard my own story. We were both white men of working-class origins who found in hospice volunteering our first opportunity to experience the life-affirming and transformative power of being present to those who are suffering. Tom has been volunteering in a hospice program at a state prison in the United States since the program began in 2010. Like Wayne, whom I described in the preface, Tom participates in the prison hospice in a double role: he is a volunteer but also an inmate, serving a nearly four-decade sentence for murder. In 2015, I interviewed nine of the volunteers in this program, all of whom had taken someone's life or been convicted of other violent offenses, including aggravated assault, sexual molestation of children, and armed robbery. By their own account, these men never would have come to hospice volunteering if they had not been incarcerated. And although their path to hospice care was, on one level, rather unlike other volunteers I interviewed, the narratives these men told about their involvement in hospice care resonated with my own experience and that of other men and women who volunteered for hospice "on the outside."

How is it that those convicted of murder, Vietnam veterans, retired state troopers, nurses, housewives, Catholic nuns, and so many others can find similar meaning in caring for dying people and their grieving family members? And what is it about hospice care that can transform some of the most inhospitable conditions of living and dying, including the infirmary in a maximum security prison, into a space for cultivating and expressing wisdom and compassion?

The founders of the modern hospice movement believed that caring for dying people opens individuals to the deeper mysteries of life and nurtures within them the virtues of patience, confidence, and compassion. Behind these possibilities is the radical principle of hospice care: regardless of who one is or the circumstances of one's life, *all* people deserve dignified care at the end of life. I believe that this principle and its related practices have profound implications for our survival and our potential to flourish as a species. It has certainly had profound implications for me, including my ability to perceive and relate to the humanity of someone like Tom.

Tom was a gentle and reflective man who shared freely with me the joys and struggles of his life. I felt a spirit of generosity and openness in him, and if I had not met him in prison, I never would have imagined he had taken someone's life. And knowing that about Tom, I treated him differently than those I interviewed outside the prison. Truth be told—*I googled him.* Before each of the prison interviews, I read online newspaper articles detailing the conviction and sentencing of each of the men I was scheduled to interview. I did this not in search of some deeper insight into the men I interviewed but as an opportunity to investigate my own fears, prejudices, and capacity for compassionate presence. I wanted to see what would come up in my heart, what I would feel in my body, and what thoughts would run through my mind as I held the present-day image of each inmate volunteer in my mind against the details of their past. I wanted to explore my own capacity to see each person I interviewed with wondering eyes, to see each as a spiritual traveler, just like me, who suffered and grieved, and who may have also known the transformative joy of caregiving.

Over a decade before I interviewed Tom, he was convicted of murder, and the details of that killing were quite difficult for me to take in. My own transformation through researching and writing this book resulted from confronting the disorientation I experienced through being in the presence of Tom and the many other individuals I interviewed for this book. These encounters challenged my understanding of who I was, my relations to others, and the interrelations among human dignity, compassion, and justice. I know that I am more than the worst things I have ever done, and my own engagement in hospice, including my work on this book, has been a path for exploring the depths of my own humanity and the humanity of those I have encountered along the way.

In our interview, Tom described himself as having lived "on autopilot" throughout his life—simply reacting to his inner and outer environment—whereas through hospice caregiving, he had cultivated the capacity to pause and reflect on his experience, opening up possibilities for responding with compassion to his own actions and the actions and needs of others. He recognized that in caring for hospice patients over the years he had "screwed plenty of things up." "In my past, I would look at it harshly," he explained. "I was *judgmental*, critical; it was a *shaming* voice." Caring for those who are dying has supported him in developing an "*awareness* voice" that accepts that his best intentions do not always translate into a skillful response and to draw on that awareness for strength to continue trying.

End-of-Life Caregiving and the Mindfulness Movement

The awareness voice that Tom describes aligns with the understanding of mindfulness made popular by Jon Kabat-Zinn, a medical doctor and key figure in what's become known as the mindfulness movement. Kabat-Zinn defines mindfulness as "awareness, cultivated by paying attention in a sustained and particular way: on purpose, in the present moment, and non-judgmentally."[1] In 1979, Kabat-Zinn began integrating Buddhist meditation practices into health care with the Mindfulness-Based Stress Reduction (MBSR) program he developed for his patients, and today such mindfulness practices are offered widely to support hospice workers and other care-givers as they attend to the needs of those who are suffering. Yet Tom did not develop such mindfulness on a meditation cushion. His transformation of being came through the relational practice of contemplative caregiving at the hospice bedside.

In recent years, there has been much interest in understanding the na-ture of compassion and how to further a more compassionate society. One expression of this interest has been the formation at several prominent universities of compassion training programs that draw on Buddhist medi-tation practices. Given all the hype around the neuroscience of mindfulness and compassion meditation these days, one might get the impression that Buddhists possess special expertise in the practice of compassion. But to cultivate compassion, does everyone need to train in Buddhist loving-kindness (*metta*) practices involving guided meditations, mantras, and visualizations? Thupten Jinpa, the longtime English language translator to the Dalai Lama and the key architect of the Compassion Cultivation Training at Stanford University, doesn't seem to think so. In the initial run of the Stanford program, Jinpa discovered that compassion training that "relies too heavily" on Buddhist meditation practices may not work so well for those who are "not temperamentally inclined to the silent, reflective approach typical of formal sitting." In the end, he and his colleagues agreed that more interactive exercises, including "two people engaging nonjudg-mentally, practicing understanding and empathy," as well as classroom dis-cussion, were "more effective in evoking the mental and emotional states we aimed to cultivate."[2]

The goal of Buddhist compassion training is to cultivate loving inten-tions, moment-to-moment awareness, empathetic capacities, and a willing-ness to extend the scope of compassion even to those we may see as enemies. As this book will show, each of these four dimensions of compassion can likewise be cultivated through contemplative caregiving for those who are dying. There is a fifth dimension of compassion that I also highlight in this book: the communal context of our care. The book is divided into five parts that correspond to these five dimensions of compassion.

Cultivating Compassion through Caregiving

My mother-in-law, Tula Tsalis, died on July 31, 2017, nearly one year to the day before I finished writing this book. Tula had had cancer for many years, and I am grateful that the circumstances of my life at the time made it possible for me to live with her and her husband for much of the final six months of her life. One of the gifts I received through Tula opening to my care was that she allowed me to be the loving adult son I did not have the chance to be with my own mother. Just a few days before she died, as I was helping her transfer to the bedside commode, Tula rested her head against my chest and sweetly stated, "John, you are a wonderful nurse." It wasn't any technical competency that elicited Tula's gratitude but the presence between us that I could serve as her legs supporting her in reverence for the integrity of her spirit and the needs of the body. What greater joy in life is there than to know this truth, that we each have this capacity to open to the loving possibilities of the moment and comfort another with such a simple gesture of compassion?

I have often wondered who I would be if I had not discovered hospice volunteering as a path of spiritual practice. What I do know is that my capacity to be present with Tula with openness, clarity, and ease was deepened through years of accompanying so many others at the end of life, beginning with Jerome in his French Quarter apartment back in 1993. In my experience, caring for those who are suffering and dying provides a powerful mirror for seeing ourselves, a space for apprehending and affirming our deepest intentions for this life, and an opportunity for maturing spiritually and expanding the capacities of the self. Over the years my care has not always been skillful, and I will share some of these moments of growth in the chapters that follow. The point of spiritual practice is not perfection but a humble commitment to show up as we can with an openness to seeing clearly, holding ourselves and others in loving regard, and learning from our experience.

Part 1, "Lineages of Compassion," reflects on the life and work of some of the key figures in the hospice movement and describes more fully what I mean by caregiving as a form of spiritual practice. All of us can dedicate ourselves to a life of compassion, but whatever our personal motivations may be, there is always a wider cultural context that encourages or thwarts our intentions from flourishing and bearing fruit. When I started out volunteering for hospice, I took it for granted that there was this thing called "hospice" that involved me going into people's homes or into nursing homes to support dying people and their family members in whatever way I could. Over time, as I came to understand more about the history of the hospice movement, I developed a sense of gratitude for Cicely Saunders, Florence Wald, and the other visionary women and men who developed the philosophy and practice of hospice care that allows ordinary people like me to accompany dying people we would otherwise never know.

Part 2, "Nourishing the Seeds of Compassion," investigates how compassionate intentions often emerge from our own experiences with grief and suffering and reveals how even those who may seem unlikely candidates for providing bedside care to the dying can flourish as end-of-life caregivers given a supportive context. Central to flourishing is a contemplative stance toward the self, a willingness to journey with such questions as who one is, what the bounds of one's compassion are, and what one is and is not willing or able to do in the face of suffering. This contemplative stance is not limited to a saintly few but is a spiritual capacity in us all. It is a process that can be unlocked by confrontations with death and suffering that shake us out of routine ways of seeing ourselves and invite us to discover and hone caring capacities we did not know were possible. Caring for the dying can be a fertile garden for our grief, a space for nourishing and deepening our intentions to cultivate compassion.

Part 3, "Caring as a Practice of Mindfulness," shows how caring for those who are dying provides a rich practice environment for cultivating moment-to-moment awareness of self, context, and other. We may begin our caregiving journey with idealized notions of what it will be like to accompany those who are dying, and fortunately for all, life is always more interesting than we expect. Crucial to the transformative power of end-of-life care is what I call the reciprocity of care. This virtuous cycle includes a receptivity on the part of dying and grieving individuals to be accompanied in this most vulnerable time of their lives, and an awareness and appreciation on the part of caregivers of those gestures of kindness and invitations to care that present in the course of what may seem like rather mundane encounters. By extending trust, those who are dying invite us to abide with, and learn from, the inevitable uncertainty and discomfort that arises in the face of dying and grieving.

The word *compassion* comes from the Latin *compati*, meaning to "suffer with," and refers to the basic human capacity to clearly see, empathize with, and respond to suffering. We often think of compassion as a rather grave matter. After all, people are suffering, and as caregivers, we are called to suffer with them. Part 4, "Unlocking the Empathetic Imagination," highlights a different view of human empathy, exploring how the fearless openness of play is central to compassionate care, taking caregivers beyond the guarded stance of pity into the spaciousness of joyful encounter. It is through a flexible and playful spirit that we affirm life, avoid taking ourselves too seriously, and encourage a mind-set that supports our growth.

Here I refer to what's been called "deep play" or "infinite play"—our capacity to move beyond the dichotomies and limited social roles that structure much of everyday life.[3] In this space, we move beyond the constraints of time and the necessity of gain, to experience sacredness in the mundane, revitalization without acquisition, and uplift in the most unlikely places. In play, we draw on creative forces that lie dormant in our lives, awaiting to be unlocked, opening us to joy, empathetic connection, and our own becoming. This playfully receptive spirit, cultivated at the bedside of those who are dying, helps explain a sentiment commonly expressed by hospice volunteers: "Even though it is a hospice and people are dying, it is a fun place to come."[4]

Compassion involves recognizing our "common humanity," the felt sense that suffering deserves a response because of the inherent value of the one suffering.[5] When a friend or member of our family is suffering, our immediate response may be to offer comfort in some way even if doing so is inconvenient or at a cost to us in the short term. But then there are those who fall outside the scope of our compassion, including those we dislike or consider our enemies. Sometimes it's our own suffering that we have the hardest time accepting and holding with compassion. An intention of compassion meditation practices is to break us out of the predictable pattern of being kind toward those we deem worthy of love and withholding kindness from those deemed "other." Sharon Salzberg, an influential figure in introducing Westerners to Buddhist loving-kindness, or metta, practices, expresses how expanding the heart's embrace in this way takes patience and creative exploration. "Perhaps you can most easily feel metta for a difficult person," she writes, "if you imagine them as a vulnerable infant, or on their deathbed.... Allow yourself to be creative, daring, even humorous, in imagining situations where you can more readily feel kindness toward a difficult person."[6]

Part 5, "Extending the Reach of Compassion," shows how such creativity and daring come with the territory of end-of-life caregiving, a natural training ground for cultivating the emotional dispositions and spiritual sensibilities necessary for extending compassionate care even to those patients and situations that may evoke physical or moral disgust. In this way, contemplative caregiving can further a compassion that is freed from moral judgments, bodily aversions, and societal stigmas, offering a healing balm crucial for our own well-being and for the maturation of our culture and society.

An Aspiration

In the course of researching and writing this book, I have come to know so many people who, like me, find meaning and purpose in caring for those who are dying and grieving. At this point, it is hard to separate the transformation I have experienced through caring for those who are dying from the inspiration and encouragement I have received from listening to my fellow hospice volunteers tell of their own joys and struggles as caregivers. What I know to be true is that we are all in this together, that our stories are both our own and part of a larger cultural bounty that we can offer to each other as a gift of encouragement, challenge, and inspiration.

A primary goal of the hospice movement has been to transform the wider culture away from fear and aversion to death toward acceptance and lay competence so that family members, friends, and neighbors develop and trust their abilities to care for dying people in their community. This book shows how hospice caregiving can help individuals from diverse social backgrounds develop the confidence and the capacity to compassionately care for those who are suffering and dying even in the face of aversion. Understanding these processes can benefit hospices and other health-care organizations in their efforts to train and support volunteers and staff in compassionate care. It can also help each of us as we care for friends or family members who are suffering or dying as we seek to learn from the many ups and downs that come with accompanying others at the end of life.

I encourage you to read this book as both a study on end-of-life care and an extended contemplation on the possibility for flourishing and living compassionately in the face of death, impermanence, and traumatic loss. To support you in integrating knowledge with your own caregiving practice, each chapter includes a contemplative exercise designed to further discussion and reflection and to evoke wonder about the possibilities of the human spirit and the meaning of a life well lived. The About the Author section at the end of the book provides more background on these contemplations, which comprise a curriculum for workshops and trainings I offer for leaders, educators, health-care providers, and family caregivers, to support your own practice and to help further a culture of compassionate care in your organization, in your family and community, and in society more broadly. May the teachings and contemplations in this book inspire your caregiving and encourage you to extend compassion in all situations where there is suffering.

PART ONE

Lineages of Compassion

*If my life ended today, I would tell you it was a happy
life—that I drew great joy from the study, from the
struggle toward which I now urge you.*
        Ta-Nehisi Coates, *Between the World and Me*

I WAS RECENTLY INVITED to a large medical center to discuss ideas
about strengthening the Physician Health and Resilience program at the
hospital. The program was relatively new, and in the first two years it focused
mostly on supporting physicians through crisis moments, such as dealing
with the death of a patient or struggling with feelings of burnout. I had
been introduced to the doctor who chaired the program as someone with a
"longstanding interest in mindfulness practice," and at one point in our conversation, she asked me, "What percentage of stress do you think is caused
by the person versus the environment?" Behind her question was curiosity
about a frequently made claim in the field of health care and wider society,
that whatever the circumstances of our lives may be, the key to our health,
well-being, and happiness is the practice of mindfulness. "Happiness is an
inside job," we are told—we could be happy if only we could relax, breathe,
and pay attention to what is happening in the present moment.[1]

Compassion, it seems, is also an inside job. Neuroscientific research in the
past two decades has revealed a link between the mental and emotional

capacities crucial to compassion and the functioning and interconnections among different regions of our brains.[2] Scientists now also understand that as adults, our brains don't just remain fixed or simply deteriorate with age but can change in response to new experiences, a capacity called "neuroplasticity." By engaging in prosocial activities, meditations on compassion, and other spiritual practices, we can nourish our compassionate intentions, deepen our capacity to read social cues and empathetically respond to the needs of others, and stretch our willingness to care even in those situations we find quite challenging. That we can train ourselves to become more compassionate resonates with the research presented in this book, which shows how we can cultivate these qualities of compassion through the committed practice of caring at the bedside of those who are dying.

But compassion is also an outside job. Our capacity to know, empathize with, and relieve the suffering of others is shaped not only by the structure and functioning of our brain but also by the structure of power and privilege in society. We experience suffering through the body, and whether it's physical, emotional, or spiritual pain, some bodies are more vulnerable than others. Furthering compassion in our world requires not only that we change our brains but that we change the conditions of society that place barriers between our wishes that others be happy, safe, and free from suffering and the realization of those wishes. In the language of author Ta-Nehisi Coates, our capacity to protect those we love from suffering is not just a question of the goodness of our intentions or the strength of our emotional dispositions but of how great the barrier is that lies "between the world and me."[3]

Some of us experience few barriers in our work of compassion. I have certainly enjoyed this privilege as a hospice volunteer, a social role that brings me into contact with dying and grieving people in a way that supports my wish to lighten the suffering of others. In hospice, the focus is holistic care for the individual and the family, and as a hospice caregiver I have the luxury of accompanying others under a model of care that affirms my own dignity and intentions to care. But end-of-life caregiving hasn't always been like this, and for many caregivers today, it still isn't.

The hospice movement was founded by doctors, nurses, and members of the clergy precisely because modern health-care systems did not support a compassionate response to the situation of patients dying of cancer and other terminal illnesses. The hospice founders addressed the "outside job" of compassion by removing those barriers and creating structures of care and new cultural practices that encouraged loving attention to the patient as a person, not just treatment of the disease. There is now greater recognition of the holistic needs of patients and their caregivers as a result of the hospice movement, yet many health-care workers today suffer unnecessarily due to time pressures, understaffing, and other barriers that stand between their compassionate intentions and the world of patients in their care. It is in such a context that training programs in mindful caregiving and self-compassion have been created that seek to address the "inside job" of compassion by providing health-care professionals and other caregivers with skills and practices for sustaining themselves and their care for others under less-than-ideal conditions.

Some believe the Buddhist-inspired mindfulness movement more or less helps individuals cope with the stresses of their lives but doesn't do much to change the underlying causes of suffering. Recent training programs by Buddhist teachers and organizations on compassion and contemplative end-of-life care do focus more on the inner rather than the outer dimensions of suffering. Yet at the onset of the mindfulness movement in the 1980s, Buddhists were at the forefront of confronting cultural barriers and extending the reach of compassionate care to marginalized groups including prisoners and gay men suffering from AIDS. In this way, engaged Buddhists have been radical religious reformers similar to the Christian and humanist founders of the modern hospice movement.

Chapter 1, "From Anglican Prayer to Secular Mindfulness," tells how the Christian physician Cicely Saunders and other wise women and men created the philosophy and practice of contemplative care, and how this compassionate work has been continued in different ways through carriers of the mindfulness movement. My hope is that the story I tell will encourage readers of all faith backgrounds and walks of life to explore their own religious or spiritual heritage as a source of inspiration in the practice of contemplative care. We are all in this together, and whether you are gay, straight, rich, poor, white, black, native-born, or immigrant—whatever your various social locations and identities may be—compassion is part of your heritage.

It's often said that those who don't remember the past are condemned to repeat it. There is certainly truth to this adage. Yet a deeper truth, I believe, is that realizing to the fullest our capacity to live wise and compassionate lives requires that we experience our caregiving as continuing a long lineage of compassion, as just a drop of kindness in a vast ocean of compassionate activity that began before we were born and will continue long after we are gone. Holding such a vast perspective can encourage us when our small selves feel exhausted and discouraged, reminding us that compassion as a force in the world cannot be dissipated or burned out, whatever struggles we may be experiencing in the moment.

In caring for those who are dying we witness the strength of the human spirit and the unnegotiable constraints of the body, the efficacy of our compassion and our utter powerlessness in the face of another's suffering, the uplifting joy of human empathy and its potential drain on the body. Grief is inherent on the path of caregiving, and at times we may try to push away our sorrow with a forceful anger or other mind-numbing intoxicants, treading water for some time before succumbing to burnout and despair. The alternative is to engage caregiving as spiritual practice, opening ourselves to a wise compassion more potent than our own sense of agency, receptive to the fullness of the moment, yet unbound by circumstance, our own timetable, or a desire to be the one who heals. Chapter 2, "Caregiving as Spiritual Practice," considers the paradox that, in caring for those who are suffering and dying, we come into the fullness of our power for compassionate presence through learning to grieve our powerlessness. How fortunate we are to live in an era with rich cultural resources to support such practice and wise foremothers from whom to draw inspiration.

1

From Anglican Prayer to
Secular Mindfulness
The Origins and Practice of Contemplative End-of-Life Care

A society which shuns dying must have an incomplete philosophy.
Cicely Saunders, "And from Sudden Death . . ." in
Cicely Saunders: Selected Writings, 1958–2004

IN 1961, as she was formulating the ideals for the first modern hospice, Cicely Saunders—an English nurse, social worker, and later physician—landed upon some essential truths about caregiving that had been clouded over by the technological and death-phobic tendencies of modern medical practice. Inspired by her Christian faith and grounded in a practice of listening deeply to the needs and experience of patients in her care, she saw how caring for those who are dying could be a path for cultivating wisdom and compassion. Saunders thereby opened herself to the contemplative dimension of end-of-life care. She discovered that abiding with those who are dying can "make us ask the most important questions of life and bring its greatest realities to our notice." A desire to serve had brought her to the hospice bedside, and she came to see that, through the *practice* of caring, we can "learn such things as to be gentle and to approach others with true attention and respect."[1]

It would be another thirty-five years before the term *contemplative end-of-life care* was coined by the American Buddhist teacher and anthropologist Joan Halifax, a key figure in the mindfulness movement as it pertains to care for the dying.[2] Today, terms such as *contemplative care, compassionate care,* and *mindful caregiving* are often used interchangeably, and it's typically assumed that to engage in such care "requires that the care provider is a practitioner of meditation."[3]

Yet Saunders, the founder of the modern hospice movement, was not a meditator, and she minced no words about it: "I've had a look at things like that and it's no good, I can't do it, so I don't try." For Saunders, daily prayer, devotional reading, and "a lot of feeling of the Communion of Saints" were what sustained her spirit.[4] Many today seem to see Buddhists as the holders of wisdom in matters pertaining to death, dying, and compassionate care, yet despite the current, widespread focus on meditation-based mindfulness, it was Saunders, a humble Christian physician from England, who inspired an international movement to integrate contemplative approaches to caregiving with all the best that science and medicine could offer.

Seeing that a mixture of Christian, Buddhist, and other religious and nonreligious influences helped create modern hospice, one is prompted to ask some questions: What was it that led Cicely Saunders to dedicate her life to creating this new approach to caring for the dying? How does the mindfulness movement relate to the model of care established by Saunders many decades earlier at the outset of the hospice movement? Does the mindfulness craze amount to old wine in new wineskins—a turning away from earlier ideals—or have the proponents of mindfulness made original contributions to the practice of contemplative end-of-life care first established by Saunders?

In order to answer these questions, this chapter uses a historical lens to explore the modern development of hospice in England and the United States. My hope is that this history will be of interest for those engaged in hospice work, especially with regard to showing that contemplative end-of-life care is a path available to people of different religious or spiritual orientations. More importantly, I hope that this background will serve to create a sense of connection, even lineage, between anyone involved in contemplative end-of-life care and the long line of such caregivers who have come before.

It takes courage to commit ourselves to a life of caregiving. By courage, I don't mean a kind of character trait that heroes have and others don't, but a quality of heart that we each can cultivate in our lives, especially when our inspiration to care has become dim. Part of what sustains me as a caregiver is the felt presence of the many wise and compassionate others whose struggles and fearless commitment to creating a better world prepared the ground for my own loving care. Personally, I have found various forms of meditation richly supportive of my own bedside care, and I feel connected to those pioneers, such as Jon Kabat-Zinn, who helped foster the connection between mindfulness practices and end-of-life care. At the same time, I have met many individuals engaged in contemplative caregiving who have never received training in mindfulness or sat on a meditation cushion, and I find it important that their experiences not be marginalized by a discussion that has perhaps become overly focused on Buddhist perspectives on caregiving and dying.

We often speak metaphorically of "standing on the shoulders of giants," which captures some of the gratitude I feel for Cicely Saunders and the other founders of contemplative end-of-life care. These wise foremothers did the groundwork in creating hospice care, and now I, and those in my care, benefit from the fruits of their compassionate action. In this spirit, may this chapter inspire in you a sense of gratitude for the visionaries in your heritage and affirm the possibilities of your own practice of compassion.

The Matriarchs of Modern Hospice Care: Cicely Saunders, Florence Wald, and Elisabeth Kübler-Ross

All of the world's wisdom traditions affirm that encounters with suffering and death can spark in us greater wisdom and compassion. A fundamental paradox of the modern era is how "progress" in terms of material well-being has come with a cutting off of wisdom. Medical and public health advances in the twentieth century have allowed many people in economically developed nations to live nearly twice as long as their forebears of just a hundred years ago, and yet, in the process, death itself has been transformed from a basic fact of life to an appalling tragedy that elicits denial and avoidance.

It was against this backdrop that, in the 1960s and 1970s, Cicely Saunders, Elisabeth Kübler-Ross, Florence Wald, and other visionary women and men sought to revolutionize the culture of dying and standards of care in modern medical institutions in England and the United States. As medical professionals themselves, these pioneers of the modern hospice movement witnessed firsthand the immense suffering of dying that arose, not simply as a natural progression of cancer or other terminal illnesses but from social conditions that inhibited medical staff from attending to dying people in the fullness of their needs and experience. As Saunders expressed in a 1958 essay on dying of cancer, "Many patients feel deserted by their doctors."[5] This desertion was not entirely or even mostly about inadequate medical care—it was about inadequate emotional and spiritual availability.

The culture of medicine in Britain had led doctors to feel powerless in the presence of dying patients and uninterested or disengaged from truly listening and attending to their concerns. The same cultural condition was dominant in medicine elsewhere in Europe, in the United States, and in economically developed societies around the world. Under the medical model established in the late nineteenth and early twentieth centuries, death became an enemy to be fought with medical technologies and pharmacological interventions that *attacked the disease* but did not *care for the person*. As medical historian Emily Abel explains, doctors "began to view death less as a human norm and more of a medical defeat" such that the "imperative to avert death increasingly took priority over the demand to relieve pain and suffering at the end of life."[6] For the medical establishment, which was overwhelmingly male in that era, death represented failure. In such a context, death was managed with silence and hidden away in hospitals, leading both to unpalliated physical pain and a sense of loneliness and isolation among those dying of terminal illnesses in modern societies.

In the United States, modern hospices emerged in the time of the civil rights movement, anti–Vietnam War protests, and the women's liberation movement. This era of questioning authority and demanding equality and democratic inclusion helped create the political opportunity for furthering more relational, holistic, and patient-centered approaches to care. It was in this context that Florence Wald, a nurse, left the comfort of her position as the dean of the Yale School of Nursing in 1965 in order to take up the work of creating the first hospice in the United States in New Haven, Connecticut. She later wrote that it was quite common in the 1950s and 1960s for doctors to "forbid nurses to answer questions from a patient about his condition," upholding what has been called a "conspiracy of silence" that denied patients the space to talk about their pain and participate in decisions regarding their care.[7] A catalyst that moved Wald to challenge the authority of doctors and work to establish more humane treatment of dying people was witnessing the suffering of a patient with advanced ovarian cancer at the hands of death-denying doctors. As Wald explains, the woman "went through hell," undergoing numerous painful and pointless surgeries because doctors could not accept their ultimate powerlessness in the face of death.[8] Central to the hospice mission is an interdisciplinary team working together to address the holistic needs of patients, an approach that could potentially transform power relations in the delivery of end-of-life care. For Wald, the hospice concept supported her vision of bringing about "a brave new world" in health care with nurses and physicians working together as equals.[9]

The values of the hospice movement resonated with the development of the "death awareness movement" in the 1960s, which stressed how death and suffering could be embraced as essential to our own growth and becoming. Most notable was the work of the Swiss-American psychiatrist Elisabeth Kübler-Ross, whose popular book based on her conversations with dying people, *On Death and Dying* (1969), offered "a new and challenging opportunity to refocus on the patient as a human being."[10] Kübler-Ross is most famous in the popular imagination for her oft-misunderstood "stages" of grief, although her international impact on the hospice movement is arguably her most profound legacy. Central to her impact on hospice care and the broader field of medicine was furthering the understanding that death and grief are more than negative experiences to be avoided at all costs and instead are essential doorways to developing wisdom and compassion.

In the late 1950s and early 1960s, Kübler-Ross in the United States and

Saunders in England were doing what had not been done before by a modern medical doctor: they listened to dying people and took their experience seriously. Saunders had worked as a nurse and hospital social worker before becoming a physician, and the gifts of her interdisciplinary training were apparent in the holistic model of care practiced at St. Christopher's, the hospice she opened outside of London in 1967. Yet the compassionate wisdom she embodied arose, above all, from her openness to loving encounters with those close to death, as well as her willingness to submit to the grief that inevitably accompanied such intimacy. "If Cicely's heart had not been touched, so deeply and so often, she would not have had the stimulus to use her mind so effectively," writes Saunders's biographer Shirley du Boulay. "St. Christopher's was the creative outcome of her pain. She had more than her share of pain; she experienced it, absorbed it, prayed and thought about it; she used it to ease the suffering of the dying."[11]

Saunders had studied politics, philosophy, and economics at Oxford University, but when England entered World War II after her first year of study, she left Oxford to become a nurse, against the wishes of her family. She pushed through her shyness and nervousness and discovered deep joy in bedside care, sensing that in nursing she had "come home." But her path was not to be so easy. Nursing during the war was physically demanding, and unrelenting pain from an injury to a spinal disc ultimately derailed her career as a nurse. She was only twenty-six years old.

Amid the suffering of the war, Saunders's personal life became overshadowed by "pain and darkness." But rather than sinking into despair, she practiced receptivity to a deeper faith and trust in the power of God's love, which she likened to "suddenly finding the wind at your back instead of battling against it all the time." She knew she needed to continue working closely with patients, so she studied to become a medical social worker, taking her first position in 1947. Although the spiritual empowerment she felt through her faith did not protect her from pain, it did open her further to loving, compassionate service. This path allowed her to discern her life's purpose, specifically through a most transformative encounter with love and loss. In her first year as a hospital social worker, Saunders "found a deep mutuality, snatched from the jaws of death," with one of her patients, David

Tasma. Tasma was a Jewish agnostic from Poland who came to England prior to the Nazi occupation of his country and was dying of cancer at age forty.[12] Saunders fell in love with David, ten years her senior, and although they only knew each other for two months, as Saunders would later explain, when it came to stirrings of the heart, "Time simply isn't a matter of length, it's a matter of depth."[13]

Saunders opened herself to knowing dying people with a degree of intimacy that was unprecedented in her day and remains unlikely today. Had she married in her twenties as she had hoped, she never would have met David and been transformed by the intimacy, and subsequent bereavement, of this brief and rather unlikely spiritual friendship. It would be hard to overestimate the depth of impact her relationship with David had on her life. It provided an answer to her prayerful question: "What do I have to do to serve?" Her love for David inspired her commitment to understanding the needs of terminally ill people and developing a contemplative approach to end-of-life care she would call "hospice." David left Saunders with £500 so he could "be a window in your home." How improbable it was—from the vantage point of 1948, and even from 1967, when St. Christopher's opened its doors—that that transformative encounter would become a window not just for Saunders but for modern end-of-life care in England and across the globe.

The Five Core Principles of Contemplative Care

Saunders revived a Christian tradition of medical care by integrating medical science with an ethic of compassion in caring for the dying. Her work has profoundly shaped the care for sick, dying, and bereft individuals through what I call the five core principles of contemplative care. The first principle is *attunement to the whole person*—recognizing that those who are dying may suffer from physical pain, as well as have social, psychological, and spiritual needs. Palliating physical pain is a hallmark of hospice care, both as an end in itself and in the understanding that relief from pain frees dying people to focus on healing relationships and attending to other matters of importance at the end of life. Saunders set the standard for the palliation of physical pain in the 1960s, not through discovering a new drug or method of administration, but through championing the view that "pain demands the same analysis and consideration as an illness itself."[14] From the outset, St. Christopher's was a place of research, teaching, and clinical care, with Saunders and her multidisciplinary team creating and sharing knowledge on best practices for holistically caring for terminally ill patients. A key aspect of Saunders's approach to understanding the syndromes of chronic pain was closely listening to patients and contemplating the meaning of their experience, a process she described as allowing listening to "develop into real hearing."[15]

Through attentive listening to patients, Saunders created the radical new concept of *total pain*, meaning the multidimensionality of pain—the physical, mental, social, and spiritual aspects—and the interrelatedness of mind, body, spirit, and a wider social context. Foreshadowing an idea that would be central to Kabat-Zinn's MBSR program for patients suffering from severe pain, Saunders expressed how fear and tension regarding physical pain exacerbates the experience of such pain. For Saunders, medicine was both a science and an art, such that skillful medical practice required "a philosophy of terminal care" that placed pharmacology within a wider perspective. As Saunders explained, she developed the concept of total pain as a "deliberate attempt to stimulate students and others to look at the various facets of a dying patient's distress, beyond the requirement for analgesics to the need for human understanding and practical social help."[16] A particularly innovative aspect of the holistic approach at St. Christopher's was the extension of care to the family and wider support network. "Their distress and corresponding need for a listener may be even greater than that of the patient," wrote Saunders. "Grief, feelings of guilt, and old, unresolved tensions may make them withdraw from real contact and communication with the patient, thus increasing the suffering on both sides."[17]

The second principle of contemplative care is that it is not simply a matter of applying technique but is grounded in *a way of being*. In the early 1960s, even as she sought to develop methods for palliating physical pain through regular administration of drugs, Saunders had the insight that the power of listening and the ability to embody a compassionate presence in the face of suffering might be as important as any medical intervention. The understanding that healing occurs not so much through what one does but through who one is in the doing, is perhaps most clearly articulated in Saunders's understanding of spiritual pain. In a talk she gave in 1965, she expressed how "the most important foundation stone" for St. Christopher's was Christ's command to his disciples to "watch with me" as he struggled in prayer and grief in the garden of Gethsemane on the eve of his betrayal and subsequent crucifixion.[18] She continued that "the command 'Watch with me' did not mean 'Take this crisis away.'" Rather, the essence of compassionate care involves caregivers "trusting in a Presence that can more easily reach the patient and his family if they themselves concentrate on using all their competence with compassion and say little to interrupt."[19]

Saunders described "spiritual pain" as resulting from feeling that neither one's life nor the universe has purpose, the sense of being disconnected from any truth greater than oneself. Here Saunders highlights the deep and pervasive anxiety and insecurity that has come to characterize modern Western societies, in which truth is increasingly reduced to fragile self-referential narratives that are vulnerable to radical doubt, particularly at times of crisis such as those faced by dying people. For Saunders, compassionate being with another in the face of such crisis involves giving an atmosphere of love and security, a holding environment in which patients and their family members can grieve, experience connection and respite, and grapple with questions of meaning and purpose. As caregivers of those who are dying, there is no requirement that one have answers or that one perfectly understand the suffering of another, only that one is prepared to show up with an open heart and a calming presence to bear witness or "suffer with" those in one's care.

The third principle of contemplative care involves responding with *reverence for the integrity of the other* in the face of whatever suffering presents in the moment. As a medical doctor, Saunders wrote several pieces on the management of various complications that may arise with terminal illness. Yet she saw it as critically important that death ultimately be viewed as "a truth to be confronted," not a "process to be managed."[20] Animating all of Saunders's work was an unshakable confidence in the human capacity to experience meaning and develop maturity through all conditions and times of our lives, including times of seemingly unbearable suffering. Those who are dying, Saunders explained, do not need "pity and indulgence" but rather to be treated "with respect and the expectation of courage." She trusted that, with loving support, those facing the end of life can "find their own way through."[21] The reverence Saunders held for the integrity of those in her care was grounded in knowing that we all will one day take our last breath. She was deeply grateful for the spiritual gifts of the dying, acknowledging that, if we are unable to receive these gifts, "we are the ones who are impoverished."[22]

The fourth principle of contemplative care is the necessity of *preparing, sustaining, and expanding our capacity for compassionate presence* through practices that cultivate self-awareness, inner calm, and insight into the needs of others. There is more than one path to self-illumination, and each of us must discern for ourselves how best to cultivate and sustain our own preparedness for compassionate presence. As a Christian doctor, daily prayer was central for Saunders in preparing and sustaining herself for a life of service in hospice care. As expressed in "Essentials for a Hospice," a pamphlet that she and her colleagues at St. Christopher's created in 1976 to support others considering becoming involved in hospice care, you should avoid caring for those who are dying "unless you really cannot help it," and only then, if you are "prepared to sweat and pray to do this." For Saunders, prayer was not so much a means for answering questions but a practice of deepening one's "readiness to live with questions" that have "no rigid answers," with "an overall confidence that there is meaning and an answer, even if it is not yet revealed."[23] Grief is inherent in the practice of end-of-life care and to sustain ourselves in this work, we each must attend to our own inner journey with clarity regarding our needs and access to sources of emotional and spiritual support.

The fifth principle of contemplative care pertains to the necessity of *cultural practices and a communal context* supporting intentionality, reflection, and ongoing contemplative learning. Our caring always takes place within a social setting, be it a family, organization, or spiritual community. Such contexts can sustain or thwart our efforts to embody a compassionate presence, stay true to our deepest intentions, and further our own growth and becoming. Abiding with those who are suffering and dying can be emotionally and existentially costly for caregivers. Drawing on Carl Jung, Saunders expressed how "real liberation comes not from glossing over or repressing painful states of feeling but only from experiencing them to the full." For Saunders, the "community of the unlike" at St. Christopher's—with colleagues coming from different faiths and denominations or having no religious commitment at all, but each having in common a reverence for each other and for the patients in their care—provided an ideal context for this process of turning toward and learning through painful experiences. In Saunders's experience, a hospice was "a place of growth," and the collective commitment of staff members to their own spiritual journey created "a climate in which others [found] it easier to make their search."[24]

A central question for Saunders was how she and her staff could "go on searching and learning with the same spirit of enquiry and strength on the medical and nursing side but at the same time give an atmosphere of love and security and meaning to people coming in much pain, anguish, and despair." The answer for Saunders was that such security would be experienced by patients, whatever their religious beliefs, through the hospice team's "mutual fellowship and the spirit of prayer, radiating out from the Chapel into every part of the corporate life" of the hospice.[25] Here Saunders speaks not of evangelism, "the desire that people should think as we do," but of staff supporting each other in developing humility in the face of death and the spiritual journey of another. The intention of the communal practice of prayer was to cultivate flexibility of spirit and a lightness of touch with each patient. "The agenda is new every time," wrote Saunders, "and our hope is that each person will think as deeply as he can in his own way."[26]

The First Phase of American Hospice: From Prophetic Voice to Mainstream Accommodation

Most of the early hospice groups that formed in the United States in the 1970s were initiated by members of the clergy concerned about the dehumanizing treatment of the terminally ill. The Reverend Ed Dobihal, then clinical professor of pastoral care at Yale Divinity School and director of religious ministries at Yale New Haven Hospital, collaborated closely with Florence Wald in establishing the first hospice in the United States. From his perspective, a hospice was "a place of ministry" and "a place for the consecration of death," yet he acknowledged that the integration of religion and science that characterized St. Christopher's hospice would not be possible for the hospice movement in the United States. America was much more religiously diverse than England, with a stronger separation of church and state. Although Dobihal, Wald, and others in the Connecticut group saw St. Christopher's as "the finest model of hospice care available," they understood that their guiding philosophy and methods of care would need to be translated to the "American culture and idiom."[27]

One concern was wider acceptance of the hospice concept in a religiously pluralistic society, where many would be skeptical of approaches to care associated with institutionalized religion. Another question was how to secure sufficient funding to establish sustainable hospice programs while maintaining true to core principles of modern hospice care developed by Saunders. As the first program in the United States, the New Haven hospice established by Wald and Dobihal was initially more successful than later programs in securing the funding necessary to keep their services separate from the wider health-care system.

The second hospice program in the United States, St. Luke's Hospice in New York City, was the first of many hospital-based programs that would be formed in the United States. The organizers at St. Luke's sought to establish a separate space for the hospice, such as a special wing set off from the rest of the hospital, but instead, a "scatter-bed model" was adopted. Under this approach, hospice staff visit patients wherever they are in the hospital, a model determined by the limited funding made available by the hospital rather than the underlying ideals of the program organizers.

The third hospice program in the United States, Hospice of Marin in California, likewise faced funding challenges, leading the organizers to incorporate as a home-health agency rather than create a freestanding hospice facility as they had hoped. As illustrated by these different approaches, hospice in the United States would not be a particular place for the care of dying people, such as St. Christopher's and the religiously based homes for the dying of earlier times. Instead, it would be a concept that could be integrated into a variety of contexts, a dynamic that would help quickly expand hospice services, while presenting challenges down the road.

The Medicare Hospice Benefit of 1982 helped legitimize and expand hospice services in the United States, although from the outset, many were skeptical regarding government support for their work. One fear was that accepting federal funding would shift the focus to cost savings and physical aspects of care and away from what was seen as the most innovative aspect in the hospice approach—spiritual care and bereavement support for patients and staff. The Medicare benefit did require that spiritual support be offered to patients, although such support was not reimbursable and, according to federal regulations, could be offered by anyone on the hospice team, including nurses or volunteers, whether or not they had training in pastoral care. Hospice care was being reshaped by the politics of the secular health-care industry such that by the mid-1980s, spiritual care was "one of the weakest hospice program elements" in the more than 1,500 programs that had sprung up nationwide.[28]

The original hospice founders have been described as "radical, religious, and reformers," motivated by personal confrontations with loss, deep commitment to holistic care, and a sense of camaraderie with like-minded peers.[29] In her classic statement on the hospice movement, published just four years after the opening of the New Haven hospice, Sandol Stoddard wrote, "In receiving the dying as significant and fully conscious members of the hospice community we are at the same time reincorporating the awareness of death into our own lives, and this is a liberating form of illumination."[30] Similarly, after becoming the director of a small hospice in the early 1980s, the Catholic physician Sheila Cassidy came to see hospice care as standing "in a prophetic relationship" to the mainstream of medical care on account of "the contemplative space" hospice creates for reflecting on moral and existential questions repressed in the wider field of medicine.[31]

The professionalization and standardization of hospice care weakened the movement's commitment to such contemplative values, with the focus on mutual emotional and spiritual support becoming seen among those starting up new hospice programs as an "inefficient use of time, given the constraints of reimbursement."[32] The very success of the hospice movement in terms of expansion and growth had compromised its prophetic voice and commitment to innovative ideals as hospice reformers were succeeded by palliative care specialists. Yet by the 1980s another religious impulse had already begun making its way into the US health-care system. This time the reformers were American Buddhists who infused creativity, innovation, and passion into the field of contemplative end-of-life care as part of a wider mindfulness movement.

The Promise of Mindfulness for End-of-Life Care

Why not try to make meditation so commonsensical that anyone would be drawn to it? Why not develop an American vocabulary that . . . recontextualize[s] it within the framework of science, medicine, and health-care so that it would be maximally useful to people . . . whether they were doctors or medical patients, hospital administrators, or insurance companies.

Jon Kabat-Zinn, "Some Reflections on the Origins of
MBSR, Skillful Means, and the Trouble with Maps"

The integration of mindfulness practice in modern health care began in 1979, when Kabat-Zinn opened the Stress Reduction Clinic at the University of Massachusetts Medical School. It was there that he developed MBSR, an eight-week course that introduces individuals to yoga, body scanning practices, and various secularized forms of Buddhist meditation, all in the service of developing mindful awareness. The program was initially offered to people suffering cancer-related pain, and it has since expanded to include people with pain or other symptoms from a wide range of difficult-to-treat medical conditions. While the initial goal of MBSR was to "reduce" stress related to the experience of chronic pain, in retrospect, Kabat-Zinn suggests that the term *reduction* is somewhat of a misnomer because the program is grounded in a "non-fixing orientation and approach." Mirroring Saunders's reverence for the integrity and agency of each person in her care, MBSR seeks to apprehend the "intrinsic wholeness" of participants, seeing each person as more than a patient, diagnosis, or ailment.[33] In the contemplative mind-set shared by Saunders and Kabat-Zinn, neither dying nor stress are problems to be fixed; rather, compassionate care involves supporting people in mobilizing their "inner capacities for growth and for healing" in the face of "a natural part of living from which there is no more escape than from the human condition itself."[34]

Both Saunders and Kabat-Zinn sought to holistically care for those in pain with practices that honored the interconnectedness of mind, body, and spirit. But there were important differences in their approaches. As a Christian physician, Saunders was explicit that the model of care she and her colleagues developed at St. Christopher's sought to integrate science and religion. With MBSR, Kabat-Zinn also sought to integrate science and religion, but in a way that "recontextualized" religion *as* science. Beginning in the early 1980s, Kabat-Zinn began publishing a series of studies in medical journals that sought to demonstrate the health benefits of mindfulness meditation. In his words, he wanted to present "the dharma essence of the Buddha's teachings" in a way that was "commonsensical, evidence-based, and ordinary, and ultimately a legitimate element of mainstream medical care."[35] His project dovetailed with the emerging dialogue between Western neuroscientists and Buddhist meditators—most notably the many meetings that have occurred between the Dalai Lama and various scientists, under the auspices of the Mind and Life Institute—such that MBSR became one component of a broad surge of interest in the connections between meditation, the brain, and health.

Kabat-Zinn's efforts in this regard have certainly borne fruit. MBSR has been applied to patient care in hospice settings relatively infrequently compared to other areas of medicine, but the widespread popularity of the program—it has been the subject of many dozens of randomized-controlled trials concerning a wide range of medical and psychiatric conditions—helped create the context for the popular reception of subsequent Buddhist engagement in end-of-life care.

The Emergence of Buddhist and Prison Hospice Programs

The late 1980s initiated a second surge of Buddhist activity in health care with the creation of three hospice initiatives that extended the scope of hospice care in important ways. Whereas cancer had been the model disease during the opening decades of the hospice movement, it was the AIDS crisis that motivated the formation of the Maitri hospice and the Zen Hospice Project, both in San Francisco, as well as an inmate-staffed hospice program at the US Medical Center for Federal Prisoners in southwest Missouri. In each case, innovative approaches were developed in response to local needs, affirming and expanding the ethical foundation and reach of the hospice movement.

By 1988, when the first prison hospice initiative in the United States began receiving patients, middle-class observers of the hospice movement had already bemoaned what they saw as the negative effect of federal regulations and standardization on hospice. Yet in elevating professionally reimbursable spiritual and psychological care above physical care as the most innovative aspects of the hospice approach, these white middle-class authors expressed a taken-for-granted privilege that pain medications and loving bedside care are readily available. Despite decades of innovations in pain control in hospice and the emerging field of palliative care, pain medications were nearly completely absent in US prisons in the 1980s.[36] In the words of Fleet Maull, a Buddhist teacher and former inmate who was instrumental in founding the hospice program at the Missouri prison, pain control was "abominable" prior to prison hospice care, with many inmates dying in extreme agony from AIDS and various forms of cancer because Tylenol was the only pain medication available. Maull, who served a fourteen-year sentence for drug trafficking, engaged in extensive networking with sympathetic health-care professionals in and outside the prison, including Kübler-Ross. He eventually convinced prison administrators to design a locked box for a morphine pump at the bedside so patients could self-administer when in pain. Introducing effective pain control, in Maull's view, "was a *radical* change in prison health care, and probably the most humanitarian aspect of the whole thing."[37]

Marginalized groups such as prison inmates have much to gain by having access to taken-for-granted standards available to hospice patients in the mainstream. To that end, in the early 1990s, Maull sought to create standards for establishing hospices in US prisons. He later collaborated with Wald in creating a prison hospice program in Connecticut, the birthplace of the American hospice movement. Wald was seventy-eight years old when she began working on an eighteen-month feasibility study for establishing hospice care in Connecticut prisons. Reflecting back on her decades of involvement in the hospice movement, she acknowledged, "When we were first trying to get hospice going, we were middle-class people focusing on middle-class people. . . . We neglected a whole segment of people from disadvantaged backgrounds . . . who can't gain entitlements without a struggle."[38] Equally important, hospice programs in prisons allow inmate volunteers to cultivate and express compassion in a context utterly devoid of opportunities to experience one's humanity through caring connections to others.

The most innovative part of hospice care is not a "part" at all, but *the approach itself*, which reveres the humanity of all involved. This core principle of contemplative care—that it's not what you do, but your way of being that heals—was central to the original model of hospice care developed by Saunders in the 1960s as well as the two Buddhist hospices that opened in San Francisco in 1987. In the words of Richard Levine, a Buddhist priest and the first medical director of the Maitri hospice, caring in the midst of the AIDS epidemic was a process through which "pain and suffering and death are once more reclaimed as part of human experience."[39] Issan Dorsey, abbot of the Hartford Street Zen Center and founder of the Maitri hospice, would himself die of AIDS-related complications within the loving community at Maitri just three years after its founding. Although the context of Maitri was quite different from St. Christopher's, Dorsey's teachings on hospice caregiving as spiritual practice mirrored Saunders's understanding of the necessity of a loving community supporting all in fully experiencing and learning from the unavoidable grief of end-of-life caregiving. As Dorsey expressed in a teaching just six months before he died, "We have created an environment that allows anxiety to be present . . . because it *is* a part of the present moment." He continued that, in hospice caregiving, as in all daily activities, the purpose is not to avoid or try to escape anxiety and fear but "to allow all that to be present and to settle with it, to allow ourselves to enter into that part of ourselves we are trying to avoid."[40]

Dorsey offered teachings on compassionate care to his fellow practitioners at Maitri with Buddhist language and imagery appropriate to the context (the Zen Center *was* the hospice), yet the focus on dying waking us up to life, and allowing space for all emotions as caregivers, articulated a contemplative mind-set held by hospice founders of other religious faiths and backgrounds. As the German hospice founder Dr. Johann-Christoph Student expressed in 1991, in the first edition of his well-circulated *Hospiz-Buch,* providing good end-of-life care requires that a caregiver "not suppress one's own fears in the face of those of dying people," but instead develop the capacity to perceive those fears "with the necessary clarity and discernment."[41] Consistent with this understanding, the sociologist John Fox has shown that "noticing how you feel" is one of the central norms distinguishing hospice volunteering from other forms of caregiving in the US health-care system.[42] In this way, hospice volunteering is a natural learning environment for practicing what Buddhist-inspired compassion training programs seek to cultivate in participants, including developing awareness of, rather than suppressing, uncomfortable emotions.

While there has been a long tradition of contemplative caregiving in hospice dating back to Saunders's early work in the 1960s, the term *contemplative end-of-life care* wasn't coined until 1996. Joan Halifax's Being with Dying training program for health-care clinicians is emblematic of a third moment in Buddhist engagement in end-of-life care, in which mindfulness-based workshops and training programs have been offered to middle-class health-care professionals as support for compassionately caring for self and others. Some see a natural affinity between Buddhist teachings on mindfulness and compassion and the hospice ideal of providing practical, humane end-of-life care. In any case, the focus of mindfulness-based training programs on engaging in practices of self-care, recognizing one's own grief as a caregiver, and being present with suffering rather than trying to fix it have helped refocus attention on the contemplative dimensions of end-of-life care embodied in the work of the early hospice founders.

CONTEMPLATION
The Practice of Encouragement

As caregivers, there will be times when we may feel disconnected from our inspiration, ineffective in relieving the suffering of those in our care, or unable to live into our deepest ideals. In these moments, we don't have to exhaust ourselves with the heroic goal of being the one who heals. We can recall that we are part of a wider whole that asks only that we embody compassion as best we are able and offer joyfully what is possible in each moment. We can trust that even the smallest drop of goodness sustains and furthers the sacredness and value of life. The goodness of our care is never in vain, and in those times when we feel discouraged, our spirits naturally lift when we remember our compassionate heritage and invite all who have inspired us to join us as we sit at the hospice bedside or wherever we may be—to share in moments of joy and to encourage us in moments of darkness.

The practice of encouragement can be approached in several ways. I list here three possibilities and invite you to consider which among these may best align with your own sensibilities and needs. Perhaps you might make a commitment to draw on one or more of these practices for a set period of time, investigating how best you can encourage your compassion to flourish even when it becomes difficult to care.

   I. **THE WAY OF PRAYER:** Many who care for the dying sustain
      their spirit through prayer. Some pray for guidance in seeking to care
      with a spirit of not knowing. Some pray for forgiveness when
      expressions of care fall short of compassionate intentions. Prayer can
      also be a practice of encouragement, opening one to divine presence
      when caregiving takes one into what Psalm 23 calls "the valley of the
      shadow of death." Are there particular words or phrases that best
      express your prayer for courage when the mind is fearful? Are there
      prayers in your own religious or spiritual tradition that speak directly
      to your own needs and experience as a caregiver? How about songs or
      passages of scripture? If you were to write a prayer of encouragement

to share with other caregivers in a similar situation as yourself, what would you write?

2. THE BLESSINGS OF LINEAGE: One way we can encourage ourselves as caregivers is to see and experience our caregiving as continuing a long lineage of compassion. What cultural or spiritual lineage or lineages make up who you are? Whose life story or legacy encourages you to continue on when the path of compassionate care is not easy?

3. THE POWER OF VISUALIZATION: Our capacity for compassionate presence is as vast as the sky, yet at times, it may seem as if the compassionate spark in our kind heart is covered with clouds. In moments such as these, when our world has become gray, when time pressures or other conditions of our caregiving are pushing us to the end of our rope, we could use the company of kind others. Drawing inspiration from a nineteenth-century African American song, "God Put a Rainbow in the Clouds," Dr. Maya Angelou explained that, as she was about to step on the stage, into the classroom, or anywhere else she was called in her work, she would bring everyone who had ever been kind to her with her, saying, "Come with me, I need you now." With this practice, Dr. Angelou never had to face hardship on her own or feel she had no help, because she was surrounded by the kindness of rainbows, even those who had long passed.[43] Who might you bring with you to accompany you in your caregiving? Whose kind face can you visualize next to you, offering encouragement in the midst of whatever clouds you might face as a caregiver? Is there perhaps a parent, grandparent, or departed friend or lover in whose honor you now care? Might you invite them in the room as a kind witness to the loving care you now provide others?

2

Caregiving as Spiritual Practice

Grief is a humble angel who leaves you with strong,
clear thoughts and a sense of your own depth. Depression
is a demon who leaves you appalled.
    Andrew Solomon, *The Noonday Demon*

IN THE SPRING OF 1998, my wife Lily and I climbed into her father's
Volvo station wagon, and the three of us set out on a fifteen-hour drive from
New Orleans to Davenport, Iowa. We were heading to my brother-in-law's
wedding and were excited about the big weekend that awaited us on the
other end of our two-day trek. The journey turned out to be a bit more than
we had expected. The rehearsal dinner, which was also a celebration of my
father-in-law Jay's sixtieth birthday, was on Friday. The wedding took place
on Saturday. Then on Sunday Jay suffered a stroke from a ruptured aneurysm
on the right side of his brain.

Lily and I ended up staying in Iowa for six weeks, sleeping most of the
time in a family meeting room on a wing of the intensive care unit. The
initial surgery to repair the ruptured aneurysm saved Jay's life, but it
compromised his ability to swallow, and he was unable to walk due to severe
neurological damage on the left side of his body. He suffered setback after
setback. Two more surgeries were necessary as a result of infections he had
contracted around the shunt that was put in to drain fluid from his brain.

Jay was an athletic man, a former track star, and he was religious about working out at the gym. But after being bedridden in the intensive care unit for a month and a half, receiving all his nutrition in liquefied form through a PEG tube, his muscles had atrophied, and it seemed his spirit had as well. Once his condition became stable enough, he was flown via helicopter to New Orleans, where he would remain at a medical center just down the street from our Garden District apartment for another six months.

Lily and I did our best to care for her father, but we were both terrified in the face of this sudden traumatic turn in his life. Jay was relatively young and seemingly in great physical condition. His stroke confronted us with the reality of how vulnerable we all are, how quickly the body can waste away, regardless of how fit we may be. But what terrified us the most were the prospects for the future. Would Jay ever walk again? Would he always be incontinent? Would he ever regain strength on his left side or swallow without difficulty? What degree of independence would he ultimately have, and what would all this mean for our own lives? Lily and I had just married the year before, and it was not at all clear whom we would become through this shock to our lives.

I had started volunteering for hospice five years before Jay's stroke. My experiences caring for Jerome and other men in their homes throughout the city had showed me I had the capacity to care and that I found deep meaning in doing so. Now life had presented me with the chance to care for a member of my own family, and I was eager to be there for Jay in any way I could. A bit too eager.

Lily and I walked to the hospital every day for those six months, visiting her father as his mind slowly became clearer and as he transitioned from acute care, to subacute care, and then to the rehab unit. As the rehab routines picked up, I took it upon myself to learn from his therapists how I could work with Jay to help him recover as fully as possible. But the force of my good intentions was out of sync with Jay's pacing. I wanted Jay to try harder. I wanted him to want to walk again as much as I wanted this for him. My judgments about what he was and wasn't doing were the machinations of my own mind, but at the time, I couldn't see my irritation as I was so blinded by my glowingly good intentions.

I was a compassionate knight in shining armor and in playing out the shadow side of this archetype, I shielded myself from the rawness of my own sorrow—the sadness, anger, fear, and brokenheartedness—and the sorrow of Jay, Lily, and others. I was hiding from these basic facts about my life and from the reality of what others were going through. In doing so, I bypassed my capacity to work with the adversity I was facing in a way that could have helped me become a more compassionate and intelligent human being. I had a strong identity as a compassionate caregiver, yet caregiving for me had not become a path of spiritual practice.

As the six months came to an end, the family created a plan for Jay to move in with his younger sister and her husband in their farmhouse in rural Louisiana, as a transitional stage before he could move, we hoped, to an apartment in some sort of residential or assisted living facility.

Jay still needed around-the-clock care to assist with dressing, bathing, and other so-called activities of daily living. We hired an aide for some of the morning care, but someone would need to attend to Jay at night as well. Lily was quite clear that she could not put a condom catheter on her father or help clean up his bottom, and so, in the end, we arranged that Lily's brother and I would alternate every three weeks living on the farm caring for Jay, taking him to his many therapy appointments, and working with him every day on the various strength and coordination exercises assigned by his speech, occupational, and physical therapists. We would try this for several months and just see what happened.

One thing that happened is that Lily and I got divorced. It was about two years between living on the farm and filing the divorce papers, and although Lily said she didn't want to get divorced, she was so enmeshed in an affair with her Tai Chi teacher and confused about who she was and what she wanted that there was no doubt that this was one door I had to walk through.

I was devastated. I had always had a false confidence that Lily and I could do anything, which expressed as a heroic arrogance in my care for her father. And I was certainly seen as a hero wherever I went with Jay. Even now, as I recount this story two decades later, I can bring to mind the proud look on my twenty-nine-year-old face as I stood there behind his wheelchair, hands on the grips, ready to do whatever needed to be done.

Around the same time that my marriage and my façade of tireless service began to crumble, one of my friends put it to me bluntly: "I miss the old John." I too had nostalgia for the old John who could tirelessly give, but it came to a point where living out this heroic self-identity was causing more suffering than the pain and confusion I was using it to avoid. After I filed the divorce papers, Lily told me, "I am grateful for what you did for my father, but I sometimes felt there was another way things could have been done." At the time, I couldn't hear either part of what she was saying. All I could hear was the wounded voice in my head pushing away both her gratitude and her pain. Instead of taking her words as an invitation for self-reflection, I wallowed in the self-serving refrain, "How could you do this after all I did for your father?"

In caring for those who are suffering and dying, we will inevitably reveal beautiful and kind aspects of ourselves as well as those places where we get stuck. That another is suffering evokes our compassion, and feeling powerless in the face of that suffering can reveal our grasping like no other experience. Such grasping, and all our struggles as caregivers, can be for us an angel that opens a heart of wisdom or a demon that burns us out with an appalling despair.

I do not judge my younger self for my grasping and irritation. And I no longer judge Lily for exiting our marriage. We both were doing the best we could with the resources we had in our lives at the time. For my part, I had an abundance of good intentions—a crucial capacity for compassionate living. But when our draw to care is not balanced by the other dimensions of compassion discussed in this book, our caregiving easily slips into self-centeredness. Herein lies a paradox at the heart of compassionate care: selfless care of the other is only possible through turning toward ourselves with an openness to explore and truly know who we are in our caring. It is as if a mirror is held up to us when we accompany those who are suffering, and to engage in caregiving as spiritual practice, we accept this invitation to see ourselves and our care with clarity and loving acceptance.

Care of the Self

Today it is widely accepted that sustained efforts to relieve the suffering of others requires a compassionate stance toward oneself. Personally, I find the necessity of caring for oneself to be true with *any* form of caregiving, whether as a hospice caregiver, teacher, parent, friend, or lover. If we don't listen to our bodies and attend to our needs, our efforts to relieve the suffering of others will eventually catch up with us and compromise our capacity to care. There is another way, the way of true compassion, which involves opening to whatever arises as an opportunity for significant learning and deepening of wisdom and compassion. I call this the path of caregiving as spiritual practice.

The notion of caregiving as spiritual practice is premised upon a particular understanding of what it means to care for the self. Contemplative care of the self, like care of the dying, embraces the fullness of the human experience, including our spirituality. By spirituality, I mean that which inspires our lives with meaning, connection, and a sense of sacredness in what we do and who we are. In one sense, caregiving as spiritual practice simply means that our caregiving is a fundamental expression of our spirituality. I think here of a question for spiritual discernment posed by the Episcopalian priest James W. Jones, who writes that "at the heart of religious experience" are not "ideas to believe or duties to perform but an awareness of a greater presence that gives meaning to our lives." The question for each of us is, "Where do *you* experience a deeper, greater presence in and behind and through your everyday life?"[1] When it is through our caregiving that we experience such depth of meaning and presence, caring for others serves as a path for our own spiritual becoming.

By this I don't mean having an instrumental approach to caregiving— that we are drawn to others' suffering *because* it is useful to our own growth and learning. Rather, it is receptivity to the fullness of our own humanity that calls us into respectful encounter with others, open to the mystery of their individuality, dignity, and becoming.

Self-care is typically thought of as something one does *after* caring for another, as a way of recovering from the stresses of caregiving. The underlying idea is something along the lines of, "I have given so much to others, now it's my time." At one hospice where I volunteered for several years, we were advised to take time for ourselves each day, perhaps by relaxing in a bubble bath, taking a walk in the woods, or enjoying fun time with our family—whatever might help rejuvenate us and release the stresses of caregiving. It is good advice to maintain balance in one's life and take a break when one's effort becomes too strenuous or one's desire to help turns into an energetic drain. Yet "care of the self" from a contemplative approach is more than a cycle of altruism, depletion, rejuvenation, and more altruism. It's not solely a process of self-*preservation* but of self-*expansion*.

"Expanding the self" refers to how caring for the dying can turn our attention to the most important matters of life and death and cultivate in us a practical wisdom that deepens our confidence and ability to respond compassionately when there is suffering. "Contemplative inquiry"—listening with the fullness of our mind, heart, and spirit—is the core practice of such transformative learning. In many contexts today, listening is approached in an instrumental way, as a charitable task we do for other people, along the lines of "lending a listening ear." Yet, for the ancient Greek and early Christian spiritualists, the "art of listening" was central to care of the self. For Plato, listening was a practice of turning inward and cultivating silence to allow insight into the order of the universe and one's place in that order. For St. Augustine, the practice of listening involved discerning the power of God at the very heart of our own being. Listening as spiritual practice is a receptive mode that allows transformation, a process that expands the compassionate *capacities* and *concerns* of the self.

Essential in caring for the dying is a spirit of "not knowing," a virtue extolled by the founders of modern hospice care as well as more contemporary Christian, Buddhist, and other ethicists of end-of-life care. The humility of not knowing opens us to see and respond clearly to the individual needs of each person in our care rather than relying on predetermined knowledge of what they might be experiencing or needing. It also invites inquiry into deeper questions of existence evoked through such encounters. How is it that I feel most alive in the presence of dying? What would my life look like if I allowed a spirit of not knowing to animate all of my encounters with others, including difficult situations I experience in my family, at work, and elsewhere? Who might I become if I kept before my eyes the reality that I too will one day be in that bed?

Contemplating the realities we are exposed to through end-of-life caregiving can at times be unsettling. In these moments, care of the self may involve calming ourselves or finding a way to ease the stress we are experiencing. Yet I encourage caregivers to consider the possibility of finding a more profound kind of "stress reduction" in the very process of acknowledging and exploring their experience. As Kabat-Zinn expresses to those who would consider participation in the MBSR program, "If you hope to mobilize your inner capacities for growth and for healing . . . a certain kind of effort and energy on your part will be required. The way we put it is that it can be *stressful* to take the Stress Reduction Program."[2] Similarly, as Father Thomas Keating writes about Christian contemplative practice, "Contemplation is not a relaxation exercise. It may bring relaxation, but that is strictly a side effect. It is primarily relationship, hence intentionality. It is not a technique, it is prayer."[3] Care of the dying as spiritual practice likewise draws on our inner capacities for growth and healing. It can become a prayerful way of being in relationship that, as the Psalms suggest, may "teach us to number our days, that we may gain a heart of wisdom."

Contemplative care of the self allows space for all that arises in the course of our caregiving, including time for reflection on our own feelings and needs. As the Buddhist teacher Sylvia Boorstein writes, the fundamental question is not whether I am happy, feeling relaxed, or stress free, but simply, "In this moment, am I able to care?"[4] Our caregiving always takes place under conditions that can support or frustrate our efforts to be present with others while also attending to our own body and spirit. Care of the self requires that we are mindful of our own needs in any given moment, but even more so, it requires awareness of how the conditions under which we care shape our chances of caring well for self and others. During the height of my efforts to care for my father-in-law, I was mostly neglecting to attend to the conditions of care—to the severity of Jay's needs, which precluded a fast recovery or any recovery at all; to the fact that my relationship with Jay fell under the purview of a more fundamental relationship, my marriage; and above all, to my own physical and psychological needs.

Care of the self sometimes means stepping away from caregiving, having a sabbatical of sorts to rejuvenate oneself and to allow for processing and integration of experience. Many spiritual traditions recommend that we start with intentions and conditions that are conducive to practice and gradually build capacity as we stretch ourselves to enter more challenging conditions of caregiving. Eventually, even under the most difficult circumstances, caregiving can be approached as opportunity for spiritual practice, for lifting up and freeing our spirit, rather than burdening us with cynicism and despair.

And what if we are not able to care well in the moment but don't have the privilege to step away? What if our work or family situation requires us to abide with those who are suffering even when our sense of love and joy in our caring is drowned out by irritation or aggression? In these moments, we can always affirm our integrity on the spiritual path by returning to the foundational practice of contemplative inquiry, of honestly seeing where we are in the moment.

Ultimately there is no distinction between care of the self and care of the other. The same practices of contemplative care that affirm the dignity of the one in the dying bed also affirm our own well-being. As caregivers, each of us will at times experience some degree of physical or emotional exhaustion. But when we allow ourselves to see with clarity our own suffering or the suffering of another, we are already inviting the healing touch of compassion. We may feel overwhelmed by grief, completely beside ourselves, not knowing how to comfort, nurture, or care for ourselves in the moment. Contemplative care of the self at such times is a gentle turning around, of allowing not knowing to flow from a place of humble receptivity, beyond the fearful struggle to power through or somehow get around the pain we are experiencing.

CONTEMPLATION
Reflecting on Our Impulse to Care

It is a natural human impulse to want to reach out and support others in their grief, and often that impulse arises for us after we ourselves have suffered trauma or loss. Compassionately caring for others does not require that our motives are somehow "pure," that we have resolved or brought closure to our grief, whatever that might mean. The question, instead, is whether we have an honest recognition of where we truly are in the moment. Have we examined whether turning toward the pain of others is integral to our own path of becoming or is instead a strategy for running way from our own grief?

Take some time to consider your own impulse to care. If you feel a strong desire to show up for others who are in pain, is that desire matched by a willingness to bring the same loving attention to the grief of your own life? Has grief become for you a path of self-illumination, or do you tend to turn away from the voice of your own pain?

Contemplative caregiving involves stretching ourselves and growing into the unknown. But at times, our own grief may be too raw. We may require time to replenish ourselves through self-compassion before we can embody a loving presence for another. What forms of care are you truly prepared to offer at this point in your life? Can you accept where you are, with honesty and self-compassion, in gratitude for what you are able to do and give at this time? And if there are ways you would like to serve, forms of care you would like to engage in that, at this point, seem beyond your capacity, how might you attend to your own growth to allow your impulse to care to flourish and bear fruit?

I encourage you to engage these questions in any way that feels most natural and helpful for you, perhaps through journaling, in conversation with others, or as part of a practice of quiet reflection. You might also return to these questions as you read through this book and reflect on how the stories of the many caregivers presented in the chapters that follow shed light on your own experience with grief and the impulse to care.

Entering a Path of Self-Illumination

The roji, *the garden path which leads from the* machiai *[portico] to the tearoom, signified the first stage of meditation—the passage into self-illumination. The roji was intended to break connection with the outside world, and to produce a fresh sensation conducive to the full enjoyment of aestheticism in the tearoom itself. One who has trodden this garden path cannot fail to remember how his spirit, as he walked in the twilight of the evergreens over the regular irregularities of the stepping stones, beneath which lay dried pine needles, and passed beside the moss-covered granite lanterns, became uplifted above ordinary thoughts.*

Kakuzo Okakura, *The Book of Tea*

The door to the traditional Japanese tearoom is not more than three feet high, requiring all who pass its threshold, whatever their occupation or station in life, to bow in humility. Grief is a doorway like this, and it can bring us to our knees. We may thrash in rage in the face of grief, feeling forsaken, deprived, unjustly singled out: Why me? Why must *I* pass through this doorway unfit for someone of my stature?

The intention of the garden path leading to the tearoom is to prepare one for receiving the simple gifts on the other side of the doorway. By cultivating presence and humility, one is prepared to move beyond the ordinary sense of self-importance and its cousin, self-judgment. Grief too invites all who enter to bow in humility to both the gift of life and to our ultimate powerlessness in the face of death. Coming through grief to a place of service requires of us a reverential attitude toward that which is given and taken and a receptiveness to the sacredness and mystery of who we are and who we may become—even through seemingly unbearable loss.

Regardless of our background, temperament, occupation, or life circumstances, we all have the innate capacity to contemplatively care for those who are sick and dying. Yet offering a compassionate presence requires that we prepare ourselves. In speaking of preparation, I do not mean the technical skills or know-how specific to a particular occupation or social role but rather the capacity to encounter another in the fullness of her being. This preparation is grounded in our willingness to explore who we are behind our doing and to lovingly hold both our good intentions and the limitations of our care in the face of the suffering and death of another. To illustrate the importance of such preparation, consider the German palliative care physician Johann-Christoph Student's description of the denial of death that was common in the male-dominated field of medicine in Germany in the 1970s.

> Presumably I enjoyed a completely "normal," unexceptional medical training like so many other physicians. I learned a great deal about various diseases, and above all, that curing such diseases was my highest objective. . . . What I learned nothing about in my training, was death, aside from making the legal pronouncement designating the time of death. My commitment to the life of patients absorbed me in such a way that I did battle with death at any cost, and feared nothing more than failure in this battle. Horrifying the thought of coming into the clinic in the morning and having to admit that a patient had died "on me" during the night before. In this way, I never really encountered a dying person. Even when I worked on a children's oncology ward, I was never able to take in that children died there! I felt compelled to simply erase the deaths of these children from my memory as if they never took place. I never saw any reason to seriously question this mind-set one inherits as a doctor—up until the death of our first daughter.[5]

Dr. Student was thirty-eight years old when his daughter Nina died from a rare infectious disease just twelve days after her birth. As he recounts, the gravity of his loss was deepened by the fact that Nina died "in one of the best children's hospitals in Europe," in the care of the "best doctors," and surrounded by the "most costly medical equipment." As a parent of two daughters who are more precious to me than my own life, I shudder to imagine Student's sense of having "failed as a father and as a doctor." Suffering a "hollow feeling of impotence and rage," he abruptly turned away from practicing medicine, cursing "a medical science that apparently was not able to maintain the life of those especially important to me."

But the story didn't end there. In 1984, four years after Nina's death, Student founded the first hospice initiative in Germany for individuals dying at home and subsequently became one of the most influential figures in developing the philosophy and practice of hospice and bereavement care in Germany. The turning point for Student was his participation in a grief workshop with Kübler-Ross. Though he signed up in the hopes of "shedding all the feelings of guilt, shame, and rage," things didn't turn out as expected. When it came down to it, Student was overcome with fear and alienation, and he was only able to engage in the workshop half-heartedly. He felt that, once again, he had failed. But it was through the imperfection of the moment that the healing could begin. As he sat in the circle with Kübler-Ross and the other participants, judging himself for his apparent inability to fully engage, something shifted. "Something pivotal took place," writes Student. "I sensed that I was also accepted and respected in this half-heartedness, and it felt as if I had never before experienced that in my life. No one other than myself seemed to judge my 'failure.' That experience gave me for the first time the sense of possibility that I could give up my own self-critical and judgmental mind-set. I saw for the first time the possibility of forgiving myself, of accepting myself even in my failure."

In that moment, the young doctor experienced what had been missing in his medical training—any form of contemplative learning, not just *about* death but *from* death and *through* grief. Through her own nonanxious and loving presence, Kübler-Ross modeled for Student how he, as a physician, could in turn offer true hope and consolation to those grieving or facing the end of life. Student considered it "the first step toward transformation and the root of the strength for further transformative steps" in a lifetime of learning. As he continued to develop a contemplative mind-set as a physician, he shifted his focus from trying to save people's lives at any cost to supporting healing in his patients whatever their medical prognosis might be—a humbler intention that transforms powerlessness into possibility on the path of compassionate care.

A Time to Every Purpose

To every thing there is a season, and
a time for every purpose under heaven.
Ecclesiastes 3:1

Like myself and Dr. Student, many people come to contemplative caregiving out of their own experiences of grief and suffering. In the hospice world, there is a general guideline of having individuals wait twelve months after a death in their own life before being allowed to volunteer at the bedside. It makes sense that space be given for reflection before moving outward to abide with those who are dying and grieving. But whether or not we are prepared to care for others is not just a question of time. Some of us have the space in ourselves to care for those who are dying even as we too are grieving, whereas for others, many years may have passed since a particular loss that still complicates our capacity to abide with those who are suffering.

Wherever we might be with our own grief, there are always possibilities for expressing compassion, although it might not take the form we had imagined. Sometimes our suffering makes us eager to jump into the thick of things, but perhaps what is right for us may be to work in the wings rather than to take center stage.

Consider Janet, a kindhearted woman in her midsixties drawn to care at the hospice bedside. Eight years before I met Janet, she had lost both her mother and her younger sister to cancer within the same month, and she was still struggling to find her way to integrate those traumatic losses in her life. Her path was not easy, but in her own way, she was finding a time for compassion.

After Janet's mother and sister died, she was eager to begin volunteering for hospice. She waited the obligatory twelve months before taking the volunteer training course, and immediately following her training she was given her first assignment. After just one visit, she realized she was not up for it. Although seven years had passed since this encounter, she remembered quite vividly how she felt "stranded" and "very alone" in the patient's room at the nursing home, unable to deal with relating to someone so close to death. She quit after the first visit. Four years later, after she retired from her work in the field of mental health, Janet went back to hospice to help out in the office as an administrative volunteer. At the time Janet and I met, she had been doing volunteer office work for the hospice bereavement program for three years.

When I asked Janet to tell me how she got involved in hospice, she warned me, "This is sort of an involved story," and then spoke for eight minutes with almost no further prompting, telling the story of how she had lost her mother and her sister. She explained how her mother had been sick with lung cancer for some time when her sister became ill and was also diagnosed with cancer. Her mother and sister lived on the other side of the country, and when she recounted how they had called her to come out to be with them, she fell silent. After a long pause, she began crying, and then apologized for her tears. "I haven't thought about this in a while," she explained.

Janet spoke of how chaotic her life had been as she cared for both her mother and sister in the final weeks of their lives. As she spoke, I could hear the sense of ragged exhaustion she had experienced at the time. She had had no space to care for her own most basic needs for food and rest, much less attend to the deeper emotional and spiritual significance of what was transpiring.

> I was running to the hospital to see my sister, running home taking care of my mother, and then my mother got back in the hospital again, then they put her in a nursing home. So, my day started at six o'clock in the morning, go to mass, visit my mother in the nursing home, go home, take care of my sister, get her ready, take her to the hospital for radiation or whatever they were going to do with her on that particular day, go home, make my sister's dinner, go back to the nursing home to see my mother.

It was in such a frenetic context that her mother passed away. Janet had been with her mother up until about two hours before she died, and she explained that, when she left the hospital, she didn't realize she would never see her mother again. She began crying again as she explained how she had had a "bad experience" at the funeral parlor when she brought clothes over for her mother. Subsequently, she didn't go to her mother's funeral, which was held back on the East Coast, 2,500 miles away from where she was still taking care of her sister. Janet expressed that not seeing her mother again had "left a void" in her. She paused and looked around the room as if she were searching for her mother, to give me a feel for how "I'm still always like, you know, where are you?"

The circumstances around her sister's death were also traumatic for Janet. She had pleaded with her sister for some time to go on hospice care, but she would not give up hope for a cure. "She was quite young, she was fifty-five," Janet told me, "and she was going to try everything that she could try." In frustration, Janet turned to her sister's doctors, begging them to end the chemotherapy, which she saw as both torturous and futile. She struggled to hold back tears, explaining how her sister died of a heart attack the day after receiving what would be her last treatment of chemotherapy. Janet once again felt robbed of the opportunity to say a final goodbye: "She was still alive when the doctor called me in the morning, but by the time I arrived at the hospital, she was gone."

As I listened to Janet recount traumatic loss upon traumatic loss, my heart broke for her. I felt the connection between her story and those of so many of us who are doing our best to care for loved ones under conditions so much less than ideal. Janet's grief was complicated not only by the traumatic nature of her mother's and sister's deaths but also by the void of care for herself in being physically separated from her home—her husband, church, and circle of friends—over a period of seven months. In such a context, even attending mass became just another thing to check off in a string of inhumanely packed days of running and doing, trying to hold everything together.

After her mother and sister died and she got back home, Janet found that her experience of her normal life changed dramatically. "My life just simmered down to a *halt*," she recounted. Finding it difficult to be with herself without "this craziness going on all the time," Janet felt moved to do something, so she signed up to volunteer for hospice. She began crying again as she told me this, her voice quivering. "For some reason or another, I thought that I *could* do this, you know, take care of people who are dying. But I'm still not ready to do it, maybe I never will be, I don't know. So, I keep coming to do the administrative work."

When traumatic losses are not integrated into our lives, the energy of those experiences does not simply dissipate with time, but instead resurfaces, often unexpectedly, reinforcing patterns of avoidance and disempowerment. Janet had done all manner of things in caring for her mother and sister, but much like me in caring for my father-in-law, she did not *take* from those experiences insight into the depth of her own being—she did not reflect on what drove her to run herself ragged, to struggle against her sister's wishes, to argue with doctors and funeral directors, and to push all this down and attempt to avoid thinking about it. Many years later, Janet was still struggling to integrate into her ongoing life her troubling experiences caring for and losing her mother and sister. As her experience of trying to sit with a hospice patient in that nursing home room had shown, she had not yet learned to face the internal void that left her feeling stranded, alone, and bereft of the resources that might have helped her be present with another dying person.

After I spoke with Janet, I wondered about her question of whether she would ever be ready to take care of those who are dying. That season may come, but perhaps it's not required. Janet herself wondered where she got the idea to volunteer at the hospice bedside, and maybe it was just that: an *idea* that may make sense for other people's lives, but not for her own. Each of our lives is unique, as are our paths to healing and embodying compassion. What's clear is that she is finding her way, as we all do, to make sense of the grief of this life and to live into her wish to be of benefit to others. There are many others like Janet who express compassion for oneself and for those who are dying by doing behind-the-scenes work for hospice or in their own families.

This chapter has sketched how caregiving can be for us a path of spiritual practice. As the stories offered illustrate, our paths will not all look the same, as the circumstances of our lives and the contexts of our care will differ.

There is no one right way to live a rich spiritual life, and there is no one right way to offer care as spiritual practice. Contemplative caregiving does not require that you are a Buddhist or a Christian or that you believe in God or don't believe in God. What is essential is the practice of contemplative inquiry that cultivates in us a humble spirit. In caring for those who are suffering or dying, we have the opportunity to express our will to do good in the world. But even more so, we are invited to open in humility to realities in us and around us that are greater than our will.

As I will discuss in part 2 of this book, our good intentions are essential to compassionate care, although to be truly of benefit to others and to sustain our capacity for joy as caregivers, our desire to do good must be balanced with a realistic view of our capacities and the context of our care. When we accompany someone dying or suffering a chronic condition such as dementia, we will confront the limits of our own care. Humbly accepting that, even under the best conditions, our care will be imperfect, is crucial for sustaining ourselves in our journeys as caregivers. Guilt, despair, burnout, and other painful states are often the fruit of our own grasping to be the one who heals, the one who serves, the one who makes things happen, instead of being a compassionate witness to another's choices and journey to death without judgment.

In caring for those who are suffering, we will touch those places in us that hurt, and unsettling doubts, fears, and questions may arise. Contemplative care of the self requires a generous opening to our grief and pain and a commitment to holding with compassion our power and our impotence, our knowing and our not knowing. It is always a time for compassion, although there may be times when the most compassionate response for us will be to remain behind the scenes and support the work of others rather than facing directly the suffering of another. In these moments, we can remind ourselves that appropriately responding to the wider context of our care, breathing in the tension and anxiety rather than blindly chasing after our impulse to do good, sustains both our capacity to care and the vast energy of compassion of which we are just one part.

PART TWO

Nourishing the Seeds of Compassion

In preparing food for the community, it is crucial not to grumble about the quality of the ingredients, but rather to cultivate a temper which sees and respects them fully for what they are.
Zen master Dōgen, *Instructions for the Cook*

THE STARTING POINT for any spiritual practice is our intention. In the case of compassion practices, this involves our wish to be of benefit to others. But where do our good intentions come from? What makes us strive to live a compassionate life rather than chasing after material pleasures or just trying to gain fame or wealth for ourselves? And when the going gets rough, what gives us the courage or resilience to continue on the path of compassion rather than giving up or burning out?

Questions like these have been around for thousands of years. More recently, social and behavioral scientists have sought to understand what kinds of experiences plant seeds of compassion in our lives, as well as what kinds of inner and outer conditions can nourish them. Some seeds are planted in childhood, including secure attachment to parents and having compassion modeled to us by those around us.[1] Our desire to express kindness to others also takes root through our experiences as adults. Oftentimes we engage in acts of compassion out of a desire to "give back" the kindness we have received from others. Many turn to hospice volunteering, for example, after a member of their own family received loving care from hospice. It makes good sense that such positive experiences—whether in childhood or later in life—can cultivate in us compassionate intentions. But it's also true that more difficult and painful experiences can sow and nourish seeds of compassion in our lives.

In popular culture, grief is typically seen as an unfortunate experience that incapacitates us and knocks us off our feet. That is certainly one part of the story. From this vantage point, grief is a kind of threat to the self that we need to resolve or somehow get over before being able to care well for others. If we are overwhelmed by our own grief, or if we repress our pain or ignore our suffering, then we certainly will not be able to respond to the needs of others with clarity and skill. When left unattended, our own needs insert themselves in our care, clouding our well-intended responses to others with pity, sentimentality, or other "near enemies"[2] of compassion.

But grief isn't just a negative state that threatens our capacity to care. Grief is fundamentally a creative act that, when nourished, intends toward integration and wholeness. Grief is a response to a broken bond. The idea used to be that healthy grieving requires us to relinquish connection to the person who has died or to that part of ourselves that was lost. But grief doesn't look like this for many of us. We don't just accept the loss and then move on. Our grief can involve continuing a bond with a loved one who has died in ways that transform our own suffering and extend compassion to others.

In some instances, this process involves offering care to others out of gratitude for the support hospice provided to a friend or family member. Chapter 3, "Becoming a Contemplative Caregiver," considers how encounters with death can inspire gratitude for that which is given, even amid the pain of loss. This chapter also reflects on the common myth about hospice volunteering that it takes a special kind of person to care for those who are dying. There may be times in our lives when we simply don't have the capacity or necessary support to be a compassionate presence to those who are dying. We may be too overwhelmed with our own grief to be there for others, as illustrated by the stories in the previous chapter. But there isn't some particular personality type or special character trait that sets end-of-life caregivers apart from others. We all have the spiritual capacity to offer gestures of kindness in the face of suffering. This process is illustrated by those who are convinced they are unable to care until they witness themselves flourishing in a supportive environment that turns their self-doubts into confidence.

There are many pathways through grief to end-of-life caregiving. Many people who lose their spouse to cancer or other terminal conditions describe their lives being completely turned upside down by grief. When their partner died, it seemed that a part of their own self died as well, confronting them with the pain of creating a new life out of the fabric of so much loss. But many people I have spoken with also describe how, through caring for a loved one and struggling with their own grief, a new part of their self was born. When we are made to confront death and loss, we often gain deeper insights into who we are, what we are capable of, and what truly gives our life meaning. This process can involve what psychologists call "posttraumatic growth." What's meant by this is that we don't just recover from grief and return to the way we once were. Instead, our struggle with grief expands our caring capacities and sense of vibrancy and purpose in life, even in the face of ongoing suffering.[3] Hospice volunteering is a powerful space for engaging grief and suffering in such a contemplative way. In chapter 4, "Transforming Our Grief through Compassionate Care," I outline several ways personal experiences with death and grief can inspire in us the intention to care at the hospice bedside.

According to a classic Zen teaching, the proper way to cook our life is through reverence for the ingredients in front of us. When tragedy or loss come to us, we may close down in self-pity and wish for it all to just go away. The Buddhist teacher Pema Chödrön reminds us never to underestimate the human tendency to try to get around the grief of life and just get comfortable.[4] In doing so, we cut ourselves off from our own creative energy and capacity for joy. There is a wisdom in letting all experiences cultivate in us seeds of gratitude and compassion. In the words of Marlena, a woman we will meet in chapter 4 who has experienced so much loss in her life, including the death of two husbands, "I can't think of anything to complain about, I mean anything that hasn't been a good part of my life." For her, the goodness of her grief is how it has inspired in her patience, an understanding of how others hurt, and a desire to care. The philosopher Judith Butler expresses the same essential truth in quite different language. With a contemplative mind-set, grieving can be "the slow process by which we develop a point of identification with suffering itself," not as "narcissistic preoccupation" but as an "apprehension of a common human vulnerability."[5] Through contemplating the realities we are exposed to through grief, our own loss can become a powerful seed for a life of compassion.

3

Becoming a Contemplative Caregiver

You do not have to get over your fear before undertaking something
new. You could just be afraid and go ahead anyway.
    Judith L. Lief, *Making Friends with Death*

AT SOME POINT OR OTHER, all who volunteer for hospice will be
asked a question by puzzled friends, coworkers, or family members and
sometimes even by hospice patients themselves: "Why do you do it?" Behind this question is a mixture of fear and awe that is commonly expressed
in statements such as "I cannot imagine wanting to sit at a stranger's
deathbed," "I could never do what you do," or "It must take a very special
person."[1] Over the decades of my hospice volunteering I've been questioned
about my motivations from all directions. The first time, it was Juliana, a
fellow graduate student. Juliana thought it was noble of me to care for those
who were dying, but she also asked, "Why don't you do something uplifting,
like tutor children?" Given our cultural conditioning around death, I understood why she would ask a question such as that—she simply couldn't
imagine that end-of-life caregiving itself could be energizing or inspiring.

A potential barrier to understanding the draw of end-of-life care is that
some of the commonsense ways of talking about what motivates people to
volunteer for hospice do not capture the experience of these caregivers. Even
the notion of "volunteering" can be misleading, since many hospice caregivers speak of themselves as being on a journey they didn't exactly sign up

for. One volunteer explained, for example, that she had never liked being around sick people, and that her becoming involved in hospice was the result of a set of seemingly chance encounters that came to her like "thorns invading my life's pruned rose garden." Hospice was not something she so much volunteered to do as something she felt fated to do as a response to a "message from the universe" delivered in part through opportunities to care for two acquaintances who had contracted AIDS.[2] Similarly, in his memoir about his experiences as a hospice volunteer, Stan Goldberg expresses the difficulty of explaining to his "nonhospice" friends what drew him to hospice. He asks, "How could I explain that the dynamics of hospice volunteering are so deeply compelling to many of us who do it that our involvement feels almost inevitable?"[3]

There has been a lot of research into what motivates people to volunteer for hospice. Underlying much of the research is what I call the assumption of saintly deviance. There is a myth that caring for dying people is so extraordinarily stressful that there must be something unique about those who volunteer for hospice. Who are these people who would sign up for something like this? What personality characteristics set them apart from others? Why do they do it?[4]

There *is* something extraordinarily powerful about hospice work. But that power will elude us so long as our questions direct us to look narrowly for some enduring trait or essence presumed to reside within the personal nature of volunteers that sets them apart from others. In my research I have found that even those who seem unlikely candidates for providing bedside care can flourish as hospice volunteers—especially if given a supportive context. Central to such flourishing is a contemplative stance toward one's own nature, a willingness to journey with a sense of wonder about who one is, what the bounds of one's compassion are, and what one is and is not willing or able to do in the face of suffering. This contemplative stance is not a substance that resides in some special people and not in others. It is a spiritual potential we all possess, a process that can be unlocked by experiences that shake us out of routine ways of seeing and experiencing ourselves in the world.

A Spiritual Capacity in Us All

Martha, a retired white woman in her midseventies, had been volunteering at a hospice in Baltimore City for over ten years. She told me that, prior to beginning at the hospice, she would have confidently stated, "I could never do that." The hospice where she volunteered had a historical connection to the church she attended, and she began volunteering only after reluctantly accepting an invitation from a priest with whom she had become friends. "He took me by the hand," Martha said, "and I thought, 'I could never do this.' I thought, 'There's just no way I can do this.'"

I asked her to clarify what was behind her immediate certainty that she was not cut out for hospice caregiving. "I thought I would be frightened or repelled," she answered, "you know, this kind of thing, and at first, we had a lot of AIDS patients, and people were so turned off, still are turned off by AIDS." But after just one day at the hospice, Martha came to see that the belief that she could not do the work simply was not true. "I just couldn't stop coming. There is something within me that keeps me coming." That something within Martha that keeps her coming back is the recognition that those suffering from AIDS are people too. "We're all human," she continued, "and at some time, we all need help, and sometimes, some people need more help than others."

Martha's shift in perspective took place within a context of support that included the confidence expressed in her abilities by the priest as well as books on death and dying he gave her that helped relieve some of her initial fears. Crucial support also came from the nursing staff at the nineteen-bed hospice house. Martha and her fellow volunteers were trained in standard precautions in caring for dying people, including those with AIDS, which calmed Martha's fears about caring for people with a transmissible disease. Several of the volunteers I interviewed indicated that they chose to volunteer at a residential hospice, as opposed to in-home care, so they would always have staff around in the case they felt they needed support. Others do not have that choice regarding where they volunteer.

Wayne, whom we encountered in the preface, had been in prison for over two and a half decades at the time I interviewed him. Like many hospice volunteers at the prison, Wayne had never been involved in any kind of care-giving prior to volunteering for hospice. He had never even heard of hospice but decided to volunteer after being invited to do so at the recommendation of the prison chaplain. He was further inspired to volunteer after an interview with the director of the hospice program at the prison, whom he experienced as open-minded and caring. But early in his tenure as a volunteer, Wayne was confronted with a situation in the infirmary that challenged him to the core. "I was up there one day taking care of this older fellow, and he messed himself, and I said, 'I can't, I can't do that, I can't change that guy, that's not me, I'm not gonna shower that guy.'"

Wayne's unwillingness to clean up the man he had been caring for didn't stem from a specific fear or risk of exposure but from his certainty about the nature of his self. For Wayne, cleaning up another man was categorically "not me." But Wayne's understanding of who he was and the limits of his care transformed rather quickly. "When I went back to my cell," he told me, "I got to thinking about it, I said, 'I wouldn't want that to be me.' I went back up and got him in the shower." Wayne still has his challenges as a hospice volunteer, but he is no longer plagued with doubts about whether he is cut out for it. Instead, caregiving for someone in need just feels like the "natural thing" to do.

In one sense, Wayne became a hospice volunteer when he signed up after his initial interview. Yet understanding how one becomes a contemplative caregiver, and the meaning of the work itself, requires that we attune to actual questions arising in the world—to how individuals shape their own becoming through contemplatively engaging suffering and testing their perceived limitations to their capacities for compassion. Wayne's willingness to bathe his fellow inmate, and through that act, his willingness to become a hospice volunteer, emerged as a practical answer to an existential question pertaining to his own mortality and embodiment. Crucial to the change in Wayne's self-narrative was overcoming a moment of crisis and seeing firsthand that he does have the capacity to care for a fellow man as a natural expression of his own goodness and desire for respectful treatment. Equally important in moving through that crisis was the positive, caring support

Wayne received from the director of the hospice program and from his fellow volunteers.

There are others, like Wayne, who do not know what they are signing up for with hospice but keep coming back after encounters that open them to a fuller experience of themselves. Another person I interviewed, Joanne, had felt a desire to volunteer in some capacity where she could be "helpful" after she retired. Living in a valley on the outskirts of Los Angeles, her primary concern was finding a volunteer opportunity that was close to home so she would not have to travel into the city. With this in mind, she went to www.VolunteerMatch.com to look for opportunities in her area. She started out tutoring in an adult literacy program at the library but quit after several months because she felt more motivated than the young woman to whom she was assigned. She tried the hospital next, but they put her in the surgery unit, which was not a good fit for her because she can't stand the sight of blood. After leaving the hospital, Joanne searched online again and came across a hospice where she completed the training program to become a direct care volunteer.

An irony here is that Joanne's primary search criteria—that the volunteer opportunity be near her home—applied to the library and the hospital, but not to the hospice. The hospice recruited and trained volunteers in her area, but after her training, she was assigned to the Alzheimer's wing of a nursing home on the other side of town. The major challenge to her expectations, however, turned out not to be the location of where she would volunteer but the experience of caregiving itself, which prompted in her a series of questions.

The hospice had a practice of pairing up new volunteers with more experienced peers. Joanne was paired with Rosa and found her to be "just as sweet and wonderful as Kathleen," the volunteer coordinator who facilitated the training at the hospice. Reflecting on the kindness and sense of presence she experienced in Kathleen, Rosa, and others at the hospice, Joanne wondered, "Where did all these people come from? They're all just wonderful people." She accompanied Rosa on her visits to two elderly women on the Alzheimer's wing. Joanne recounted, "We went just before lunchtime, met them, fed them lunch, took them for a ride on their wheelchairs and talked to them and held their hand. You know, I just did whatever [Rosa] did. I mostly watched because I didn't have any experience with this." Joanne told me that she and Rosa laughed and talked at the end of the visit—"and then I went to my car and sobbed. I thought, 'How could I do this? How can I do this?'"

In her first encounter as a hospice volunteer, Joanne was shocked by the suffering of residents on the Alzheimer's wing, but even more so, by the beauty of the loving care she witnessed. Her sense of awe for the compassionate care of her fellow hospice workers inspired confidence in her own capacity for growth. This was reflected in her shift from the doubtful subjective tone—how *could* I do this?—to a more committed inquiry—how *can* I do this? She continued the weekly visits to the nursing home with Rosa. "After a while, something in you just kind of turns around and I guess that you look at it different," she said. "You have a different perspective of what you're seeing, and it becomes fun."

I asked her to tell me more about her experience of "sobbing" after the first visit at the nursing home.

I had never volunteered for hospice before, so I never experienced what these people are living on a day-to-day basis. And especially in the Alzheimer's wing. It might have not have been so bad if I had been on the other side of the assisted living facility, but to go straight into this wing was, it was a culture shock. I was just amazed. And I think that I was also amazed at the way that the caregivers were so wonderful with them. And the woman I went with who was training me she was just so wonderful. And the whole—I think, it was the combination of the condition of the people with the way the caregivers were, was just so emotional. It was unbelievable.

Joanne went on to say that her expectations about the nursing home had been way off: she thought it would be like visiting her grandmother—maybe knitting, reading a book, or watching a movie together. She had a sense of humor about the mismatch between her expectations regarding what it would be like to volunteer for hospice and the realities she experienced on the Alzheimer's wing of the nursing home. Two years later, she was still volunteering for hospice, caring for individuals on the Alzheimer's wing and with no intention of stopping. She continued on with hospice, not despite, but precisely *because* what she encountered was beyond her expectations. "It never ceases to be sad," she says, but something in her has "turned around." Witnessing both the suffering of the residents and the manner of being of her fellow hospice caregivers had enlarged her perspective, drawing her to return again and again each week.

Martha, Wayne, and Joanne volunteered in quite different contexts—a residential hospice serving many patients with AIDS, a prison infirmary, an Alzheimer's wing of a nursing home. Yet all had discovered through hospice caregiving that they were capable of being a loving presence in the face of suffering. Crucial for each of them in "turning around" and stretching themselves into this work was a positive social environment that drew them back to the hospice bedside and supported them in expanding their understanding of their own capacities.

CONTEMPLATION
A Life Well Lived

No one takes on a volunteer role or any other activity because they want to end the day in tears. Yet I invite you to pause for a moment and consider: Is there any activity worth our sustained engagement that will not, at some point, evoke sadness or other uncomfortable emotions? There are many messages in the wider culture about having fun and enjoying the good life. But when and where in your life do you find the deepest meaning and sense of joy? Based on your own experience, what have you found that makes for a life well lived?

Take a few minutes to sit quietly with these questions and just observe what arises in the form of memories or thoughts that might be running through your mind or emotional reactions or sensations you may be experiencing in your body. There are no right answers here, so just observe with a nonjudgmental awareness what is alive for you in this moment.

If you find it helpful, you might jot down a few notes now or come back to these questions later as an inspiration for journaling or quiet contemplation. Perhaps these questions might also inspire conversation with members of your family, friends, or colleagues.

Returning the Gift of Care

Among those I interviewed for this book, it was relatively uncommon for individuals to have come to hospice volunteering through the recommendation of a friend or acquaintance, as had Martha. The exception was at the prison, where many volunteers in the hospice program came through the recommendation of the chaplain—even though most, like Wayne, had no prior experience as caregivers. I met a few volunteers like Joanne who were simply looking for an opportunity to volunteer and came across a call for hospice volunteers either through the internet or through printed advertisements in newspapers or church bulletins. But the majority of those I interviewed specifically sought out hospice volunteering, and typically that draw was due in part to a death or other loss they had experienced.

Many come to hospice volunteering as a natural human response to repay kindness. When someone we love is dying, even the smallest gesture of kindness can be transformative. Zemira, a forty-seven-year-old home-health aide, had been volunteering for hospice for just under a year when she and I met. She explained how, about four years earlier, her mother had died on hospice care, and that she had been the primary caregiver for her mother for the last six months of her life. Zemira said that caring for her mother had been one of the most transformative experiences in her life. She felt deep gratitude for a specific hospice nurse who responded to her and her mother in a way that allowed Zemira to experience a sense of calm in what had become for her a "crisis situation." Things started getting difficult for

Zemira as her mother's pain, nausea, and confusion increased, so late one night she called the hospice and spoke with the nurse.

> I'm not sure what I was looking for when I called, but she was in pain, it was very scary, she was throwing up, it was just very scary. And instead of saying something like, you know, "take two of this, and do this," she read me this poem about forgiveness, forgiveness of ourselves, that you know we do the best we can, forgiving others for all of the things that are going on with them. And I remember so distinctly that at that time, the minute she said that, all of my anxiety and everything that was going on just sort of, it melted, it just lifted. . . . I was able to go back into the room, and be with my mother and be present with her with *all* of the other stuff that was going on.

Zemira was a waitress at the time of this encounter. After her mother's death, she began working as a home-health aide, dedicating her life to compassionately caring for others through her employment and through volunteering for hospice. She told me that she had come to think of caring for someone who is dying as "some of the most powerful, greatest work that a person can do." Not everyone experiences the depth of transformation Zemira described in her life, although her gratitude for the compassionate care that the hospice offered and the desire to give back is a common experience drawing many to volunteer for hospice.

Another woman I interviewed, Paula, age sixty-four, referred to hospice workers as "angels from heaven" during her experience caring for her mother as she died of lung cancer. Paula had felt overwhelmed with gratitude not only for how they helped her mother but also for how they helped her and her sister during their mother's dying process and during their bereavement.

A Mormon with a deep faith, Paula believed that after her mother died, she was directing her to volunteer for hospice. She described how her mother came to her in dreams. She recounted a particular dream that pointed to a more mystical link between her mother and her draw to hospice volunteering.

I had tried to get a GED test and I passed all four tests, but I couldn't pass the math. And I took it again, and I took it again, and I took it again, and then finally I gave up. And in this dream, my mom came to me and had a report card, and said "Sit down, sit down, I want to show you this, I brought you something, and it's important." And I looked and it had all of the classes I took, and next to it there was a line for a grade, and there were no grades, but down underneath the math, it had all of the classes that I took and tested. It had "Life," and on the line next to it, it had a big A. So when I got up, you know, when I woke up that day, I thought, "Oh wow, I guess this is telling me don't sweat the small stuff, there's more important things in life."

The next day Paula picked up the newspaper. "There was an ad that just stood out, brighter than life," she recounted, "and it said 'Hospice volunteers, we're looking for hospice volunteers.'" Sensing her mother communicating with her, she called the hospice and signed up for the next training class, which began with the volunteer coordinator asking, "What is hospice?" Paula's first thought was that "hospice was all about death." But the volunteer coordinator explained, "Hospice is about *life*, the remaining part of someone's life that they have left, and that they can still keep their dignity." Paula was astounded. "I just went, whoa, *life*, that fits in with the dream," she told me. "My mother has been guiding me to this, and I just knew I was supposed to be there."

Our capacity to care is often unlocked through confrontations with death, grief, and suffering in our own life. When we care for a dying loved one, our suffering as the caregiver may at times be greater than the suffering of the one in our care. In these moments, even the smallest gesture of kindness can be quite healing. Family caregivers often wish to volunteer for hospice after their loved one dies to extend the same loving support they received from hospice to others now facing similar situations. Such reciprocity that extends kindness beyond the original giver and recipient of a gift has long been a foundation of human society. In this way, our grief and compassionate intentions are central to the very fabric of what makes us human. The next chapter explores additional ways grief can become a pathway to compassionate care, and how extending compassion to those who are dying can, in turn, be integral to exploring and healing our own suffering.

4

Transforming Our Grief
through Compassionate Care

*There were some dreams in which she would appear to me very happy
and dancing and turquoise jewels in her neck and ears and around
her head, and I think in that dream and all the feelings that came
with that, she was giving me so much permission to enjoy life.*

Carmine, hospice volunteer

CARMINE WAS TWENTY-SEVEN YEARS OLD when she arrived in
the United States in 1979, and she felt inspired by the opportunities that
became available to her to learn a second language and complete her
schooling. She earned a certification as a massage therapist and then a degree
in nursing, but her joy in learning was also marked by sadness. Having grown
up in a poor, rural community in Nicaragua, she only had a sixth-grade
education before coming to the United States, and she described how not
having access to education was in some ways "more painful than other
things about poverty." The sadness she felt was in realizing more fully the
education that had been missing in her childhood, and which was still
unavailable to her family back in Nicaragua. Most significant for Carmine
was "the luxury to look inward" and to bring an energy of kindness toward
the many painful experiences that had shaped her and her family's lives. She
was on a path of transforming the grief and trauma of her life, and in time,
caring at the hospice bedside would become integral to that journey.

Carmine was fifty-two years old when she and I first met in San Francisco. At the time, she had been volunteering for hospice for four years. She was drawn to hospice after caring for her mother-in-law at the end of her life. "I was ready to do something like that," she said of the experience, "and I didn't know why I hadn't realized that before." She described having a readiness to attend to the needs of those who are sick and dying, because in the community where she grew up, many people died at home, and even as a young child, she would help in one way or another when a family member or neighbor was dying.

Many of Carmine's childhood experiences with death and caregiving were traumatic due to the political violence in Nicaragua in the 1960s and 1970s and the lack of access to basic medical care in her community. Her first encounter with death was the murder of her fifteen-year-old cousin. Carmine was about six or seven years old at the time. "I don't remember feelings, I don't remember my thoughts," she told me. "I just remember being awakened and taken with my mom and going and I remember the picture of her." She described being led through tunnels and into a dark room lit only by candles, seeing her cousin lying in a white dress with blood still oozing from the place in her neck where she had been shot. In recounting these memories, Carmine wondered if her cousin may have still been alive. No doctors were there attending to her dying relative.

These memories of her cousin's death were traumatic for Carmine, but "the greatest pain," she said, was in losing her little brother, Enrique. She was eighteen years old at the time, and though she knew that death was a fact of life, she resented that Enrique died. "Some seed sort of got planted because in my opinion and maybe in the opinion of many others, certain deaths were kind of what could be called like 'premature' because they were kids that were dying because of lack of medical attention." In her brother's case, simple antibiotics and hydration likely could have saved his life, but neither the resources nor the medical knowledge was there.

I first interviewed Carmine in 2004 and then again in 2012. Over the course of that time she had come to realize that healing the traumatic losses from her childhood was an "unconscious motivation" for becoming involved in hospice. Volunteering for hospice was "a way of allowing more openness, more ability to open to feelings of loss" in her life. Part of her healing came through caring for patients who, like her, were "transplants from other countries" separated from members of their own families. She felt a deep spiritual healing in her first year at the hospice through caring for an elderly man from El Salvador. Carmine understood that care for this man was also care for members of his family back in El Salvador who were not able to be with him as he was dying—a painful situation she understood quite well. "In being present to him, I'm doing it for a lot of people," she told me. And through the privilege of offering such care, she experienced the flowering of a seed that had been planted in her childhood, a way of honoring her cousin, little brother, and other members of her family, including her mother who died after Carmine had immigrated to the United States.

Two years after she started volunteering for hospice, Carmine traveled with her husband to Nicaragua to visit the cemetery where her mother and other family members had been buried. This was the first time she had been back to Nicaragua since immigrating to the United States over two and a half decades earlier. At the cemetery, she felt her mother's presence guiding and supporting her in coming "face-to-face" with all the grief and trauma she had been carrying in her life. "We were having a problem finding the place where my little brother had been buried," she explained, "and I found that I was giving up, but then I had my hands on the cross of where he was buried and we hadn't seen it, and it was as if my mother was there guiding for that." Her mother's healing presence also came to her in dreams. In some, she saw her mother watching over her before ascending and gradually disappearing in the clouds. In others, "she would appear to me very happy and dancing and turquoise jewels in her neck and ears and around her head." In these ways, Carmine felt her mother blessing her life, and offering her permission to "go on and have my life with all the pains and also the joy and happiness that I can touch and experience." For Carmine, volunteering for hospice nourished this "inner movement" of connecting with her mother and watered compassionate seeds planted in her childhood. "All the way through my life is going to be an opportunity of service and honoring," she said.

As I listened to Carmine speak about how the death of her little brother had planted a seed that would later flourish in her care at the hospice bedside, I heard a more universal story being told—one that is also expressed in my own life, in the life of Cicely Saunders, and in the lives of many others I interviewed. When we know the pain of trauma, tragic loss, or injustice, our natural inclination is toward healing, to make right in some way what has been fractured by grief. In this way, our care can be a legacy to our grief, a path for continuing a bond with someone we hold dear.

Making Things Right

Susan had been volunteering at a hospice in upstate New York for seven years. She explained that she became involved in part because of a sense of guilt she had carried for many decades after having turned away from her father as he lay dying. "I was in my twenties when he was near death," she recounted. "I *ran* from the situation, and I think I never have forgiven myself for that, and I mean, it just *scared* me because, I mean, death was on him, and I remember I just couldn't wait to get out of the room—I just couldn't handle it. I just turned the other way and ran." Susan sensed her father had forgiven her, although she felt a draw to somehow make right what she was unable to do for him years ago by helping others who were dying in similarly lonely situations. She specifically requested to be sent into hospitals as opposed to visiting hospice patients in their own homes, where there is typically greater social support from the family.

Similarly, Christina was volunteering for a hospice in Berlin, Germany, and she explained how her motivation for becoming involved was connected with an experience in her early twenties when her grandmother died. "I just didn't have the ability, I couldn't do it," she said. "Everything just made me so anxious, and I think I really did just turn my back on her." Christina deeply regretted having abandoned her grandmother at the end of her life, but rather than becoming paralyzed by guilt or blindly driven by it, she consciously drew on the dark emotions surrounding her grandmother's lonely dying as a well of inspiration to "somehow make things right by helping other people who are dying."

About a year after his mother died, Manuel started volunteering for a hospice in Los Angeles that provided care for residents on an Alzheimer's wing of a nursing home. His continuing bond with his mother, who also suffered from Alzheimer's, became for him a powerful source of compassion for others who struggle as he did to care for a dying parent under less-than-ideal conditions. Manuel carried a sense of guilt for how he had been unable to care for his mother as he had wanted to and felt he should have. He and his wife had been caring for his mother in their home for several years, but when she fell and broke her hip, her doctor told him that his mother would need around-the-clock care. Throughout the interview, Manuel kept coming back to the current situation for many Hispanic families living in the United States, where the traditional pattern of adult children caring for elderly parents at home was becoming less and less a reality. Although he understood the caregiving challenges facing Hispanic-American families, including his own, his decision to put his mother in a nursing home left him with tremendous guilt. "No matter how well they treat you, you're not with your family anymore," he explained.

Manuel sensed that the loneliness of being in the nursing home precipitated his mother's quick decline, and his heart went out to others who had to make the rough decision he and his wife did. His sense of guilt for not being able to be there for his mother as he had wanted to became a bridge connecting him to others in their grief and suffering. He expressed how volunteering in memory of his mother kept him from "drowning in this emotional sea of suffering" that pervades the Alzheimer's unit. Manuel's ongoing grief was both the motivation to reach out to others and a source of strength allowing him to put his good intentions into action, even in the face of realities that were difficult to witness.

Others spoke of entering hospice work as a path toward "making things right," not in relation to a personal sense of guilt but through spiritually integrating traumatic losses from the distant past into conscious, embodied awareness. Frau Lang, a German woman in her fifties, explained how her mother had collapsed and died suddenly and unexpectedly in her apartment. Not long thereafter, Frau Lang sank into a depression in which she ruminated on the possibility that her mother did not die a natural death.

She indicated that this was her greatest fear. The fear seemed to have deeper roots in her family history and uncovering them was part of what ultimately brought her to hospice work.

Between 1939 and 1945 the Nazis killed roughly 200,000 to 250,000 institutionalized mentally or physically disabled people through medical experiments, lethal injections, gassing and starvation.[1] After her mother died, Frau Lang learned from a friend of the family that her grandmother had been murdered in the Nazi "euthanasia" program. "This was never mentioned in my family," she told me. "It was taboo." Her eyes teared up as she recounted how she had contacted the Federal Archives to request her grandmother's medical files. They indicated that she had been "all but starved to death" and then succumbed to an "artificially induced pneumonia." It was symbolic for her that she signed up for the training course at the hospice on the same day she received her grandmother's files and was able to verify "a topic that had always silently reverberated in the background."[2] After learning what the Nazis had done to her grandmother, Frau Lang was drawn to accompany others in their final moments of life to offer them a different kind of send-off. In her words, she entered hospice work as a spiritual path for "making right" the murder of her grandmother.

Others have given of themselves to make right the neglect or mistreatment of dying people because of stigmatized conditions such as AIDS. Jimmy had been in prison for nearly three decades when I interviewed him. He recounted that in the late 1980s several men were dying from AIDS, "and they didn't know what to do with it, so they *isolated* them." Sick inmates were kept in two dorms at the prison that Jimmy described as being "like a dungeon." According to Jimmy, inmates were left to die alone in their cells because the nursing staff was terrified that if they touched them, they might contract AIDS. Even without such fears, he explained, all prisoners back then were basically treated like "scumbags." Jimmy witnessed how, in some cases, care was explicitly denied to particular inmates because of the stigma of their crime. He described, for example, how a man two cells down from him was left on the floor "laying in his own puke and blood for two days because of *his kind*—he shot a cop, and they didn't like that." Jimmy held the conviction that nobody should be treated that way. He explained how he and another prisoner, Mike, who also became involved in the hospice program due to these experiences, would ask the guards to let them into the cells of these dying men to help clean them up and comfort them in any way they could. Some officers who "had a little bit of compassion" would let them in to help, but others would not, because "whether he was suffering or whatever, that was their punishment, part of their punishment, that was the way they looked at it. So that's kind of where I got involved in hospice."

Discovering Our Capacity to Care

We often don't know what we are capable of until we are put to the test. This dynamic is especially the case when someone we love is dying. Given the fear and aversion to death in the wider society, many of us go through life just assuming that it would be too difficult or frightening for us to care for a dying person. We might imagine it would be too stressful or depressing to watch someone we love suffer and wither away. But often we discover that we do have the confidence to care for someone at the end of life and experience deep meaning in doing so.

Richard was the son of a Presbyterian minister, and he explained how different experiences in his life had led him to think a lot about death and dying. There had been several deaths in his immediate family and circle of friends over the years, and for Richard, "each encounter with death or dying in my life stands out as an important experience." A turning point for Richard came when his older brother lay dying of AIDS-related complications. Richard was thirty-five years old at the time. "I discovered just how important it was to me to be there with him," he said, and also "how difficult it was for other members of my family who loved him just as much, to be with him." In caring for his dying brother, Richard found that he had a spiritual draw to be present with others at the end of life as well as a sense of confidence in his capacity to do so with ease. After his brother died, he turned to hospice volunteering, first in Boston, where he was living at the time, and then in California after he moved out west.

Richard had been volunteering for hospice for eight years when he and I met, and he mused at how people are often "very impressed with someone who works in hospice," especially when that person is a man. When a member of the family is dying, it is typically women—wives and adult daughters—who take on the bedside care. But for Richard, caring for those who are dying was just a normal part of his life, the way coaching a Little League team or volunteering at a soup kitchen might be for others. More and more men are discovering that end-of-life caregiving is something they can do and want to do. Today, about one in five hospice volunteers are men.

One reason more women volunteer for hospice than men is that wives tend to outlive their husbands. Carol was forty-eight years old when her husband died of leukemia, and a year later she began volunteering for hospice. She was sixty-three at the time I interviewed her, and she had been volunteering for hospice off and on for the fourteen years. About seven years after her husband died, she took a break from hospice volunteering to care for her mother as she was dying. She discovered that she was able to care for her mother in a way that her siblings could not.

"They distanced themselves," she said. "They were in her room, but they were talking all about everything else—construction work or sports or— and I would watch them and I was like, 'Don't you see, our mother is dying, she's not going to be here!' And they weren't able to focus on her." Through caring for her husband, Carol had developed an inner strength that allowed her to "get close to death." As she put it, "You're not afraid to be real." What allows Carol to abide in the midst of suffering is a spiritual sensibility that draws her to care for those who are dying even in the face of her own fears. As she explained, through attending to her dying husband, she was opened to a mystery: "In somebody's deep pain, there can be a shining light going through. You know those feelings come up, like 'I wanna run out of the room,' but you don't, because there's something going on here, *beyond* beyond—it calls you there, to be here."

Samantha likewise lost her husband to cancer, and she described how caring for him up until his last breath gave her a "gift" that her friends simply could not understand—an irresistible draw to accompany others at the end of life and the capacity to experience joy in those encounters: "When I first started coming [to the hospice], right after my husband died, they said, 'You'd have to be crazy, you just spent six months with somebody day in and day out who was very close to you. Why would you want to throw yourself into that? Go out and have fun. Do something that's going to make you happy.'" But, she explained, caring for hospice patients *is* enjoyable for her and gives her a sense of vibrancy, which she described with a bit of humor: "My motto is to hang out with the nearly dead and fully alive because they are the true people. They're not living on automatic."

I have met many individuals like Samantha who experience joy in end-of-life caregiving, not as a special or charitable activity they go out of their way to do but as a practice integral to their lives. Perhaps more than anyone I interviewed, Marlena embodied such joy. It was a sunny morning in May when I met her, and from her living room window you could see a small Gothic-style church at the end of her street along the Hudson River. "This is my little church over there, isn't it sweet?" she said. Marlena had been involved in her church for more than fifty years, and she joked that the church "belonged" to her, pointing to its significance as the organizing element of her social life and as a symbol for her deep faith in God. But the central motif in the narrative she told about her life came from the river. "I've always been a caregiver," she explained, waving her hand across the front of her chest to illustrate how caring for others has "flowed" through her life since her childhood. At age seventy-three, she reflected back, "Maybe God put me here for that reason. I do think that sometimes, that's okay, okay by me."

As the oldest of seven children, with an eight-year gap between her and the next oldest sister, Marlena grew up caring for her younger siblings. She was eighteen years old when her father died, and that same year she helped deliver her youngest brother. She married young, and then her first husband died of cancer, leaving her a thirty-four-year-old widow with three young children. After her husband's death, she began a career as a private duty nurse and then took two years off in the late 1970s to care for her mother full time in her own home after her mother had become ill from cancer. After her mother's death, she continued working as a private duty nurse, and then two years later she began volunteering for hospice when the first hospice opened in her area. Twenty-one years later, she was still volunteering at the same hospice. Throughout that time, she had also cared for dying family members and friends, including her second husband, whom she cared for full time in their home before he died of cancer. Marlena explained that what brought her to hospice was the focus on the needs of the family and the caregiver, which she found were often greater than the needs of the patient.

The death of her father, her first husband, and her mother were important turning points in Marlena's life, and she spoke of these "little twists" in her life as formative experiences through which she developed a deep understanding of the needs of dying people and their family members. For Marlena, grief had not been a tragic imposition on her life but was a doorway to developing wisdom and compassion.

> I can't think of anything to complain about, I mean anything that hasn't been a good part of my life. Cause I always felt my life has been kind of interrupted at points, you know, I lost my first husband, I was a widow, nine years, then I remarried—and then *he* got sick and, you know, so my life has been not straight through like some people, marry John and away they go and he gets pensioned and they ride off happily ever after. And I think maybe that's made me a better volunteer because I've had a lot of things in life that have been hurting. I think that that helps. You gotta understand other people's hurt, don't you?

Marlena radiated joy as she spoke of her life and work with hospice, and her sense of gratitude included the many experiences that had been quite painful. "You just seem to get wiser and more patient," she said. "*I* seem to find that." She spoke of her varied experiences caring for others, often occasioned by the illness and death of someone in her family, as the means through which she had become "an expert" in the kind of holistic care hospice offers. The expertise Marlena refers to is not the hands-on skills of nursing but the capacity to see realities others cannot and to find meaning and abide calmly in situations others try to avoid.

CONTEMPLATION
Who Would You Be without Your Grief?

Grief can disrupt our lives, and at times, we may suffer the seemingly unbearable weight of loss and the wish for our grief to end. But pause for a moment and consider this question: "Who would you be without your grief?"

I often ask this question when I give workshops and talks on caregiving, and I typically get responses such as this: "Without my grief, I would be a much less interesting person." We often think of grief in terms of loss, but we can turn this around and ask, "What part of yourself would you lose without your grief?"

I'm not talking about glossing over or sugarcoating the pain of grief but of contemplating who you have become through the pain. Has the experience of grief given you a sense of purpose and the inspiration to further loving care in the world? Has the pain of loss opened in you a creative and compassionate spirit, a willingness to explore who you may become in and through your grief?

Take a few minutes to sit quietly and allow yourself to register any thoughts that might be running through your mind or any emotional reactions or sensations you may be experiencing in your body in response to these questions and to the stories you have heard in this chapter. There are no right answers here, so just observe in this moment what feels true to your own experience.

If you find it helpful, you might jot down a few notes now or come back to these questions later as an inspiration for journaling or quiet contemplation. Perhaps these questions might also inspire conversation with family members, friends, or colleagues.

Exploring and Learning from Caregiving and Grief

Hearing of the many losses Marlena has experienced, some readers might feel sorry for her or feel fortunate not to have had to go through what she has experienced. Certainly no one would wish to be widowed with three young children at the age of thirty-four. But is it really so unfortunate to know grief, to be familiar with one of the most basic and unavoidable parameters of the human condition?

This question was central to the narrative that Kerstin, another woman I interviewed, offered in explaining what drew her to hospice care. Kerstin had been volunteering for three years at a residential hospice in Berlin when I met with her in her home in one of the wealthier parts of the city. As a forty-two-year-old psychotherapist in private practice, she explained that caring for dying people is important work that receives too little attention in German society. But she was unapologetic that, first and foremost, her draw to volunteer for hospice was to learn about matters she had not yet experienced in her own life. "I've had the good fortune to this point in my life," she explained, "to have never lost someone close to me—parents, siblings, children. I've never been emotionally undone by grief. And so, I thought, okay, it makes sense, even if you can't really get around the grief, but to try to take something in before you get hit so close to home, so you have some sense of what it's like for someone at the end of life, what it's like for the family members, so it's not completely uncharted territory when it does come your way."

In speaking about her draw to hospice work, Kerstin, like many hospice volunteers, used the metaphor of *journeying*—entering "uncharted territory"—to express how caring for dying people was integral to her emotional and spiritual becoming. Unlike Marlena, however, who knew grief and suffering intimately and who was brought to hospice work out of a sense of wholeness "flowing" through her life, Kerstin came to hospice volunteering precisely because death, dying, and grief were foreign to her—"all Greek to me," as she put it. In a sense, her decision to volunteer for hospice was similar to expectant couples who take birthing classes rather than waiting until the contractions start before beginning to reflect on the conditions under which they would like to deliver their baby.

Michael, a sixty-four-year-old soft-spoken man, likewise came to hospice volunteering to explore uncharted territory, although the circumstances of his life were different from Kerstin's. Michael got involved in hospice several years after his father died. He told me that it was the lifelong silence in his family around his father's chronic illness and suffering that had ultimately brought him to hospice caregiving. "I come from a family that was militantly nonreligious and nonspiritual," he explained. "Both my parents were Jewish by birth and both explicitly left that because they did not like it, so my brothers and I were raised with no spiritual background at all, and I was feeling like I really missed something." His father had had multiple sclerosis for several decades. "We all lived with it," he said, but his parents "never talked about it, about the illness and what it meant to them and the family." Michael referred to the weight of that silence as being "like a stone in my heart." He was drawn to volunteer for hospice with the hope that "maybe hospice work would be something that would help me come to terms with my own parents' attitudes about death and dying and their health." A decade later, he continues to volunteer for hospice twice per week and has found hospice work a profound avenue for offering loving attention to others and deepening his own sense of calm and quiet in his life.

David was dying of cancer when I interviewed him, and he too had entered hospice work to chart new territory in his life. There was something poignant in my asking him what had drawn him to hospice eight years earlier, as he now stood at the threshold of receiving care at the residential hospice where he had offered bedside care for so many years.

David began volunteering for hospice when his dearest friends asked him to be the godparent to their children. He said, "I looked at the covenant and I wanted to know how I could live into that covenant, *more completely*, and be an example for them. [Caregiving was] total territory that I really hadn't had time for, because I'd been concentrating so much on my work." He told me that he had accomplished other goals he'd set for himself, especially as a businessman. But as a devout Christian, he felt an emotional and spiritual void from a lifetime so narrowly focused on employment. It left him feeling unprepared for caring for his godchildren as he wanted to and believed he could. He began volunteering for hospice with the intention to cultivate the caring capacities he would need as a godparent. After years of caring for dying people, David referred to hospice as his "private vocation, the second vocation in [his] life." It was the means by which he had learned how to care for others and experience sacredness in human relationships.

This chapter has examined three connections between grief and contemplative caregiving. We grieve in response to loss, yet when our grief brings us to care, we have the opportunity to:

- find healing
- develop confidence in our readiness to care
- explore and learn from our experience

In these ways, grief is not a passive response to what has been done to us but rather a generative act that can transform even the darkest energies that touch our lives.

Grief can be the doorway to compassion. It can focus our attention, shake us out of routine ways of seeing ourselves, and invite us to discover and hone caring capacities. We can emerge from the crucible of grief with the capacity to wonder more deeply about impermanence, mortality, and our connection with others. This process of expanding the concerns and capacities of the self resonates with research showing that grappling with traumatic losses can change one's priorities in life, deepen confidence in one's caring capacities, and create a willingness to explore new ways of being.[3] Painful experiences can be made fruitful in our lives when the conditions are present that allow us to turn toward those experiences and be ripened by them. As the diverse pathways through grief to hospice volunteering indicate, the bedside of those who are dying is a powerful space for contemplatively engaging grief and suffering integral to a path of compassionate service and a life well lived. Part 3 continues our inquiry into such possibilities through investigating how the context of hospice volunteering supports caregivers in journeying with uncertainty, flexibly adapting expectations to meet the needs of those in their care and learning from their own emotional reactions and judgments that arise in the course of accompanying others at the end of life.

PART THREE

Caring as a Practice of Mindfulness

When you're using the toilet, let that be the most important thing in your life. . . . Each act is a rite, a ceremony. Raising a cup of tea to your mouth is a rite. Does the word "rite" seem too solemn? I use that word to jolt you into the realization of the life-and-death matter of awareness.
Thich Nhat Hanh, *The Miracle of Mindfulness*

ONE OF THE most important figures in popularizing the practice of mindfulness in the West has been the Vietnamese Zen master, poet, and peace activist Thich Nhat Hanh. Looking at the titles of some of his books—*The Miracle of Mindfulness, Being Peace, Present Moment Wonderful Moment*—one might get the impression that mindfulness practice is about feeling peaceful, calm, and healthy. Thich Nhat Hanh acknowledges that mindfulness meditation can be beneficial to one's health and well-being. Yet he also writes that these benefits "cannot be considered as ends in themselves" but rather "are only the by-products of the realization of mindfulness."[1] So if it's not getting blissed out, what exactly is mindfulness? And how might caregiving be an ideal context for engaging in such a practice?

Mindfulness meditation practices that have become popular today come from Buddhism, a religion that began in India over 2,500 years ago and that has since spread and been adapted to other cultural contexts throughout Asia and more recently in the West. Yet in contemporary Western societies, mindfulness is typically presented as a secular practice grounded in the language of modern psychology and justified in terms of scientific research. As it has been applied in health care and other sectors of society, mindfulness is typically described as "non-judgmental, present-centered awareness in which each thought, feeling, or sensation that arises in the attentional field is acknowledged and accepted as it is."[2] Given this shift in framing, some have questioned whether current understandings and applications of mindfulness are consistent with the ethical foundation and conceptual underpinnings of authentic Buddhist teachings.

There is validity in this critique. Buddhist mindfulness practices were not originally intended to be in the service of individual improvement but rather in that of spiritual liberation. They were not supposed to soothe the ego or bolster the self but promote a more selfless way of being in the world—a way thought to match the impermanent and interdependent characteristics that Buddhists take as intrinsic to all life and being. Likewise, mindfulness practices were understood to be fundamentally relational. In popular culture today, mindfulness is typically presented as a solo endeavor, most often with the image of a serene individual (usually a white woman) sitting alone on a meditation cushion. Historically, mindfulness has been practiced in communities and, in particular, in the context of a student-teacher relationship through which the teacher serves as a mirror reflecting where the student is clinging to ideas or stuck in harmful patterns. The teacher encourages the student to see her true nature as open and spacious— not just on the meditation cushion but in all circumstances of life. The American Zen master Robert Aitken writes that a trusting relationship with a teacher is of utmost importance to avoid mindfulness becoming "only a sterile practice in concentration, with no movement toward realization and beyond."[3] For a glimpse of what Aitken means by realization, consider the text inscribed on the *han*, a wooden instrument used in most Zen temples and monasteries to call practitioners to the meditation hall: "Great is the matter of birth and death. All is impermanent, quickly passing. Awake! Awake! Don't waste this life."

In contrast to the sense of urgency in the Buddhist call to awaken, the secular mindfulness movement often appears rather superficial—more a kind of sophisticated self-soothing than a practice with the power to transform our lives and societies. That said, I do not think that Buddhist monasteries or temples are the only places where the transformative power of mindfulness is being practiced. The bedside of a dying person is similarly a context for waking up to what Thich Nhat Hanh calls "the life-and-death matter of awareness."[4] In this sacred space of human encounter, there is also a kind of teacher-student relationship; many hospice caregivers will tell you that dying people have been their greatest teachers. Such a dynamic has certainly been the case for me. Those who have allowed me to accompany them in their final days and weeks have supported me in learning how to let go of preconceived ideas about my role. They have given me the chance to study how to be with another without being driven by emotional or physical reactions based on past experiences or personal likes and dislikes.

Mindfulness meditation can serve as a powerful complement to caring for those at the end of life and at any point in life. At times we may feel irritated, fearful, or impatient in the course of caregiving, and practices that calm and focus the mind can help put a gap between having a thought or feeling and reacting to it in a way that would work against our intention to care. Meditations that focus attention on the breath are one method for developing such nonjudgmental, present-centered awareness. When a thought or feeling arises, we can simply label it as thinking, let it go, and then return the attention back to the breath. Developing the capacity to witness what goes on in our mind without being driven by all the background chatter is a crucial capacity for caregivers.

But caring for another requires not only awareness of what's going on inside us but also insight into what's going on around us, and most important, what the needs and wishes are of those in our care. In this regard, contemplative caregiving can also serve as a powerful complement to mindfulness meditation. For both Buddhists and those practicing secular mindfulness, many people, especially after they've established a regular practice for several years, hit a point where they begin to wonder if their meditation is continuing to deepen and to bear fruit off the cushion. This may be a sign that a more dynamic context for one's practice would be a welcome challenge. If you have learned to be aware of typical sounds that occur during meditation (birds singing, the hum of an air conditioner turning on and off, family members or neighbors moving around or talking), can you also be aware of and accept the much more unexpected occurrences common to end-of-life care—family members arguing in front of their dying loved one or a patient asking questions: "Am I going to die?" "Why me?" "What does the spirit of my grandmother expect of me?" For those of us who enjoy the fragrance of burning incense during meditation and have perhaps extended our mindfulness of smells to passing unpleasant scents of trash or body odor, can we affirm the deeper commitment to stay present amid the smells of food, urine, and chemicals in a nursing home or while helping to clean someone who is dying?

Hospice volunteers bring to the bedside an intention to care and a willingness to attune to the needs of others and sometimes also a romanticized view of what it will be like to accompany others at the end of life. When our expectations are not met, we may hold more tightly to the way we wish things were, creating a mismatch between our compassionate intentions and the skillfulness of our actions. The alternative is to release our expectations and journey with the inevitable uncertainties of dying, grieving, and caregiving. Chapter 5, "Flexible Mind, Caring Mind," illustrates how the ethical framework of hospice care provides an ideal context for practicing such mindfulness. The foundational view of hospice care is that the wishes of the dying person and her family members, not our own, guide our care. As caregivers, we try to listen without judgment as we compassionately witness this human journey toward the threshold of life and death. As with formal meditation practice, contemplative caregiving can be a path for realizing the truth of impermanence, nonduality, and the interconnectedness of life, all of which can be experienced firsthand as we journey with others on a path that we too will one day travel.

Mindfulness practice can transform our lives, and for transformative learning to take place, there must be discomfort as ideas and beliefs central to our understanding of self and others are called into question. Perhaps the most important support for volunteers in abiding with the discomfort and uncertainties that arise at the hospice bedside is the atmosphere of trust extended to them by dying people and their family members. Chapter 6, "The Reciprocity of Care," examines the importance of such trust. Rather than developing set routines, trying to always be cheery, or setting rigid parameters of how to care, the most powerful step a caregiver can take is often the simple act of recalling that one has been given a gift of welcome to be with a person in their sacred journey toward death.

5

Flexible Mind, Caring Mind

"IN THE BEGINNER'S MIND there are many possibilities, but in the expert's there are few." This pithy teaching from Shunryu Suzuki's *Zen Mind, Beginner's Mind* offers a powerful reminder of the need for flexibility and receptivity in compassionate care.[1] Many hospice caregivers will tell you that their patients have been their greatest teachers. Oftentimes encounters with one's first patient stand out as particularly powerful teaching moments. On that day in 1993 when I first visited Jerome, he invited me to have lunch with him, so we went into his kitchen and prepared turkey and avocado sandwiches. "Look at that avocado smiling at me," Jerome mused between bites. I looked over, and it was true. There it was, a joyful smile peeking out from between two slices of bread, there to be seen by all with eyes of wonder. And there I was, learning to see and enjoy the beauty of what I would have likely missed in another context—gratitude for the kindness of avocados.

I visited Jerome every week for the last three months of his life. On most of my visits, we were alone in his apartment. In the final weeks of his life, friends would come by to see him, and it seemed many of these visitors were quite anxious. Many young men were dying, and the community was gripped by grief and terror as it witnessed so many loved ones suffer this stigmatized death, not knowing whom it would take next. Jerome knew he was an object of fear. And I understood that the most essential care I could offer was to embody as best I could a nonanxious presence. For the most part, I felt calm when I was with him. As a straight man stepping into the gay community in this limited role as hospice caregiver, I didn't have the same fears or depth of grief as Jerome's other visitors. But one day I had my turn.

During one of my afternoon visits, a hospice aide came by to check in on Jerome and give him a shave. At this point, Jerome was spending most of his time in a hospice bed set up in the living room, and so the aide just inclined the head of the bed and got to work. She was quite efficient. She managed to shave Jerome without exchanging a word aside from the initial hello and explanation of who she was and what she came to do. Sitting in the chair in front of the bed, I just watched quietly while she lathered Jerome's face and took care of business. After she left, Jerome and I picked up our conversation where we had left off. And then he asked if I would massage his shoulders. He indicated that there was some lotion in the drawer of the end table at the head of the bed, so I walked around behind him, opened the drawer, and took out the lotion. And then I saw it just sitting there on the top of the table—the box of disposable gloves.

In all the weeks I had been visiting Jerome, it had never crossed my mind to put on gloves. But there they were. The hospice aide had brought them, and I saw her put on a pair before shaving Jerome. So I assumed I should as well. I reached into the box and grabbed a pair. Jerome heard me putting on the first glove, and in a despondent voice he said, "You don't have to put those on." I stood there for a moment, unsure of what to do. And then I got scared. Jerome couldn't see my face, but I winced in embarrassment as I put on the other glove. I couldn't speak. I slowly put a dab of lotion on my gloved fingers and began massaging his shoulders. Jerome hung his head under the weight of my touch. I did as well, as I witnessed how my own fear and discomfort had placed a barrier between us.

Recently I completed a training program to become licensed as a certified nursing assistant (CNA). Early in the course, the instructor, a registered nurse, spoke of what she called "overgloving," the tendency among some nursing staff to wear gloves for any kind of patient contact. She asked students in the course, "How many of you have ever gotten a massage? Did the massage therapist wear gloves? How many of you have ever gotten your haircut? Did the person wear gloves?" The training program focused on the competencies and skills needed by CNAs to assist with the many tasks of basic nursing care, yet the instructor reminded us that human touch, more than anything else, is the most essential dimension of our work. "How unfortunate it would be," she continued, "if you went through the day checking vital signs without ever actually touching a human hand." She suggested how healing it can be for patients to receive a five-minute back rub in between all the medical contact, and then, as if speaking directly to me, she offered, "But sometimes it might be better to *not* give a massage than to give a massage with gloves on."

It was wise practice for the aide to wear gloves while shaving Jerome. But it would have been better for me not to massage Jerome that day than to do so as I did. My touch, in silence, was harmful for Jerome, feeding into the stigma that people with HIV/AIDS are untouchable. The problem wasn't that I wore gloves when I didn't need to, but that I couldn't relate directly to my own fear. Mindfulness isn't some magic state where we no longer feel fear, anxiety, or other uncomfortable emotions. It's about seeing with clarity what's going on inside us and around us *and* being able to respond in a manner consistent with our intentions.

My intention was to be a loving presence in Jerome's life for those few hours each week that we were together. But my compassion was limited by dualistic thinking. Jerome knew I didn't need to wear the gloves to massage his intact skin. My rational mind knew that as well, but I was too terrified not to. With beginner's mind, there would have been other possibilities that honored both my fear and Jerome's need for human touch. The essence of beginner's mind is the nondualistic flexibility to see such compassionate possibilities. How might my touch have felt, gloves and all, had I paused in mindfulness for a moment, come around to the front of Jerome's bed, and owned my fear rather than shrouding it in oppressive silence?

Releasing Expectations

Hospitality is not about what you do, it is about who you are becoming.
  Father Daniel Homan and Lonni Collins Pratt, *Radical Hospitality*

The dominant conception of a good death in the mainstream hospice movement includes dying people sharing deep feelings and engaging in life review. Allowing space for patients and their family members to talk about their experiences can support healing, yet some individuals come to hospice work with romanticized notions of what it will be like to listen to dying people reflect on their lives or to help family members work through the grief of losing a loved one. In many instances, the practice of mindfulness as a caregiver means letting go of such romantic expectations and simply being present to the situation as it is.

Many volunteers I interviewed indicated that they had to release their expectations of what it would be like to care for hospice patients, given the actual needs of those they encountered in the course of their work. Diane had been assigned to hospice patients at a nursing home in upstate New York. I interviewed her two years after she had completed the volunteer training, and then we spoke again five years later. By that time, she had stopped volunteering for hospice to care for one of her closest friends who had been diagnosed with colon cancer. At age sixty-six, she reflected back on her five years as a hospice volunteer. "I definitely was drawn into volunteering in part because I thought that life review was really important as a part of readying for dying," she said. "But," she continued, "one of the things I learned right away in nursing home contacts was that this didn't necessarily become my job, and in fact, was rarely my role. I did love hearing stories from patients, but probably half of the patients I met were quiet and may or may not have been aware [that I was there]." Listening in this context "involved being a lot more present and flexible about expectations." Diane expressed a deep reverence for the many people she encountered through her hospice work, including those who were unable to speak. "[I never] felt that the talking and friendly nature of some relationships was any better or more important than the time I spent next to a sleeping patient," she emphasized.

Amy, age forty-nine, volunteered at the same hospice in upstate New York. She and I had gone through the volunteer training session together about a year before I interviewed her, and she referenced a line directly out of our training manual: in order to do this work, "you have to have really big ears." She clarified, however, that for her, listening did not necessarily imply having a conversation. Instead, you listen "not just for the auditory things, you listen visually, you listen *subliminally*, and that openness I think is very important." She originally signed up for hospice with the intention to do home visits, but she ended up visiting patients in the hospital two mornings each week because that was where the volunteer coordinator indicated was the greatest need. Amy was assigned to patients in two hospitals, and in her first eleven months as a volunteer, she accompanied over one hundred individuals in the final days of their lives. She approached these encounters with openness and reverence: "I love the spirits of the people that I see and meet, no matter what state they're in."

Quite often volunteers find deep meaning in listening to the fears or life stories of dying people and their family members, yet, as Diane and Amy quickly discovered, at the very end many individuals simply do not have the energy to carry on conversations. And even when they are able, some patients or family members may not wish to talk about their experiences, and instead may request that volunteers run errands, watch TV, or do other mundane things. Tonya, a retired nurse, had been volunteering for hospice for eleven years, and two of those years were spent caring for a patient who confronted her with the limitations of her own preconceived notion of what a "peaceful death" should look like. Whereas Tonya had expected that they might occasionally engage in "quiet conversation," she described how the patient "didn't want to stop and even recognize the fact that she was dying, that her body was slowing down." At the time, Tonya thought that the woman was just "running from death." She found being in her presence "unsettling because it wasn't peaceful."

She wanted me to *push* her in her wheelchair to a meeting, push her here, push her to the aqua festival, push her to, you know, she wanted to go to the fairgrounds. Mind you now, she's probably fifty-something pounds and can't stand up on her own, and she wanted me to take her to the health food store, because she was going to eat right, you know. And it was just like, I wanted to be a little more realistic about things. I mean that's me putting my values on things and I would get a little frustrated with myself, in spite of the fact that I know I was being judgmental and not just *assisting* her. I mean I had to deal with me.

Caring for this woman over a period of two years repeatedly held up a mirror for Tonya to investigate why the experience made her uneasy, with a sense that she wasn't doing it right. In hindsight, she laughed about her journey with this woman, who just kept going and going, and then died in a way that reflected the preferences she had been expressing all along: "She went to a meeting, . . . laid down for a nap, and died." Tonya had experienced this woman as "demanding and controlling," yet in the end, she explained, "I had to deal with me." The caregiving experience came with a dawning realization: "I'm not as nice as I'd like to be." Despite her view that this woman was a "control freak about [dying], instead of just going with the flow," in the course of time, Tonya came to see that it was her own attempt to control how this woman lived her final months of life that was the source of her frustration.

Kerstin likewise explained that her understanding of what it means to accompany a patient had changed considerably over the course of her three years as a hospice volunteer. In her experience, what is most essential to accompanying others at the end of life is "leaving your expectations at the door." She came to the insight that "you never know upfront what your role really is. . . . It's not always so clear who actually wants me to be there. . . . It's more often the case that it's not the patient at all but the family who need support, so at first you really have to check things out and ask yourself, 'Who am I primarily here for?'" She laughed and added, "You show up, but maybe someone doesn't want you there at all. So again and again you have to find out what your place really is." Several volunteers spoke about the suffering of family members being even greater than that of the patient, a dynamic I have also witnessed on many occasions in my work as a hospice volunteer.

But the biggest change Kerstin described concerned her expectations about listening and spirituality. "When I started out, the spiritual component was for me personally the most important aspect, and I simply thought that when someone comes to the end of their life that they would automatically have the *need* to come to terms with the meaning of their life, to engage in life review, and perhaps also be engaged with spiritual questions like, 'What comes next?' 'Is this really the end, or does life continue?' 'Is death just a transition?'"

She had a good laugh at herself regarding the assumptions she had about the needs of dying people. Experience had taught her that "for many patients, what really matters are quite practical issues, just being there, offering support, but not necessarily regarding spiritual matters." She admitted that sometimes she felt a sense of disappointment that it was not possible to talk to this or that patient about deeper questions of meaning, but "that is my issue, and that has nothing to do with the patients I am caring for."

Witnessing Emotional Reactions and Judgments

Giving good care as a hospice volunteer does not require that one do anything in particular, such as engaging patients in life review or getting them to talk about their feelings. Instead, it requires that the caregiver herself becomes more flexible, open, and receptive to the actual needs of the other, beyond preconceived notions of good and bad, proper and improper, right and wrong. This insight ties in with a central principle of hospice care: what matters most are the wishes of hospice patients and their family members, and no matter what comes, volunteers and staff should not pass judgment on those entrusted to their care. In the everyday talk of hospice volunteering, this principle is referred to as "listening without judgment," and it is seen as central to the quality of care volunteers offer. But it would be naïve to think that one can simply decide once and for all not to have judgments. What happens when volunteers feel irritation and a sense of judgment at the hospice bedside? How do hospice caregivers work with such discomfort?

One possibility is that one may feel a sense of judgment but not express it to patients or their family members. Sociologist Arlie Hochschild calls this process "emotion work," managing one's emotions according to the implicit "feeling rules" that direct how one is supposed to feel and act in a given situation.[2] In some contexts, it may be skillful for volunteers to control their display of verbal and nonverbal behaviors to avoid potentially harming the patient or family member. At a training session at a hospice in Virginia, for example, a story came up about a family that arranged a viewing of their baby in which the dead baby was displayed sitting up in her playpen surrounded by her toys. The imagined scene elicited "a communal gasp of horror" among the trainees, but the hospice director quickly interjected, "If your patient's family expresses a similar wish, you *cannot* gasp. Your jaw *cannot* drop open. You are there to help, not to impose your own tastes and preferences on them."[3]

Caring for dying people gives hospice volunteers the opportunity to practice seeing that things are not always as they appear, or that what at first appears is not all there is. "I don't judge everything according to appearances. Appearances aren't everything," explained Frau Schneider. She had volunteered for hospice in Freiburg, Germany, for over nine years, and she indicated that a benefit of her long-term engagement in hospice was that it had allowed her to gain this "wisdom." Rather than jumping to conclusions, through her experiences with hospice, she has developed the habit of pausing and asking herself, "My God, what is this person really going through at the moment?"

Similarly, Zemira explained how end-of-life care challenges caregivers to practice taking a broader perspective than they normally take in everyday life. She had recently had a patient whom she described as a "really prickly" woman, and her initial reaction was "Ugh, I don't like this person." But then she stopped herself and became interested in why she had this reaction, "and so I watched myself doing that, and changing, watching my feelings and how I was reacting to that." She continued, "This was not a woman who had a particular style that I like, she wasn't a warm fuzzy. I like warm fuzzies, warm fuzzies are great for me, I do very well with that, and she was *not*." But rather than reacting blindly to her aversion or simply trying to stuff down her feelings, she explained how volunteering for hospice opened in her a curiosity to understand "what might be behind" the woman's hard exterior, which she said was "a new question" for her. "I think most of the time we see someone we don't like, we say, 'Ugh, we don't like them,' and that's the challenge to say, 'What really is going on here?' And '*Why* maybe is this person doing this?'"

Manuel described a situation in the nursing home where he witnessed family members arguing with each other in the presence of the patient. He acknowledged that he felt "a small grain" of judgment toward the family, because he could see that the turmoil in the room was upsetting the patient. Yet he kept his thoughts to himself, stating, "It's not my place to say anything. I can't say anything. Even if I felt it, even if I had a reaction where I could say, 'Why are you arguing over the patient? Can't you see he's getting upset hearing you argue?' I really can't say anything, because it's none of my business." Referring to the distinction between having a thought and expressing one's views, he continued, "Can I have an opinion? Yeah. Can I be judgmental? No."

Here Manuel was not simply submitting his feelings to social norms, but instead, his decision to witness quietly this family dynamic in the face of his own discomfort was grounded in a more spacious view: "You don't really know their situation." Manuel's humility and generosity of interpretation with this struggling family was linked to his own family's recent experience of doing their best to care for his mother, who died on that same Alzheimer's wing of the nursing home. In this way, his quiet witness in this situation was an act of compassion not only for those struggling family members but also for himself—for the dedicated yet imperfect care he had offered his own mother.

CONTEMPLATION
Loving Our Imperfect Care

I invite you to think of a time when you were not at your best as a caregiver. Perhaps a particular encounter comes to mind in rich detail, or maybe the specifics have faded but what remains is a sense of guilt, embarrassment, or shame for what you did or did not do as a caregiver. If more than one memory comes to mind, that is fine, but eventually choose one particular experience for this practice. If quite painful experiences come to mind, you might begin this exercise with less painful memories as a way of trying out the process. In any case, trust your own sense of what is best for you in this moment.

There are three parts to this contemplation. First, begin by describing in detail precisely what took place. You may find it helpful to write down those details or speak them to a partner who listens as a silent witness. Whatever approach you take, imagine that a video was taken of what took place, and based on your memory, simply describe what one would see on that video. In other words, describe the scene from the perspective of an outside observer. Perhaps it was a time when you fought or argued with other members of the family in front of someone who was sick or dying. Just describe the scene as it appears without prior interpretation.

Second, after you have written down or told someone the details that would be captured on the video, imagine what kinds of judgments someone might make about the person they saw in the video. We are often our harshest critic, so perhaps you don't have to imagine judgments one might have but instead it may be judgments you have actually felt about yourself based on the memory. If that is the case, try not to evoke the intensity of the feeling but instead express those judgments in the third person. For example, "This person is being disrespectful by arguing in front of the patient," or "This person is being controlling by trying to force food onto someone who no longer wishes to eat."

The third part of this contemplation involves taking the stance of a compassionate witness. Rarely do we care under the best conditions, so for this part, describe the wider context that shaped what took place in that video. Perhaps you were exhausted beyond words, pressed for time, worried about finances, feeling stuck in old relational patterns, or grieving losses you could not yet fully imagine. And perhaps none of these dynamics would be apparent to an outside observer watching that video. All he would see is our short temper, our prickliness, our irritability. There is always more than meets the eye, so describe with the energy of a loving friend what that person in the video was going through at that time. If necessary, stretch yourself to truly feel compassion for the caregiver in that video.

INTEGRATION

The realities of dying will inevitably bring into relief the limits of our care. Humbly accepting these limitations—that even under the best conditions our care will be imperfect—is central to the practice of compassionate care. Whether we are the caregiver or we are witnessing someone else, use this three-part exercise to notice what is taking place in the outside world (what would be recorded on the video), hear the emotional reactions and judgments of the mind, and then release the grip of those judgments through taking on the energy of a compassionate witness. And when we do not know the story behind the suffering we see in the video, we can practice softening our judgments with the gentle reminder: "My God, what is this person really going through at the moment?"

Hospice work can be transformative for caregivers because it provides opportunities for releasing expectations, journeying with uncertainty, and contemplating one's experience beyond the dualistic categories that limit perception and structure much of everyday life. As with formal meditation or other mindfulness practices, contemplative caregiving can be a means to expand one's sense of possibility, to see relationships and moments in a new light. Being perfect is not required of us as caregivers. Instead, our perfection is found in our willingness to witness our reactions and judgments and to stretch ourselves to live into our deepest intentions to care. Signing up to care for those who are dying and grieving is asking for a mirror of awareness to be held up to us. Contemplative caregiving involves a willingness to look into that mirror with a loving curiosity that, in turn, extends outward to those in our care.

As caregivers, we may at times accompany those who grate on us, or we may be asked to enter situations or witness dynamics that will turn our stomach or bring up irritation or anger. Compassionate caregiving does not require that we like those in our care or that we like what we are being asked to experience. No one likes the smell of an open tumor or the scene of family members upsetting someone close to death. Yet we can abide with it all as a loving witness to what is going on around us and churning around inside of us. Taking the compassionate stance of a witness allows for a generosity of interpretation, not jumping to conclusions about the meaning of another's behavior and thereby putting up a wall. Instead, we can use our own reactive and judgmental mind as an opportunity to move toward another, as well as the self, and to inquire more deeply into what he or she may be experiencing in the moment.

We may never know for certain what another is experiencing or precisely why they are responding to their current situation as they are. Contemplative caregiving, instead, involves recognizing that things are not always as they appear, and that what appears is not all there is to see. This stance invites us to continually open ourselves with curiosity to the mystery of the human encounter. In chapter 6, we move on to explore the basic fact that something has made possible our participation in that mystery in the first place. In opening their lives to our presence, dying people and their families offer us a gift of relationship. Recognizing this fundamental truth, we can return again and again to experiencing contemplative caregiving not as a one-way street but as a reciprocal relation of care.

6

The Reciprocity of Care

*The dying so often have an openness and simplicity which call forth
the same qualities from those who try to help them. We are debtors
to those who can make us learn such things as to be gentle and to
approach others with true attention and respect.*

Cicely Saunders, "And from Sudden Death . . ."
in *Cicely Saunders: Selected Writings, 1958–2004*

SUSAN, a sixty-six-year-old women suffering from chronic kidney disease
and diabetes, had a matter-of-fact air about her. We had one brief encounter
during her time at the hospice. I knocked on her door, entered and
introduced myself, and asked if I could visit with her. She seemed reserved,
but said yes, her face devoid of emotion when she spoke. I pulled up a chair
and took a seat on the right side of her bed. I had only been in Susan's room
for a few minutes when Carla, the nursing assistant, entered and asked me to
help move Susan up in the bed. Carla reclined the head of Susan's bed and
elevated the foot end to make it easier for us to lift Susan with the drawsheet.
While Susan was reclined, legs elevated, she asked, "Am I going to die?"
Without pause, Carla leaned over Susan and her voice took on a patronizing
tone of concern as if talking down to a child: "Oh, well, that's not for us to
know. Sometimes people come in here and get better, but only God can
answer a question like that. Susan, do you want to see a chaplain?" Susan
immediately turned away from Carla and looked up at the ceiling in a stare
and firmly said, "Just sit me back up." After we had gotten Susan sitting up,

Carla said, "Just let me know if you want to see a chaplain," and then she left. This interaction took place in just a few seconds, and then it was over.

I moved around to the other side of Susan's bed. Susan continued to stare at the ceiling. After a few minutes of sitting quietly, I asked, "Do you feel you are dying?" Susan made and held eye contact with me. "I want to die," she said. After a pause, she continued, "But I don't know if I will be able to." Hearing her fear, I responded, "We don't know exactly when, but I have confidence you will be able to die quite peacefully when it's time." She closed her eyes. I sat quietly with her for another few minutes. My shift was at an end, and so I told her that I was going to go. I reached out to hold her hand briefly before I left. She tried to lift her hand and apologized for having limited movement in her arm. I reached down, and we held hands for a moment. I thanked her for allowing me to meet with her and said I would be back at the hospice in a couple of days. "I would be happy to see you again," I said, "and I would be happy if when I came in again, you were no longer here." We held eye contact. I thanked Susan for allowing me to see her good heart. She thanked me in return.

Before I went home for the night, I wrote in her chart that Susan had asked if she was dying and indicated that she appreciates honest communication about her condition and reassurance that she will be able to die when it is time. When I returned to the hospice four days later, Susan was gone. I was told that she had died peacefully that morning. I expressed to the nurse who told me this that I was happy for Susan that she was able to go. "Yes," she said, "Susan had wanted to die for a long time."

When I knocked on Susan's door, she allowed me in. Such a simple gesture on Susan's part, and so common we might easily take it for granted. And then as Carla and I were adjusting her in the bed, Susan made another gesture, an invitation to accompany her with a most intimate inquiry: "Am I going to die?" Just five words, a question, posed in the midst of one of the most routine interactions at the hospice. How often do we go through our days missing the fullness of the moment, taking for granted the gestures of kindness and invitations to care that come to us and then quickly pass?

Contemplative caregiving involves the practice of seeing the power each moment offers for healing and connection. It is an invitation to not live on autopilot or otherwise reduce one's care to fulfilling a preconceived role or expectation. Carla and I both heard the spiritual dimension of Susan's question as well as the fear with which Susan asked it. Carla met Susan's fear with pity, apparent in her infantilizing tone and in declining Susan's invitation to journey with her in the shadow of death, suggesting that such work was the purview of another, outside her role as a nursing assistant. In response, Susan withdrew the invitation to enter her inner world and, in staring at the ceiling, allowed herself to be tossed and turned on the drawsheet like a spiritless body.

There is nothing inherently uncaring about asking a patient if she would like to see a chaplain. Perhaps Carla was following protocol at the hospice of informing patients about the availability of chaplains when questions regarding death come up. Yet in this situation, Carla's question violated the trust Susan had placed in her and me to abide with her in her journeying. I too responded to Susan's inquiry with a question, but one that sought to reopen the space for her concern. I heard in Susan's question a surfacing of fear, and in asking if she felt she were dying, I let her know that I could bear with her this fear. I didn't know how Susan would respond to my question, nor did I know the nature of her fear. I suspected that she was afraid of dying, only to learn that she was afraid she wouldn't be able to die. What I did know is that Susan had entrusted the space with her inner stirrings, and that I was willing to receive the kindness of her trust and be present with her in that space.

As caregivers, we often see ourselves as the initiator of compassion, the one making a difference in someone's life. Contemplative caregiving begins from a different premise, a recognition that we each create the ground for the action of the other. This chapter investigates what I call the reciprocity of care, a virtuous cycle that makes possible the transformative potential of contemplative caregiving. By opening in trust to our care, those who are dying support our own learning and growth through the inevitable ups and downs of the caregiving journey. Mindfulness practice at the bedside includes recognizing our indebtedness to those who open themselves to receive our care.

An Immediate Atmosphere of Trust

Trust is the foundation of all caring relationships. Crucial to forming and sustaining trusting relationships is attentively listening and responding to the needs of those in one's care. Hospice programs often stress the importance of volunteers building relationships of trust with patients and their family members through embodying a calming presence and simply sitting and listening with a truly open heart. Some hospices seek to facilitate trust with patients by trying to closely match the interests and personalities of volunteers to the needs of specific patients or family situations. Efforts in this direction include assigning just one volunteer per family to facilitate a sense of rapport and continuity in care, recruiting more men as caregivers in order to match male volunteers with male patients, and establishing veteran-to-veteran volunteer programs with the understanding that common life experiences in the military help volunteers build trust and a sense of camaraderie with veterans receiving hospice care. The importance of common life experience as a basis for building trust may be especially crucial in prison infirmaries, where staff and other outsiders are often viewed with suspicion by inmates. As Fleet Maull, founder of the first prison hospice initiative in the United States, suggests, "Inmate volunteers are likely to have a distinct advantage over nonprisoner caregivers since they can identify with the heightened suffering attendant with dying without family support and with the shame of dying in prison."[1]

Matching patients and volunteers based on their backgrounds or similarities, and other efforts to build trust with patients, all have their place. Yet many involved in hospice speak of a less mediated kind of trust that can emerge from authentic encounter—a more fundamental openness and hospitality that creates the space for other forms of intimacy to appear. As one study attests, individuals at the end stages of a terminal illness often have "dispensed with any possible social etiquette that may have slowed the development of their friendships," allowing hospice caregivers to form intimate and often immediate bonds with complete strangers.[2] As Sandol Stoddard expressed in her classic statement on the hospice movement, dying people "drop their masks and do not worry any more about inconsequentials."

She continues that, as caregivers, "the usual walls and barriers of our own perception have a way of crumbling quietly, very nearly vanishing in such situations. . . . So it is for each of us, living and dying when the usual systems of elaborate defenses are stripped away."[3]

The dispensing of social etiquette can, of course, lead to a different result. Consider, for example, my brief encounter with a patient named Rick. As one of few male volunteers at the hospice where I met Susan, the nursing staff often hoped I would be able to connect with male patients. On one occasion, a nurse took me into Rick's room, and upon being introduced to me, Rick promptly stated, "I'm not into any new dealings, because I'm too sick to deal." I was slow to accept this initial invitation to exit, so he made the next one a bit more emphatic by simply pointing to the door. I got it that time. At some point, all who volunteer for hospice will experience having one's offer of care denied. And yet even experiences that may feel like rejection can be responded to with a spirit of reciprocity, trusting that the patient knows best what he needs in that moment. The general experience, though, is one of being received with trust and an invitation to care.

David, who had volunteered for many years at a hospice in San Francisco, had a deep reverence for the invitation to care that dying people extended to him through what he called "an immediate atmosphere of trust." He explained that for care and community to be possible, "it's just so purely simple that there has to be trust, a sense of safety and trust." He continued, "One of the things hospice taught me was deep listening, just listen, cause I think that's what people want, people want to be heard." Here David pointed to a tragic irony he saw in American culture. In his experience, dying individuals "can't always be heard if they're at home with their family. . . . Sadly, at the time of death, in our culture, trust starts to diminish. The very moment, the very time that we need to rely on and to depend on honesty and integrity and people believing us is the time when all that starts to be questioned." In such a context, hospice volunteers may play a unique role in being present to dying folks in ways that friends and family may not be able to given their own attachments and concerns. In this way, David honored the importance of what he brought to the hospice bedside as a volunteer—his openness to authentic encounter. Yet in speaking of the immediacy of trust, he recognized the primacy of the trust and invitation to care extended to him, at the outset, by residents at the hospice.

Hospice brings together individuals from diverse social milieu and makes possible intimacies that would be unlikely in other settings. Richard explained that some residents at the hospice where he volunteered had been homeless for much of their adult lives, and he contrasted the quality of care these individuals received at the hospice with how they had been treated on the streets. He described how his fellow volunteers were quite loving to the residents at the hospice, although he acknowledged that those same individuals most likely "walk[ed] by homeless people on the street in the same way everyone else does." Richard was grateful for the hospice setting, which he saw as creating the context where he could care for those who were suffering rather than simply turn the other way and avoid their predicament. There was an "unspoken kind of agreement" at the hospice, he said, in the sense that volunteers offered their care and dying persons opened themselves to receive that care. In his mind, there was no question that the residents did more to make that exchange possible.

Richard's awareness of such an agreement resonates with the experience of Sam, a seventy-seven-year-old white man who had been volunteering for a hospice in Baltimore City for sixteen years at the time I interviewed him. Sam recounted one of his first experiences with hospice, pointing to multiple boundary crossings—most notably of race and social class. Sam said of one hospice patient whom he visited:

> He lived north of North Avenue, and I drove for about four or five blocks without seeing a white face and I began to wonder if this was precisely my calling to be a volunteer. And I parked the car and this young black man comes to the edge of the deck and he says, "Brother, is that a new Ford?" And he knew that I was from hospice to see that chap, and I felt so at home and safe. I mean they knew that this white fellow wouldn't be stopping here unless he was heading in to see this man who was a hospice patient. I mean, they didn't know me, but they knew that I was a part of hospice.

Sam had been visiting this man in his home for several months when, during one visit, he asked if Sam would pray with him. "And I almost started to cry," Sam said. "I mean, such a masculine fellow asking another man to pray with him, and I am not a minister or a priest, so it was a very powerful moment."

Hospice volunteers are invited into liminal spaces that are not bound by the conventions of culture and everyday life, yet those spaces are already somewhat socialized by the trust placed in the institution of hospice. In this way, one is out of his or her normal element yet held in immediate trust by others. In Sam's words, this creates a feeling of being "at home and safe" in uncharted waters. As his experience likewise illustrates, the experience of being held in trust in the midst of multiple uncertainties and boundary crossings is the outer ground that invites hospice volunteers to relate to the often unsettling emotions of care in potentially transformative ways.

"Disorienting dilemmas" are central to transformative learning.[4] Yet when demands exceed the resources and support available to meet them, we tend to experience situations as stressful and potentially threatening, undermining our capacity to learn from and be transformed through discomfort. Those same situations, however, can be received as workable learning opportunities when they occur in a supportive context that allows for open exploration without the debilitating experience of feeling overwhelmed. Such is the context of hospice, where even those with no prior end-of-life caregiving experience, like Sam, can be transformed through encounters at the bedside. The supportive framework of hospice allowed Sam not only to meet and befriend someone from a different race and background than him but also to establish such intimacy that they could pray together. Such a situation prompts one to ask, "Who is taking care of whom?"

CONTEMPLATION
An Infinite Debt

In *Works of Love*, Danish philosopher and Christian existentialist Søren Kierkegaard writes that love is the utmost a human being can give to another.

In offering our love, we become "infinitely indebted" to the one who opens to receive our offering.[5] Reflecting this dynamic, the immediate atmosphere of trust dying individuals extend to hospice volunteers opens a space for compassion to become unbound from the everyday habits of heart and mind that often limit possibilities for human connection.

I invite you to pause for a moment and consider your own works of love, your own experience of vitality and joy on account of the myriad of others throughout your life who have allowed you to express care and compassion. To whom are you indebted in this way? Where do you experience an atmosphere of trust that allows your love to find expression?

Alternatively, in what areas of your life do you help create an atmosphere of trust that supports others in expressing compassion? When you are sick or in need, how receptive are you to receiving care? When you are nearing the end of life, will you fight to remain "independent" and resist being a "burden" to others? Or will you give others the gift of receiving joyfully their compassionate care?

Follow your own inner voice as you work with these questions, perhaps as starting points for engaging others in conversation or as inspiration for journaling or quiet contemplation.

Journeying with Uncertainty

We can try to control the uncontrollable by looking for security and predictability, always hoping to be comfortable and safe. But the truth is that we can never avoid uncertainty. This not-knowing is part of the adventure."
Pema Chödrön, *Comfortable with Uncertainty*

In the situation of contemplative end-of-life care, both the dying person and the hospice volunteer bring their hopes, fears, vulnerabilities, and strengths to the encounter. Under the right conditions, each person can be engaged in the process of becoming—be it wiser, more confident, more skillful, more compassionate, more whole. In this way, contemplative caregiving first and foremost involves *journeying with*, rather than *providing a service to*, those in one's care.

Entering the room of a dying person is a journey into the unknown for the hospice caregiver, just as the dying process is a journey into the unknown for the patient. Opening oneself to uncertainty at the threshold of life and death is a basic requirement for hospice caregivers, since it is through embracing uncertainty with an attitude of not knowing that loving attunement to the needs of others becomes possible. And it is also through such openness and willingness to experience disorientation and discomfort that hospice volunteers allow themselves to be transformed through this work.

The process of opening to uncertainty is not all or nothing. Some volunteers, particularly those new to end-of-life care, may attempt to bring some degree of routine into spaces that might otherwise be experienced as overwhelmingly open. Tim began volunteering for a hospice in upstate New York shortly after retiring from his career as a state trooper. He had had no prior experience providing bedside care, and being just two months into his work with hospice, he was understandably nervous about what he might experience. At the time of our interview, he was still caring for his first patient, and he explained how he brought the newspaper with him on each visit to the man's home. He spoke of having established the "routine of reading" to the patient, indicating how the newspaper helped him bring some degree of order to the anxiety-producing situation of not knowing what to say to a bedridden stranger who had difficulty expressing himself verbally. Tim continued, however, that on his last visit, there was a disturbance in his routine due to a crisis in the family that was upsetting to the patient. "But once this gentleman was able to communicate his concerns about a family situation," Tim said, "then he calmed down and I was able to read a newspaper to him and try to get him back to a more—to a routine at least that I know." Notice that the emphasis here was how reading the newspaper was a source of comfort *for himself*: "a routine at least that I know."

Not all hospice volunteers need to rely on something as concrete as reading the newspaper to feel a sense of routine, but each can be certain of encountering the edge between what's familiar and what pushes their boundaries in terms of comfort. Joy, a thirty-two-year-old case worker at the Department of Health and Human Services, said that part of what she loved about hospice was that it gave her a break from the high pressure and repetitive nature of her job. At work, she had "too many caseloads, not enough time," whereas as a hospice volunteer she was able to be with each patient without pressure to get something done and then move on to the next thing. She described her hospice volunteer experience as follows: "Everything just stops, and I find that when I leave I have a peace about me." She had been volunteering for hospice for two years when she and I met, and she explained how she "got her foot in the door" by bringing her dog with her when she visited patients in the nursing home. Her dog had been through all sorts of canine training, so her volunteer coordinator allowed her to use him as a "therapy dog" on her visits with patients. The residents enjoyed the show her dog would put on. "It helps me [too]," she explained, "because you're new at it, and I was nervous, but I had my dog and it worked out *wonderful*." She went on to say that if she didn't have anything to talk about, having her dog with her allowed her to easily connect with residents at the nursing home with whom she might otherwise have a hard time relating.

On one occasion, Joy did not have such great success bringing her dog on a visit to the home of a hospice patient who was near death. She recounted how the man would not release his "death grip" on her dog's leash. Fortunately, there was a home-health aide present who was able to get the leash out of the man's hand. The patient let out a terrifying groan, and Joy was "sweating bullets" as the aide, "a big, big guy," peeled the man's hand off the leash, an experience that clarified for her the edges of her "comfort zone." Joy spoke with her volunteer coordinator about the experience, and since then, none of her assignments had required her to be alone with patients. At the time of our interview, she was visiting a family that had an infant on hospice care, and although she was going into a private home, the parents were there, so she "always had some kind of lifeline still." Similarly, nursing homes were a safe zone for her because, as she explained, "If something goes wrong, I can hit the bell and I'm going to have a nurse right there."

Sam liked how hospice volunteering "stretched" him in ways that developed his caregiving capacities, even as he, like Joy, bounded the care he offered—in his case, not by requesting situations where others would always be present but by only taking on male patients. For a decade and a half, Sam had been visiting patients in their own homes. He explained, "Well don't you think that if I go into somebody's home it's a lot easier if I am talking to another man?" At stake here was not so much his relative level of comfort conversing with men compared to women but instead, "the whole situation" of caring for an embodied other. He continued, "If a woman needs something or has to go to the ladies' room, I mean the whole situation—I really don't want to have any distractions or any misunderstandings." He described his choice to visit only male patients as "common sense," and the general approach, if not the specific practice, was common among several volunteers I interviewed.

Common Sense and Uncommon Sense

Common sense in the context of hospice care refers to informal, practical understandings used by hospice workers to direct behavior in the absence of formal guidelines. At an acute care hospice where I volunteered for three years, the nursing staff routinely expressed to volunteers their commonsense understandings regarding which patients were and were not appropriate for volunteers to visit. Most often such advice took the form of suggestions to avoid the rooms of certain patients, particularly those carrying contagious pathogens, such as MRSA. And then there was Carl, who suffered from face and neck cancer. There was a large open tumor covering the entire right side of his head that was gradually engulfing his face. When I met Carl, the tumor was just beginning to reach his right eye and the right corner of his mouth. He wore a bandage wrapped around his head and neck to keep the tumor from oozing blood onto his pillows. An aide explained that the bandage also helped to contain the smell of the tumor. In reality, it only contained the sight, and even so, only incompletely. The nursing staff had generally expressed to volunteers that "there's no reason for you to go in there," yet one evening Nadine, an aide, suggested that Carl might enjoy my company.

Nadine and I had a good rapport, and she always seemed to know when there was an opening for me to connect with a particular patient. "He doesn't seem to be a talker," she said, "but if you go in and interact with him, who knows what you will get." I was warned about the smell of the tumor and advised that putting a drop of lavender essential oil under my nose would help. It didn't. The smell was thick and unpleasant. Carl apologized for his appearance and the smell, and I responded that I would gladly sit with him if he would have me. I visited Carl a few times before he died. He allowed me to massage his feet, and at his request, I read him essays by Emerson on friendship, self-reliance, spiritual laws, and gifts. He did not talk much, and largely, he explained, because of the discomfort of the bandage that was tightly wrapped around his chin. But he was quite receptive to all I had to offer, and we quickly developed a sense of meaningful connection to each other.

The bandage around Carl's head and the smell of the tumor kept many would-be visitors away. Being in Carl's presence was not difficult for me, but given the smell, I could understand why someone would not have wanted to enter his room. Yet it would have been a shame if the commonsense idea that volunteers would not want to interact with someone so disturbing to the eye and nose had led Nadine to refrain from suggesting I go visit Carl or had dictated my decision whether to care for him. His hospitality was a far stronger antidote than any essential oil, and I'm grateful he allowed me to spend time with him. The context of hospice provides the chance to act from common sense, and sometimes that is what's called for. But it also challenges us to act from the uncommon sense of pursuing intimacy outside of our normal social boundaries; it allows for the possibility of connecting to people and situations that our cultural and personal backgrounds might otherwise forbid.

The hospice was an acute care facility, so patients were typically only there for a few days or at most a couple of weeks. Carl was one of the exceptions. So was Buddy. They both were at the house for over three months. But I only visited Buddy once. He had been a heavy smoker and was at the hospice because he was having difficulty breathing due to lung cancer. I had seen Buddy's name on the census for several weeks before I decided to enter his room. I was told by an aide that he was "a loner," but I thought I would knock on his door anyway. Buddy invited me in, and I took a seat next to his bed. He began speaking about why he was at the hospice. He explained that he loved to smoke and would right then if he could. He also told me where he was from and what kind of work he had done. That was about it for the conversation.

Buddy was on oxygen and he spoke with great difficulty, but even worse, talking made him hack. It pained me to see him suffer, especially on account of small talk with me. He was watching a television show called *Ax Men*, a documentary reality series highlighting the dangers of working in the logging industry, so I sat there in silence and stared at the screen with him. I found the television loudly oppressive and the dialogue and hypermasculine plot rather tortured, so I felt a sense of relief when the aides came in to help Buddy go to the bathroom, signaling an opportunity for me to exit the room. Buddy was at the hospice for another two months, but I somehow never knocked on his door again. I would have visited with him again had he rung the call button and asked for company, or if Nadine or another staff member had sensed that I should go see him. I occasionally asked an aide about him, and perhaps I comforted myself with the common under-standing that he was a "loner." After all, his door *was* typically closed. But for my part, I knew it was my own discomfort that kept me from wanting to enter his room, and on any given night, there were always other patients at the house for me to visit. In this case, I relied on the commonsense feeling of my comfort zone.

The language of a "safe zone" or a "comfort zone" is a spatial metaphor pointing to the connection between place and the embodied emotions of care. I do not judge myself for walking past Buddy's closed door, just as I do not judge my fellow volunteers who avoided Carl's room. Each of us has our own idiosyncrasies regarding whom we are drawn to and when and where we feel out of place. But a comfort zone is not simply a space that hospice volunteers become aware of and seek to remain in. Even if that were one's intention, it would be hard to pull off given the surprises that are quite common in end-of-life care. The metaphor of a comfort zone can best be understood as a starting point to work from as we stretch ourselves over time ever more deeply into the uncertainties and possibilities that arise in the course of caring for dying and grieving people.

This chapter has examined *the reciprocity of care*, a virtuous cycle in end-of-life care that includes a receptivity on the part of dying people to being accompanied in this most vulnerable time of their lives. Our efforts as caregivers to build trust with patients through nonanxious presence, silence, and nonjudgmental listening are integral to giving good care. Yet offering these precious gifts depends first on the generosity of dying people to allow us to enter their inner world. As we seek to live into our intentions to express compassion, we are indebted to those who extend to us these gestures of kindness and invitations to care.

Caring for someone who is dying is an experience fraught with uncertainty and change. There may be sounds, sights, and smells, as well as troubling thoughts and emotions that lead us to doubt our capacity to care. We may pull back in self-protection at different points, trying to bring some degree of order to the potential chaos of accompanying those who are dying. Yet it is precisely when we confront the unexpected that opportunities to learn and grow appear. Seizing those opportunities requires both a commitment to the practice of mindfulness and a context supportive of our exploration. Hospice volunteering provides such a context for learning from the inevitable uncertainties of caregiving at the end of life. Central to that context is the atmosphere of trust dying people extend to hospice volunteers, inviting them to approach whatever arises with spacious awareness and a spirit of contemplative inquiry. And very often, that invitation includes something unexpected—a sense of lightness, play, even flirtation. Part 4 takes us more deeply into this mystery, examining how a playful spirit and the light touch of contemplative care are central to empathetic connection.

PART FOUR

Unlocking the
Empathetic Imagination

Without imagination, true empathy is not possible.
Ira Byock, "Imagining People Well" in *Awake at the Bedside*

IT'S A NATURAL HUMAN RESPONSE to do whatever we can to help relieve the suffering of another. But as those who are dying show us, the experience of compassion comes not only through our doing but through our willingness to relate as a person, beyond a prescribed role or call of duty. We enter a relation of compassion through empathizing with the unique experience of the other and allowing ourselves to be touched by her humanity. Without empathy, there can be no care, only charity, service, or, at worst, pity.

When we feel pity for another, we separate ourselves in self-protection. Pity is what happens when our concern for another is colored with fear, whereas compassion naturally arises when the concerns of our heart are softened by empathy. When we engage another with empathy, there is a willingness to put ourselves in her shoes, to feel into what she is feeling from her perspective. But how can we empathize with one who is dying when we have not been there ourselves? How can we put ourselves in the shoes of those suffering from dementia, cancer, or any other affliction of the body and mind if we have not been personally touched by such experiences?

An important aspect of empathy is that it can't be forced. As C. M. Davis writes, empathy is "indirectly given to us. . . . When empathy occurs, we find ourselves experiencing it, rather than directly causing it to happen."[1] Perhaps one of the greatest ironies of the medical field is how the standard training of professional caregivers, which focuses on diagnosing and treating diseases, can undermine rather than nourish the empathetic willingness of caregivers. For this reason, some suggest that in training doctors, there is no need to teach empathy, but instead only to preserve the innate human capacity to imagine the suffering of another.

Empathy is not a discrete skill, such as how to take vital signs or how to dress a wound, but rather a moral capacity intrinsic to what makes us human. And although empathy cannot be directly taught, our empathetic imagination, a creative and fundamentally playful sensibility, can be fed and given space to flourish. Caring at the bedside of those who are dying is one context for cultivating our innate potential for empathy. Through such practices as becoming curious about the experiences of others, deeply listening, and offering ourselves without pretense, each of us can expand our awareness of the humanity, individuality, and worldview of others, even those we may consider strangers or enemies. Part 4 of this book reflects on this process of extending compassion through an underappreciated quality of empathy—its rootedness in play.

We treat empathy with too much seriousness and not enough reverence. To get a sense of what I mean by this, we need only look at discussions on how to nourish empathy in children and then get curious about why we seem to believe adults are so different. It is through play that children become social, and by social, I mean empathetic. Through role-playing, children practice imagining the experience of another. Free play feeds a child's natural sense of discovery and wonder about the world. Similarly, encountering all that is with a reverential attitude of wonder captures the essence of contemplative caregiving, which is as much about affirming the possibility of meaning and joy as it is about relieving suffering. Chapter 7, "Caring with a Playful Spirit," examines play as a fundamental drive for transcendence and meaning, that we are always more than the suffering we may experience in any given moment. Just imagine if we were to approach parenting solely as a process of relieving suffering. Our children would become quite neurotic and distrustful of our efforts to care. And as any child knows, an adult who is willing to play in complete freedom and imagination is an adult who cares. Are we courageous enough to let go of our own serious agenda as end-of-life caregivers and experience the joy of being fully alive whether the one in our care may live another ten minutes or another ten years?

Chapter 8, "Offering Spiritual Friendship," reflects on empathy as an encounter of equality. In hospice circles you will often hear folks talk about helping another die "with dignity." Typically, dying with dignity implies that one is able to die as much as possible on one's own terms, that one has the autonomy to make one's own medical choices and other decisions regarding one's care. While respect for autonomy is crucial to compassionate care, so too is equality. Suffering creates an asymmetry in the relationship between the giver and recipient of care, and redressing this imbalance of power is central to compassionate care. Dignity in our care emerges, above all, from our willingness to engage the other from a place of mutual vulnerability, recognizing that it is only but a span of time that determines whether we are the one beside the dying bed or the one in it. In offering spiritual friendship, we recognize that we each are the guardian of the other's soul, giving and receiving tenderness in an unending chain of human empathy.

7

Caring with a Playful Spirit

EVA ROSENTHAL worked in the fashion industry in her hometown in Germany before fleeing to England to escape persecution under the Nazi regime. Many of her family members perished in the Holocaust. After the war, Eva settled in the United States, where she married, worked, and raised a family. Eva was eighty-four when she was admitted to hospice care, and during the intake, she requested a volunteer who could read to her a book she had recently acquired on the history of her hometown. I was assigned to another patient at the time, but given my fluency in German, the volunteer coordinator asked if I would be willing to visit with Eva. I gladly accepted.

It was mid-May when I met Eva in her apartment in a retirement community in the adjacent county. When I arrived, I was shown in by a middle-aged black woman named Corinne who brought me to the living room where Eva was sitting. Eva offered me a seat and then asked Corinne to bring the "professor" some tea and cookies. When I had spoken with Eva on the phone prior to our first visit, I could sense she liked that I was a university professor, so I dressed for the occasion, wearing a linen jacket, a pressed shirt, and slacks. What I discovered upon meeting her was that I liked her eyes. Eva's vision was declining, yet her eyes glowed with life. She was quite stunning.

As it turned out, I only read to her a few pages of the book. Eva enjoyed the reading, but hearing about her hometown prompted her to tell me of her life. She spoke about being a model in the 1930s, the circumstances of her escape from Nazi Germany, and her emigrating and building a life in the United States. Hanging high on the walls in her living room were large portraits of her adult children and grandchildren. I asked if I might bring a tape recorder on my subsequent visits to record her life stories to pass on to her family. Tea and cookies for the professor, and a witnessing of life stories became our courting ritual that summer.

I had visited Eva about every other week over the course of three months when she popped the question: "Would you like to marry me?" It was just weeks before her death, and at this point, she lay feeble in bed, her radiant blue eyes framed on one side by the large bruise on her right cheek from a recent fall on the way to the bathroom. I smiled, kissed her forehead, and replied, "I would have very much liked to marry you." I paused, and then playfully continued, "But I'm already engaged." That evening, I told my fiancée Andrea of my afternoon out, and she delighted in the loving affection between Eva and me.

The following week I spoke with Eva for the last time. Since she lived about an hour away, I routinely called as I was on my way, just to be sure she was up for seeing me. This time she was too weak for company and asked me not to come. She told me she loved me. I responded that I loved her as well. When I hung up the phone, I sensed that this would be our goodbye.

Some believe we have forgotten how to care for the dying in modern societies. But perhaps even more so, we have forgotten how to play. Several years after my time with Eva, I was asked by a staff member at another hospice to contribute to their blog on hospice care. Happy to do so, I submitted a one-thousand-word essay on the centrality of play in end-of-life care that included the above story. The woman who invited me to write the blog was uncomfortable with what I had written. "I have taken the liberty of editing the piece so that it does not lead someone to misinterpret what a volunteer does and doesn't do," she explained. Her edits were many and included deleting Eva's proposal and my playful response. In its place, she had written, "She told me how much she valued our time together—that I was like a son to her." I withdrew my submission, and not only because Eva never said those things. The edits drained the life out of the piece.

I have accompanied many dozens of individuals at the end of life, and each relationship and encounter has been unique. In one sense, there was nothing special about my care of Eva. On my visits, I engaged in two activities often seen as central to the hospice volunteer role—I listened without judgment as she reviewed many experiences from her life, and in the process, I helped her create a legacy for her family in the form of tape-recorded stories. Yet the essence of my care for Eva had nothing to do with these activities. Instead, it was my opening to the playful spirit that animated our encounters.

The flirtatious edge in how Eva and I related to each other went beyond the constraints of time or the necessity of gain and moved into a sacred space where there was nothing to win or lose, only love to be experienced. Caring is an art, and as musician Stephen Nachmanovitch suggests, "For art to appear, we have to *disappear*." He calls this process "deep play" or "total immersion in the game."[1] In the world of hospice, this stance is referred to as "just being there" or "not having an agenda."[2] But caring well at the end of life is not just a negative stance, showing up without an agenda; it involves the positive force of engaging another with a playfully receptive spirit that expresses a fearless openness to the possibility of joy, love, and growth in all stages and times of life.

Should I feel embarrassed that a dying woman in my care more than twice my age asked if I would like to marry her? The response of the administrator who took issue with my blog post suggested as much, implying that in my encounters with Eva I had stepped over "the boundaries that are so critical for all hospice workers." In her view, if Eva had thought of me "like a son," that would have been okay, but somehow the particular question she asked was beyond the pale. In a literal sense, Eva's proposal was an impossibility, both ethically and practically. Yet those working in end-of-life care often speak of the necessity of attuning to the metaphoric dimension of language, how the symbolic communication of dying people "evokes their life experiences."[3]

Eva had been a model during the Nazi rise to power, a time when her beauty was socially recognized even as her basic humanity and right to exist was threatened by Hitler's regime. And now she lay there, bruised and dying, a condition experienced by many in contemporary society as an indignity, an affront to one's personhood. Eva's proposal was not literal, but in the realm of deep play. She was finding her way into what Diane Ackerman has described as "a refuge from ordinary life, a sanctuary of the mind, where one is exempt from life's customs, methods, and decrees."[4] As caregivers, we can rejoice in the freedom of such play.

Central to the companionship I offered Eva was an affirmation of her timeless beauty and unconditional worth. Feeling into this fundamental acceptance, she trusted she could playfully propose to me as she did, calling forth in me a compassionate response that was likewise in the realm of subjunctive possibility. Neither was this form of exchange idiosyncratic to our relationship. Another hospice caregiver described, for example, how once, when she was bathing a patient, the woman asked if she "would like to be her mother." "I could very much imagine that," she responded, because "in that moment I felt my deep affection for her and experienced myself as if I were in fact her mother."[5] Such expressions of intimacy, of playing *as if* a relationship were otherwise, affirms the human capacity for transcendence, meaning making, and connectedness in a fragmented, painful, and chaotic world.

When we respond to a dying person with a playful spirit, we affirm the wholeness of the person, that she is more than one who is sick or one who is dying. We likewise affirm our own wholeness and capacity for authentic encounter. Play takes us beyond the guarded stance of pity into the spaciousness of joyful encounter, offering both a respite from taking ourselves too seriously and a mind-set that supports our own growth. I call this approach the "light touch of contemplative care." It is animated by a fearless openness to the possibility of the moment, allowing spacious inquiry to carry us beyond the parameters of what we might have imagined or expected.

The Light Touch of Contemplative Care

Playing is what we are doing when we do not need to gain something from a situation.
    David R. Loy and Linda Goodhew, *The Dharma of Dragons and Daemons*

The role of hospice volunteer has the widest latitude among all members of the interdisciplinary hospice team. In some contexts, volunteers may assist with the physical care of patients, including toileting, bathing, and dressing. Such was the case at the prison and three other hospices where I conducted interviews. In the other hospices in my study, assistance with these activities of daily living was solely within the purview of nursing staff. Volunteers who go into the private homes of patients may assist with housekeeping or running errands, depending on the needs of the family and the willingness of the volunteer to engage in such activities. Perhaps most importantly, home volunteers provide much-needed respite care for the spouse of the patient or other family caregivers so that they can take a couple of hours for themselves while the volunteer sits with the patient.

In all contexts, listening and being a friendly presence are seen as central to the role of direct-care volunteers, which sometimes can involve supporting family members in their grief or listening to any fears patients may have about death and dying. Depending on the condition and needs of the patient and family, volunteers may also read, watch TV, or play cards or other games with patients and their family members. Sometimes families request that a volunteer "sit vigil" at the bedside to pray, meditate, or otherwise offer a calming presence in the final days or hours of a patient's life. While there are many ways a volunteer may fulfill her role, the art of contemplative care is less about what you do and more about who you are in the doing.

As illustrated in the previous chapter, some hospice volunteers develop routine ways of caring at the hospice bedside, whereas maturing as a caregiver involves releasing expectations about what we should be doing and move beyond habitual ways of seeing and being. Caring with a light touch means approaching whatever we do with a spirit of empathetic inquiry as to whether our offering of support is attuned to the needs of the patient, or if there might be a more skillful alternative. One consequence of caring with a light touch is a sense of humility and personal growth for the caregiver.

Sister Pauline had been volunteering at a hospice in Baltimore ever since it was founded by the convent two decades before I interviewed her. She used to drive to the hospice herself, but about five years earlier, she realized that her declining eyesight made it so she could not drive safely, so she began traveling to the hospice with Martha, who lived near the convent and frequently visited the sisters there. Sister Pauline described herself as a "pastoral visitor" and indicated that Martha was a "volunteer," although she clarified that "we do the same thing." The two of them go to the hospice one morning per week for about two hours. After checking in with the nurse, they each take a floor of the hospice and go room to room visiting and praying with patients.

I interviewed Sister Pauline and Martha at the same time, and both indicated that volunteering at the hospice over the years had profoundly affected their lives. They explained how hospice care had brought them in contact with people they would not otherwise have had the opportunity to know so intimately in their daily lives—homeless individuals, intravenous drug users, those of other religious backgrounds, those dying of AIDS. As Martha stated, through these encounters, she had become "a much stronger and much more understanding person."

Sister Pauline described how her engagement at the hospice had broadened her "intercessional life," referring to her evening prayers at the convent. She indicated that she knows every patient at the hospice by name, so when she and her sisters pray for patients in every room of the hospice, she has a vivid image in her mind of who each person is. But both Sister Pauline and Martha described how over the years they had come to see that their role at the hospice was much wider than they had originally imagined, and that what they had learned was how to attune to what each individual needed in that moment. Sister Pauline explained that, beyond praying with patients, her role was simply "to be here" and to "think of the *little* things," like offering someone a drink of water. Martha added that the pain medications patients receive often cause constipation, and that she sometimes assisted the nursing staff by holding patients on their side when they were given suppositories, an experience that was "humbling" for her and for which she was deeply grateful.

Both Martha and Sister Pauline described hospice care as a "vocation" or "calling" in their lives, and one that they had come to approach with a light touch born of their experiences being with so many different individuals in the final moments of their lives. I asked them to tell me of an experience that would indicate the significance of hospice work in their lives. I could feel their joyous grief as they recounted story after story of particular patients who had touched them deeply, often through a spirit of playfulness. Martha spoke of James, an African American man with AIDS who had come to the hospice from the penitentiary. "I would take him out on the porch to smoke," she recounted, "to see the girls passing by, and I had come in, and he had done the same thing to Sister Pauline apparently. We'd come by his room and he would say, 'Hey Babe!'" Sister Pauline laughed at how James had flirted with her in this way, remembering how she and Martha would often bring James candy, an expression of the sweetness with which she held him in her heart. Martha came to think of James as a friend.

Sister Pauline also told of how she playfully connected with another young man dying of AIDS through the romantically symbolic act of bringing him flowers. Christopher, a gay man whom she described as "handsome," was quite receptive to Sister Pauline's gifts. "I loved him and used to bring him daffodils, and camellias, and little snowdrops. And I said, 'You know, these are for you.' . . . He was just dear and very flowery in his speaking, you know, and he said, 'Oh, you stole my heart!'" Sister Pauline restated her love for Christopher and her appreciation of his "flowery" response to her gift, acknowledging how those who die at the hospice "go on in your memory, they live on in your contacts with them."

Sister Pauline and Martha opened themselves to the individuality of each patient in their care, and in the process became much lighter and more imaginative in how they understood the spiritual gifts they had to offer. Many patients were quite uninterested in having a nun pray with them, yet a drink of water, a smoke on the porch, a piece of candy, a bouquet of flowers—these could all be offered as the highest form of prayer. Yet in speaking of the "light touch" of contemplative care, I do not mean insisting on keeping things light or using fun to try to shy away from suffering. Instead, the gentleness of our care is born of a fearless openness to the fullness of life, including moments of joy and moments of seemingly unbearable suffering, as well as the absence of imposing our own hopes and fears on the situation.

Although agendas can differ quite a bit in their focus, they invariably come with a sense of rigidity, whereas the light touch of contemplative care is spacious, receptive of whatever needs be. When we as caregivers are driven by fear, we often act out of our own habitual style of trying to calm anxiety and gain a sense of control or ground under our feet. For some of us, fear may lead to tightening around doing a certain task or activity. For others, fear can lead to being driven by an agenda of *being* a certain way, whether serious, solemn, funny, or upbeat. Central to the art of contemplative care is the capacity to modulate our energy in any given moment in a way that is both authentic to our own being and attuned to whatever needs may be presented by those in our care.

From Helper Persona to Authentic Encounter

Consider the experience of Tom, an inmate volunteer, whom we met in the introduction to the book. Tom is quite witty and playful in spirit, and in each of my interactions with him at the prison, I have been struck by his sense of joyfulness in being alive. Tom's sweetness of spirit is clearly a gift he brings to the hospice bedside, yet, as with each of us, when we become driven by fear, our greatest gifts can become distorted and lead to unskillfulness in our care. Tom vividly described his nervousness and apprehension as he was heading down to the infirmary for his first shift as a hospice volunteer. It was late at night as he was about to take over for his fellow volunteer, Alton, and running through his mind was the fear that there would not be enough time for Alton to fill him in on what had been going on with the patient on the previous shift. He was also having doubts about whether he was "good enough" to do this or whether he was going to "mess things up." In the face of these fears that had put knots in his stomach, Tom got off to a rocky start with the hospice patient, Charlie.

Tom clapped and rubbed his hands together as he described how eager he was to do something helpful for Charlie. "Hey Charlie, how ya doing, buddy? What can I do for you?" But he quickly learned that Charlie wasn't interested in his helpfulness. Charlie was dying and he was angry about it, and no amount of upbeat energy or willingness-to-do-for on Tom's part could change that reality. "He's dealing with his illness, his liver's shot, his skin is yellow, his eyes are yellow, his stomach is distended, and I mean, he's dealing with pain, and he's dealing with a lot of stuff," recalled Tom. "And amongst all that, he's dying. And here *I* am . . . to help him, but at the same point in time, I'm *excited* to help him. Well, I'm bringing a happy energy there, and he's not happy. He's dying. It's like two opposing viewpoints. And so . . . they *clashed.*"

Tom's shift at the infirmary was from 1:00 a.m. until 7:00 a.m., and what he learned during those first six hours at the hospice bedside profoundly shaped how he came to approach being with those who are dying. In his eagerness to be helpful, Tom asked again and again if he could do this for Charlie or do that for him, whether he wanted the TV channel changed or more ice in his soda. "It seemed like every time I opened my mouth, I was getting scolded," he said.

Tom eventually relaxed around his nervous desire to be helpful and was able to sit quietly, just occasionally chatting with Charlie until he fell asleep. Charlie slept for a few hours, and upon awakening just before Tom's shift ended, he apologized to Tom. "I just wasn't in a good mood and I just took my anger out on you," Charlie said to him. Tom described how much better he felt upon hearing Charlie's apology. "What I really allowed him to do was *vent,*" Tom said. "I was a safe person for him to dump that on. And I *learned* that. I learned . . . that I was an emotional dumping station for him. And, that's a good thing. . . . I allowed myself to be there so he could just, throw his junk out at me. Get it out of him so he could like, if you will, do his emotional housekeeping." Tom described how letting go of his upbeat helper persona allowed the two of them to form an authentic connection where they could be real with each other. This bond included sharing moments of fun together and times of irritation and anger in the face of the physical and spiritual pain of dying in a prison infirmary.

What Leads to Caring with a Heavy Spirit: Hopes, Fears, and Proselytizing Agendas

> *The friend who can be silent with us in a moment of despair or confusion, who can stay with us in an hour of grief and bereavement, who can tolerate not knowing, not curing, not healing and face with us the reality of our powerlessness, that is a friend who cares.*
> Henri Nouwen, *Out of Solitude*

As we saw in chapter 5, contemplative care can be transformative as we explore and learn from the discomfort and emotional reactions we experience in the course of caregiving. But not all caregivers take a contemplative approach. Rather than developing awareness of what is going on for them internally, some try to suppress the difficult emotions that arise at the hospice bedside. This heavy-handed approach undermines the quality of our care, for when we as caregivers cannot abide with the fullness of our own experience, we compromise our capacity to offer true companionship to others.

Mindy, a thirty-five-year-old Asian American computer analyst, had a rough first three months as a hospice volunteer. She had cared for two patients up to that point, both with dementia, and one of them had died shortly before our interview. She had only seen the man twice, and both times he was experiencing a lot of pain, which was difficult for Mindy. "I've never been with someone in so much pain," she told me. She explained how, on her last visit with him, just two days before he died, he was in such agony that she reacted with a request that was an effort to mitigate her own discomfort. "I just asked him to smile, to smile for me. And he did! It was a quick smile . . . and that was it." Mindy's strategy of trying to elicit an emotional response from the patient for her own benefit, asking him to smile *for me*, was linked with another sentiment she expressed, that she was "trying to stay positive for him." But Mindy did not *feel* positive. Being in the presence of individuals with dementia elicited terror in her. She explained that her biggest challenge in volunteering for hospice "is just the fact that there's no cure for this awful disease that just eats your mind, you know? It's something that just eats you up until you just can't function, until the mind does not function, does not communicate with the body anymore." Since she started volunteering for hospice, she has been gripped with the fear that her parents, now in their sixties, might one day get dementia. She tries to push this fear away by redirecting herself with the thought, "I'm just hopeful that maybe there'll be a cure someday."

Mindy's strategy for suppressing fear involved trying to be upbeat or telling herself or the patients in her care to think positive thoughts or at least feign a positive appearance. But a smile was not all she tried to get from those in her care. There was a more fundamental agenda that brought Mindy to hospice work and shaped how she related to those in her care. Mindy had no background or particular interest in end-of-life caregiving for its own sake. Instead, it was her recent experience of religious conversion that sparked her interest in attending those who are dying. "I've only been a Christian for about two years, but I've been pretty passionate about it lately," she told me. "And so obviously when I signed up for this hospice I actually was thinking about talking to someone about God in hopes of . . . if they don't believe in God, in hopes of bringing them close to God before they pass on." Mindy explained that when she asks patients, "Do you know who God is?" she finds that, in their dementia, they can't understand her question or stay focused on answering it. This dynamic is hard for Mindy, so she tries to comfort herself with the thought, "Hopefully they believe in God." More generally, she explained, "I try not to get too attached to the patients. . . . It's like I go there, I do my job, and when I leave I don't think about it, I try not to think about it, I just detach myself."

Caring for those with dementia can present unique challenges to caregivers. Yet the difficulties Mindy faced as a hospice volunteer resulted more from her own religious zeal and lack of attunement to her own emotional needs than from any challenges she faced in meeting the actual needs of patients in her care. Hospice organizations are quite clear that it is inappropriate to try to convert a patient to one's own religious beliefs, and in this way, Mindy was an outlier among the many volunteers I interviewed. There was just one other volunteer I talked with who shared Mindy's evangelical mission, and she too engaged the same heavy-handed strategy of trying to manage her own emotions and the emotions of those in her care.

Connie, a white woman in her midsixties, had been employed on the administrative side of a hospice for several years, and then, following a health crisis in her own life, became involved as a direct-care volunteer at the hospice where she worked. Her shift into volunteering eventually resulted in her taking over the role as volunteer coordinator at the hospice when the former volunteer coordinator resigned. Connie had been in her capacity as volunteer coordinator for just a month when I contacted the hospice to inquire about conducting interviews with their volunteers.

Connie expressed an interest in learning how to better recruit and retain volunteers. The hospice had been founded by an order of nuns, and she indicated that over the years, they have had "a subset of very committed volunteers" as well as some temporary volunteers who are completing internships for seminary. "Others," she said, "burn out or some do it for a while and then they aren't committed." Connie was particularly interested in recruiting fellow Christians to volunteer at the hospice because, in her mind, to do this work, it is essential to have "pure motives." She referred me to a book by Rick Warren titled *The Purpose Driven Life*, which according to Connie outlined "what the Christian heart should look like." She explained that she volunteered "out of gratitude for everything that God has given me and because I truly love other people," emphasizing that "when you come across committed Christians, you will find this kind of motivation." Pointing to her evangelical intentions, she asked rhetorically, "How can we bring others to our faith if we don't have that attractiveness in our own life?"

During my time at the hospice, I had the opportunity to witness Connie interact with several patients. One of those patients was Harriet, a ninety-four-year-old African American woman. Upon entering Harriet's room, Connie walked around to the far side of her bed, put her hands to Harriet's face, and asked, "How are you today, my little girl?" Harriet nodded, but did not speak. Connie then bent over Harriet, cupped her face in her hands and kissed her right cheek numerous times. She then looked into Harriet's eyes, their faces only inches apart, and asked again, this time in a near whisper, "How's my little girl today?" Harriet nodded and stated quietly, "I'm okay," to which Connie retorted, "I want to hear you say you're terrific." Harriet nodded again, but this time without speaking.

Connie told me that her role as a volunteer involved being "completely focused on the patient," yet in this encounter, she sought a display of emotion from Harriet that was quite out of sync with Harriet's needs and much more about her own need for assurance and emotion management. In my observation, Connie's kisses and requests made Harriet quite uncomfortable. In any case, Harriet did not kiss back, nor did she meet Connie in her request to tell her she was "terrific." And despite any good intentions Connie may have had, a white woman referring to a ninety-four-year-old African American woman thirty years her senior as "my little girl" indicates a form of infantilization, a malignant expression of care that does not affirm the dignity of the care recipient. When Connie left Harriet's room, she repeated this style of interaction with the African American patient in the adjacent room, pointing to a general pattern in how she sought to manage the emotions of bedridden patients and her own emotions as a caregiver.

I found it difficult to witness Connie interacting with patients in this manner. It was likewise odd to hear her speak of her role as volunteer coordinator. She was suspicious of a Buddhist workshop that a prospective volunteer was about to attend, suggesting that a committed Christian approach to volunteering is "a different perspective from the Zen approach to spirituality focusing on terms like 'meditation' or 'contemplative' or 'existential.'"

Contemplative care is not inherently Buddhist or "Zen," and as we saw in chapter 1, the contemplative origins of the modern hospice movement are Christian, not Buddhist. Many of the volunteers I interviewed self-identified as Christian, and although most did not use the language of "contemplative care" to describe their volunteering, they articulated the necessity of developing self-awareness and engaging in deep listening to discern the actual needs of patients in the present moment. They also eschewed imposing their religious views on those in their care.

Sam, a devout Christian, had volunteered for sixteen years at the same hospice as Connie, and as we saw in chapter 6, he was quite moved when a patient in his care asked if he would pray with him. Yet he was clear that as a hospice volunteer "you can't in any way advocate this approach to religion or any approach or even a nonapproach, it's just not discussable.... You have to be absolutely passive to what the patient wants." This is a gentle approach that, in his mind, "takes a certain maturity."

Similarly, Susan, who described herself as having "a strong faith," expressed that she is careful to avoid bringing up religion with patients. At the same time, she is receptive to patients talking about anything they might have on their minds, including religion. During her six years of hospice volunteering in two hospitals in upstate New York, several patients had initiated conversations with her about religion. She described one encounter with Lucille, a woman at the very end of life, who told Susan of the comfort she felt in being loved by God and "the help that she had gained from him, this feeling that he was with her." Susan recounted how both she and Lucille began crying as they "felt the true presence of the Lord" in their midst. She described the moment as "comforting and joyful" for Lucille, and a "top-of-the-mountain experience" for herself as a caregiver. Lucille died just a few days later.

Some hospice administrators have spoken of the difficulty of "managing overtly religious volunteers,"[6] potentially confirming a view expressed over three decades ago that the "intensity" of hospice volunteers' religious views "may give clues to the degree that individuals may impose their own value system on others."[7] Yet the issue is not whether a volunteer has a strong religious faith but whether or not their care is grounded in the patient-centered principles of the hospice movement. Frau Fuchs, for example, had been engaged in a hospice initiative for four years in a rural area of the Black Forest region of Germany, and as a Catholic, religion played a vital role in her motivation to engage in this work. Yet, like Susan, she explained that she only talks about religion if the patient initiates. She drew on a musical metaphor: "We are second violin, the dying person is the first violin, and we are the accompaniment and always remain in the background." Frau Fuchs found this metaphor a powerful reminder that skillful care at the hospice bedside involves a light touch, requiring her to attune to the wishes and needs of patients and their family members without the interference of any agenda of her own, religious or otherwise.

CONTEMPLATION
A Playful Spirit of Compassion

Play is a receptive mode of being, a fundamentally other-oriented stance that deepens empathy and invites a compassionate response. As anyone who has engaged in the world of improv knows, entering with others into the space of play requires attunement to their needs, receptivity to their leads, and awareness of the boundaries of what's possible.

The hospice volunteer occupies a fluid social form allowing her to take on various energies and imagined roles as she attends to the needs of those in her care. Her playful spirit can perhaps best be captured with the openness of the question, "Who shall I be for this person in this moment?" Is it the warmth of a mother, the affirmation of a lover, the companionship of a sister, or the honesty of a friend that is most needed in this moment?

Reflecting on your own caregiving practice, whether at the end of life or in another context, have there been times when you engaged in "as if" relationships with someone in your care, perhaps being "like a friend" or "like family" to a patient? From your perspective, were these relationships healing or otherwise beneficial to the patient, and on what grounds could you discern this? And in your experience, were these relationships uplifting and meaningful to you as a caregiver? Alternatively, in what contexts have you or might you experience such friendships or family-like relationships as burdensome or emotionally draining?

After you have had some time to think through and possibly write down reflections on your experience, you might join with one or more caregivers in your field to discuss your responses.

In this chapter, I have used the idioms of a light touch and a playfully receptive spirit to describe the empathetic approach of contemplative care. These idioms point to a process of attuning to the uniqueness of this moment, with this person. Health-care organizations have various rules and regulations to guide the actions of staff and volunteers, norms about what one should and should not do. Such norms can help ensure the integrity of care, for example, by protecting patients from volunteers with proselytizing intentions. Yet flourishing as an end-of-life caregiver requires more than fulfilling a prescribed set of tasks and refraining from others. Skillful care requires the capacity to discern "the right way to do the right thing in a particular circumstance, with a particular person, at a particular time."[8] Contemplative caregiving at the bedside of those who are dying is a context for expressing and developing such empathetic and practical wisdom.

When we feel empathy for another, we naturally want to help relieve her suffering. And as caregivers, we may see ourselves as engaging in very serious work. At such times, it can be helpful for us to relax around our desire to make a difference, and perhaps especially when someone is dying. As Zen master Shunryu Suzuki has said about spiritual practice, "What we are doing here is so important that we should not take it too seriously."[9] When we release ourselves from the tight energy of the helper persona, we open to receive another on her terms, which might be surprisingly playful. Play is a fundamental refuge in the face of all manner of suffering, and a powerful language for communing with another in a spirit of equality, trust, and beauty. Sometimes the voice of one's suffering, and the offer to join in transcending it, even if only for a moment, may come in the form of a proposal of marriage, an exchange of "flowery" responses, or an invitation to be someone's mother. The question is whether we as caregivers have the inner freedom to enter such spaces, to accept another on her terms, in her language, in the light of her creative genius.

8

Offering Spiritual Friendship

You and I are here [so] open your heart now and
pour whatever you please into the ears of a friend.
Aelred of Rievaulx, *Spiritual Friendship*

CYNTHIA, the patient in room 220, had pressed her call button, so I headed down to see what she needed. She was sitting up in bed when I entered her room, and as I approached her to deactivate her call button, she looked at me nervously, trying to read my name tag. "What department are you from?" she asked. I told her I was a volunteer, and as I was about to ask her what she needed, Carrie, a nursing aide, entered the room. Cynthia needed to use the bedpan, so I assisted Carrie by gently holding Cynthia to the side while she got the bedpan under her. Carrie asked if I would stick around in case she needed me to help pull Cynthia up in the bed after she was done, so I walked to the far side of the room by the door and waited, out of Cynthia's sight.

As Cynthia sat on the bedpan, she and Carrie had quite a conversation. All the talk centered around eating and voiding. Cynthia seemed quite anxious, repeating herself that she wasn't eating much and didn't have much of an appetite and that she was eating "at odd times." "Is someone recording how often I eat and what I eat? Could someone confirm or ensure that I eat three meals a day?" Carrie tried to assure her that she had nothing to worry about, and that she could eat whenever she wanted.

Cynthia seemed concerned about continuity in her care, asking Carrie whether nurses coming from one shift to the next were aware of what had taken place on the prior shift. Again, she spoke in terms of eating and voiding. "If I am eating my meals at off times, would the girls coming in at night or in the morning have any clue as to whether I had already had my three meals that day?" Over and over she expressed concern in the form of the question: "Where does one end, and the next one begin?" It seemed she was referring to the ending of one day and its three respective meals and the beginning of the next.

After Cynthia was done on the bedpan, Carrie called me over and we got her back up in bed. Cynthia was ready for breakfast, so I took her order of a small egg and cheese omelet, half a muffin, and orange juice. Returning from the kitchen with her food, I pulled up a chair and sat down as she ate her breakfast. She chatted about eating, about her routines around eating, and about working as a receptionist, and she mused about where she had seen me before. I told her I was in her room two weeks earlier when her son was visiting, and I had stopped in to say hello. She assured me that that wasn't it.

When she had had enough of her omelet and muffin, she indicated that I could take away the tray. As I got ready to leave with her dishes, something in the tenor of her talking changed; things got exciting. Sensing the shift, I crouched down at the end of her bed with tray still in hand and listened as she mused again about food, about the pain in her arm, about how she no longer had an interest in reading, about how she had been married for forty-eight years, about how things had worked well with her husband. It started to dawn on me that what she was saying about beginnings and endings had to do with more than tracking staff shifts and meals.

She again asked, "What department are you from?" I started to listen behind and between her words, trying to sense into the needs or desires that might be prompting her questions. Once my focus shifted in this way, she held eye contact and immediately dropped all the nervous talk. She now spoke slowly, more deliberately, and with greater ease. She dropped the coded talk about meals and voiding and began speaking about how the pain in her leg was "respected" by staff at the hospice and by her family, and that *only* her physical pain was acknowledged. Speaking about members of her family, she said, "They feel sorry for me because I am in pain, but I feel sorry for them because they don't believe in anything." After listing the various denominations she was brought up in, she explained how she couldn't talk to anyone in her family about the importance of God in her life and how she was going back to the religion of her earlier years. They just shut down. She explained how her faith has always been there throughout her life and how it is there for her now, but no one in her family could go there with her. She repeated the phrase "so be it" over and over as she recounted the isolation she felt in her spiritual journeying. So be it. Amen.

I had met Cynthia's husband at the hospice a few days earlier, and he had told me about the terrible pain Cynthia had in her left leg because of a shattered bone, recounting in precise detail how the injury had happened. Cynthia spoke to me about the pain as well, but in a wider context. The pain is the one constant in her life, she said, asking, "How much pain should one person be able to endure?" On several occasions, she expressed, "I know what you here at the hospice are trying to do [i.e., palliate pain], and I respect that. That all makes sense to me." But, for her, pain was not just some *thing* to be palliated; it was a process that turned her inward, to questions of the spirit. She used the phrase *soul pain* to distinguish another kind of pain that was more excruciating than the pain she felt in her left arm and left leg—the spiritual pain that was not acknowledged by hospice staff or her family members.

"Where does one end, and the next one begin?" Cynthia felt herself in an in-between state, not quite dying or ready to die, at least not while she still had these unanswered spiritual questions. At the same time, she was aware that something had changed and that she was beginning to exit this world, as indicated by her lack of appetite and her lack of interest in reading. She wondered again if we had met before—"that's why I asked earlier if you were studying theology." She asked my name again, so I wrote it down along with the phrase "the volunteer department." I handed her the paper, and then after reading my name aloud, she took some notes on the paper, stating, "I have my method." She then reached out to shake my hand, expressing gratitude that we had met, along with a wish: "I hope our paths cross again."

We each have our method of revealing our soul's journey to ourselves and to others. Once I got quiet and was able to attend to what was on

Cynthia's heart, to the "soul pain" beneath her anxious talk, the meaning of all her fears about her continuity of care became clear. Cynthia was asking that I witness her spiritual journey, the continuity that had run through her life, and recognize that the pain was not the only "constant" in her life. She knew she was more than her physical pain and wanted that perspective to be shared and affirmed. Beneath all her anxiety about having her meals logged and recorded by staff was a more fundamental question of whether others could hear who she was and accompany her on this journey to the threshold where this life ends and what comes next begins.

This chapter explores an empathetic way of being with another that I call "offering spiritual friendship." We typically think of a friend as someone who knows us well and with whom we share some kind of history. Cynthia and I were not friends in this conventional sense of the term. I had only met her two weeks before, and this conversation was our only substantive interaction. Spiritual friendships are not defined by their longevity or by the level of detail with which we know one another. An offer of spiritual friendship might occur in a single interaction, even in just a passing moment.

Friends are those with whom we can trust our deepest thoughts and struggles, knowing that we will be received with empathy and love. For the transcendentalist philosopher Ralph Waldo Emerson, it is these qualities of truth and tenderness that elevate friendship as the "masterpiece of nature." Friendship demands a quality of reverence, of recognizing the mystery of the other who, in Emerson's words, is never ours to possess but will remain "a stranger in a thousand particulars, that he may come near in the holiest ground."[1] In offering spiritual friendship, we see the other with fresh eyes, unbound by the weight of the past or by fixed assumptions about who they are. The other may reveal specifics of their life to us, but as a spiritual friend, we don't need intimate knowledge of another's personality, their likes or dislikes, who they were or what they may have done in the past. When another entrusts themselves to our care, all that is required on our part is a willingness to listen, empathetically, with patience, to hear the soul's journey unfold before us.

The twelfth-century Cistercian monk Aelred of Rievaulx spoke of spiritual friends as "guardians of the soul" who, through pure intention and empathetic witness, "rejoice with my soul rejoicing, grieve with it grieving."[2] Aelred is one of a long lineage of contemplative authors, including Aristotle and Cicero, who distinguish such friendships for the good from human bonds toward other ends, such as pleasure or personal gain. For all of these authors, spiritual friendship is a relationship of mutual disclosure and support. As I described in chapter 6, there is reciprocity in relationships of contemplative care, although as caregivers, our intention is to empathetically witness another's life journey, a one-sided offer of spiritual friendship. Still, as a spiritual friend, we encounter the other in a spirit of equality.

Sterbebegleitung, the German word for end-of-life care, means accompanying or being a companion to a dying person. The Latin roots of *companion* refer to "one who breaks bread with another," pointing to a condition of equality between the giver and the recipient of care. The notion of accompanying, or journeying with, is also expressed in the Latin root of hospice (*hospes*), which connotes both "host" and "guest." The most fundamental human equality is that of our mortality, and it is this mirror of a more universal journey, behind the idiosyncrasies of this or that person's dying, that reflects back how the one dying is as well the guardian of our own soul.

Friendship and the Weight of the Past

Those who are dying often have a desire to embrace each moment and deeply connect with others. As one hospice nurse explains, "The families who I work with are in a time of their lives where they are open to a supportive stranger. All the layers of fluff that we ordinarily use to buffer us from others are stripped away." Hospice nurses, she suggests, are "safe strangers" with "no history or emotional obligations attached," and this "frees the person who is ill and the family to be how they want to be, and allows hospice caregivers to enter into very real human dramas."[3]

Hospice nurses and nurse's aides frequently do form affectionate bonds with those in their care, although it is hospice volunteers whom many believe are uniquely situated to connect deeply with patients and family members. As sociologists Michael Leming and George Dickinson write, hospice volunteers have "the double benefit of being identified by the patient and family as being knowledgeable but not having the professional status that can create a social distance." In their capacity to abide at the hospice bedside "without emotional involvements or professional entanglements, the volunteer can support the patient and family members as can no other participant in the social network of dying—'stranger and friend' at the same time."[4]

Social psychologists conceptualize friendships as being based on diverse interdependencies and a relational history of unique and shared interpersonal norms and worldviews.[5] These features that are understood as the building blocks of personal relationships are absent in the immediate, short-term, and relatively one-sided self-disclosure that emerges in hospice volunteer-patient relationships. As Kerstin, a home volunteer in Berlin, explains, a type of friendship can form between patients and volunteers precisely because the relationship is unencumbered by the emotional baggage that comes with the relational histories shared by family members and friends.

> I don't share a past with patients, and we won't have any long future together either. And of course, because of that I don't bring any sense of hurt from the past, which as you know doesn't necessarily make family relations or relations among friends any easier. In life, there are all these ups and downs that we associate with others, whereas as a hospice volunteer there is this luxury that you don't bring any baggage with you, you don't weigh down this relationship with anything from the past, and instead are simply able to remain in the moment.

Kerstin described how relating to others free from the weight of emotional baggage transformed the hospice bedside into a powerful contemplative space for cultivating an abiding calm in her life. As she explained, "For me, quite simply, being present in the moment is a capacity that is helpful in just about every area of life, and hospice volunteering creates the perfect context for practicing this capacity." Similarly, Frau Lang described experiencing greater vitality and joy in life on account of being allowed to enter sacred spaces of trust with dying strangers. She spoke of the tremendous possibilities these "relationships that develop out of the present moment" provide for "seeing oneself anew, creating oneself anew, and taking in the present moment." Abiding in the space between suffering and joy, death and life, and stranger and friend enlarged her perceptual world and her capacity for joyful, loving presence. She considered "staying in the present moment" as her primary focus during hospice work and sought to "also live that out in other areas of life."

Frau Lang spoke of herself as a kind of "neutral person" in relation to those in her care, not in the sense of being emotionally detached but in the sense of there being a freshness to the relationship that allowed for honest communication and the possibility for compassionate care. She illustrated this process with the unique role she played in a family where such communication had not been possible. The patient was a man in his seventies, and it was clear that he was dying. "This was denied, negated by his wife, the fact that he did not have much longer to live," she explained. "It was the typical situation where one person won't let the other one go, these habitual patterns or relationship structures that inhibit that." She described how "the wife was still cooking for her husband, even though he didn't want to eat anymore. But somehow if she kept on cooking, you know, that was a guarantee that he would *keep on living*." Frau Lang laughed with compassion at the absurdity of the situation. "He would eat just to please his wife, you know, these little lies and mutual deceptions." Witnessing the suffering in this family touched her deeply, and she often felt the impulse to speak frankly with the couple of the painful dynamics she saw in their relationship. Instead, she patiently visited the man until one day an opportunity opened for a healing conversation.

> The man's son had sent him a photo album of pictures from his life, and one day when the wife was out, he used the photo album as a means to reflect back on his life from the view of this final stage, as a way of speaking the truth that he was dying and to have or develop some closure with that. It was clearly very important to him to be

able to express this as a fact, and he could say this to me as a neutral person what he never could have said had his wife been there.

The healing the man experienced through this exchange resulted from having someone with whom to speak truthfully about his life. Being freed from the weight of his past allowed Frau Lang to arrive in the role of witness in a way no one else in his life could. But the past is not just a heavy burden; it can also be "weighty" as a source of deep meaning and inspiration for compassionate action when the richness of our own biographies is met with a creative spirit.

Empathetic Imagination and the Warrior's Compassion

Military heroes are not born; rather, they have been trained in the group, socialized, and internalized the military moral code to 'protect our own.' Courage, empathy, a sense of efficacy, and valor are salient motivating factors.

    Samuel P. Oliner, *Do Unto Others*

Sam, a veteran, experienced deep meaning in his weekly encounters at the hospice bedside, yet even when he felt an intimate connection with patients, he saw his role as more "formal" than a friendship. In his words, "I'm going to give you my best shot. I'm going to give you my best attention. And I'm going to try and make you as comfortable and have our meeting as enjoyable as I can make it, but we're not going to be friends." But when I asked directly if he felt he had ever become friends with a patient, he responded immediately that he had. He had formed a friendship with a patient named Louis on the basis of their common experience as naval artillery officers. Louis was a "fascinating guy" who had "worked on some really ancient range finders," Sam explained. His only regret in caring for this older gentleman was that he hadn't met him ten years earlier.

A sense of shared identity and commonality of interest or experience can further a bond of friendship in a caregiving relationship. But such a fraternity as Sam experienced with Louis is an unusual basis for compassionate care because of the rarity of such connections for most hospice volunteers. Reflecting back on his sixteen years with hospice, Sam indicated that developing a friendship with a patient based on common life experience was almost akin to "winning the lottery." In other contexts, such fraternal bonds were more common. Alton, a Vietnam veteran who had been incarcerated for nearly three decades, indicated that most of the guys he and his fellow volunteers had cared for through the hospice program at the prison had been veterans. He found it deeply satisfying to help them in their final days. Beyond the greater frequency, the way Alton spoke about the nature of the bonds he formed with the men in his care differed from how Sam spoke about his friendship with Louis. Sam and Louis were a generation apart, and based on Sam's account, their conversations were not so much about combat experience as they were about a common interest in how the technical aspects of naval artillery had changed over time. In this way, their friendship could have just as well been centered on conversations about antique cars or darkroom photography.

The bond Alton felt with his "brothers" was at an existential level and did not necessitate talk. As he explained, most of the Vietnam veterans he cares for through the hospice program "don't really want to talk about their situations over there." "But," he continued, "just knowing that he was there, and knowing what he probably went through, you have a little more sympathy and compassion for [him] I think, having been there yourself. . . . He's part of the same story, part of my story, part of his story."

Alton knew the horrors of war firsthand. "There always seems to have been a survivor's guilt," he told me. "I came back, thirteen of my high school [friends] *didn't* come back." Alton felt "blessed" to be able to care for his fellow veterans, and the blessing was how compassionately caring for others was part of his own journey of healing. "I was drawn to hospice as a way of making amends to my experiences in Vietnam," he said. "This program soon became obvious to me that it was what I needed to do, not only for myself and my own sanity but for all my friends and brothers I lost over there. There were seldom opportunities to say goodbye or bid farewell. They are like bookends to the same saga: Vietnam on the front end, and hospice on the trailing end."

Alton had been a squad leader for part of his time in Vietnam, and his grief and survivor's guilt was tied up with the ambiguity of not knowing what happened to the men in his unit who were evacuated after having sustained injuries in combat. "After they were taken away to a medevac hospital or wherever they went," he explained, "you never saw them again, you never knew whether they passed away, whether they got sent home, or whether they went to some convalescent hospital in Germany or Japan— wherever they'd take these guys for different injuries. . . . Even though I can't remember their names, I still remember their faces, and I remember the situation, and remember all the circumstances that we were in together." The suffering caused by a lack of knowledge about what happened to the men in his squad and not being able to say goodbye to them can be understood in terms of "ambiguous loss," which has been described by psychologists as a "particularly stressful kind of loss because . . . there is no possibility of closure."[6] As with some of the subjects detailed in chapter 4, who found in end-of-life caregiving a way of "making right" traumatic losses from the past, Alton experienced serving as a hospice volunteer in the prison infirmary a path for gaining a sense of closure in relation to his missing squad mates from Vietnam.

Central to integrating traumatic losses and bringing a sense of coherence to one's life's journey is shifting blocked energy through imagining and taking actions that, in a spiritually embodied sense, alter how a story ends. Hospice volunteering became such a path of healing for Alton. Volunteering in the prison infirmary "has kind of gotten me back on track with guys [I lost in Vietnam]," he told me, clarifying that they were "not the same guys, but in the same situation." Caring for veterans in the prison infirmary allowed Alton to complete a memory symbolically, caring for his fellow inmates *as if* they were the injured, perhaps dying, young men from his squad who had been flown out and lost to him more than four decades earlier. In this way, caring at the hospice bedside lifted a burden he had been carrying for most of his adult life. Such is the creativity of the human spirit and the power of contemplative caregiving.

Bill was a fifty-four-year-old Vietnam veteran who volunteered for a hospice in upstate New York. Like Alton, he expressed an empathetic imagination that linked his combat experience with his willingness to accompany others at the end of life as a hospice volunteer. From Bill's perspective, to be there for others when they are dying, "you need real grit, you need to have a side to you that you can always fall back on, you need an inner something that's impenetrable, that's indestructible." His experience of wartime losses in Vietnam were connected to both the source of his inner strength and the deeper "push" he felt to care for others at the end of life.

A few years before Bill began volunteering for hospice, he started visiting three members of his church who were sick, including a fellow Vietnam veteran—Frank—who was nearing the end of life. "We just hit it off right away," he explained. "He was ex-military and so was I. We both went to Vietnam; he was in the Air Force, I was in the Marine Corps, kidding back and forth about that." Similar to how Sam spoke about Louis, Bill described Frank as "the finest old gentleman I ever met in my life, just a nice man. He was one of those people that you meet him and you like him right away." He continued that Frank was unable to speak during his last several visits with him, but "when you start heading down the road, it's all about who's here to be with them, it's important that somebody is there. They don't necessarily need to say anything, they just gotta be there." Bill connected his willingness to be there for Frank and the other two members of his church back to his experience in the Marine Corps. "When I was in the Marine Corps, the one thing they stressed was teamwork," he told me. "These three people I was [caring for], I came to think of them as my team, and you never let a buddy down. You know, he really is, he's my buddy now, so that might be why I'm here at all. I get something because of that, you know, my buddy's in trouble. And I'm going to walk that final mile with my buddy."

I asked Bill what he liked least about volunteering for hospice, and he stated it matter-of-factly: "In the end, it's that I'm going to lose a friend. That would be probably the thing that I least like about the whole situation." But Bill also said that volunteering for hospice was similar to going into combat: "You go into it with your eyes open. This is what I do here, that's what I'm in business for." For Bill, each patient he encounters as a hospice volunteer is his "buddy" whom he will accompany on that final mile, expressing an "as if" subjunctive mind-set similar to Alton's, but with a wider level of reach to include *all* in his care, not just his fellow veterans. In this way, Bill creatively extends the military code to protect our own into a warrior's call to be there for all he encounters.

CONTEMPLATION

Being a Spiritual Friend

Offering spiritual friendship may sound like a lofty goal, but being the guardian of another's soul is always a beautifully down-to-earth way of being. When we show up at the bedside of someone who is dying—or in any other encounter in our lives—we don't wear a mantle announcing that we are arriving as a spiritual friend. Spiritual friendship is a quiet, understated offering.

For this practice, observe and experiment with shifting patterns of interaction in your everyday conversations with others. If you are currently involved in end-of-life caregiving, consider not starting there but with relationships in your family or with friends or others where you are not involved in some kind of helping capacity.

When we interact with others, many of us shift the focus of attention to ourselves, even when we think we are expressing interest in the experience of the other. When someone speaks the pain of their grief, for example, a common response is to say "I know how you feel." But in offering spiritual friendship what matters isn't what *I* know about another's experience, but how I can be a presence that supports her in more deeply knowing and honoring her soul's journey.

For the next couple of days, just observe how common it is in conversation for you to shift the focus of attention onto yourself. If someone says, "I'm having a bad day" or "I'm exhausted," do you respond with "Yeah, me too" (a shift from their experience to your own), or do you invite them to speak more deeply about what's going on in their day? If you observe that you often shift the focus of attention to yourself, experiment with slowing down, allowing for silence, and refraining from immediately jumping in after someone speaks and observe what happens. How do others respond to even subtle shifts in your behavior and mind-set? How do you feel as you allow for greater clarity and intentionality in your interactions? Notice any insight into your own patterns of thought, feeling, and interacting. And notice also your power to shift those patterns with a spirit of mindfulness.

Being a spiritual friend is not about technique. It's not about doing this instead of that. The essence of spiritual friendship is a sincere interest in the lives of others and a willingness to attend with patience to their heart's concerns. In observing yourself in interaction with others, become mindful not just of your outward listening skills but of the inner state of your heart.

Central to the joy of volunteering for hospice is the possibility of offering to someone the loving energy of a close confidant without carrying the baggage of emotional patterns or history of hurts that often characterize more conventional friendships or family relationships. As contemplative caregivers, we can cultivate in ourselves the capacity to offer these same qualities of tenderness and freedom from attachment when we care for others within our own circle of family and friends. Stretching ourselves in this way is a lifetime commitment, and in part 5 of this book I illustrate how I have sought to offer spiritual friendship in my family and elsewhere as if I were at the hospice bedside.

Caring is fundamentally a creative act that engages what I call our empathetic imagination. An example of such loving creativity is the warrior's compassion expressed by veterans caring at the hospice bedside, an unspoken bond of kinship, empathetic connection, and responsibility for the well-being of others as if they were one's brothers or sisters whose lives depended on one's courage and altruistic love. As we will see in the final part of the book, contemplative caregiving can support us in extending the reach of compassion even wider than such familial bonds and feelings of friendship to include a sense of shared humanity even with those who have harmed us or evoke disgust or those we may consider enemies.

PART FIVE

Extending the Reach of Compassion

"Compassion is not something we can turn off and on," wrote a Jewish doctor as she laid out the challenge she faced when she found herself caring for an unreconstructed Nazi patient. "Do we develop compassion only if the patient is morally, philosophically acceptable to us?"

Constance Putnam, *Hospice or Hemlock?*

AT A CONFERENCE a few years back, I gave a talk on the radical principle that underlies the hospice movement: no matter who shows up in that bed, we attend to them with loving care. In this way, hospice care can cut through all the stigmas of society at large—all the variations on the worldview that some are deserving of human kindness and others are not. In my talk, I spoke of how, at a hospice in Germany, some volunteers have struggled living into this ethic when occasionally an old, unreconstructed Nazi or Holocaust denier would end up in the hospice bed. I invited all in the room to contemplate who would be the most challenging person for them to see show up in that bed, and, to the extent that they affirmed the hospice ideal, to consider how they were cultivating themselves, so that they could, in the best way possible, accompany that individual in his or her dying as they would any other person.

Our oldest daughter, Ariana, who was nineteen years old at the time, spent the day with me at the conference, which focused on hospice care in prisons. As Ariana and I were driving home from the conference that day, she reflected, "I wasn't one of those people who stigmatized prisoners and looked at them like they were less than human. I just never thought about them." In that moment of reflection, Ariana acknowledged one of the ways we often dehumanize others—by simply going about our lives and not allowing ourselves to see the suffering of others and consider how we might help bring relief. Currently over two million individuals are incarcerated in the US each year. I invite you to think about them, to hold them in your mind and heart. Although this book only scratches the surface of the structural flaws in our prison system and the issues faced by those who are incarcerated, my hope is that the stories about inmate hospice volunteers in the book will serve as a prompt for exploring the terrain and edges of our heart's embrace of others.

Compassion and empathy seem like such personal processes, yet whether we acknowledge another's suffering and allow our heart to be touched is also shaped by the cultural context of our lives. The sociologist Arlie Hochschild uses the term "empathy maps" to express how our relative position in overlapping structures of oppression and privilege in a global world order influence "who we feel empathy for, and how hard we try to feel it."[1] Similarly, the philosopher Judith Butler speaks of a "hierarchy of grief," how politically motivated cultural frames set limits on "who counts as human" and whose grief and suffering we acknowledge as real.[2]

We don't have to look far to see the power of these concepts. As I write these lines in early July 2018, over two thousand children are being detained in Brownsville, Texas, some under the age of five, separated from their parents by the US government.[3] Over the past weeks, commentators on television and social media have bypassed the trauma caused by separating these children from their parents, with the president of the United States himself tweeting that there is no suffering, only "phony stories of sadness and grief" made up by Democrats to "help them in the elections."[4]

In contrast, a participant at a meditation retreat I attended recently offered a prayer for the separated families, stating how the detained children were not the children of others, but were her own children. As I heard this prayer, I thought of the words of Jesus expressed in Matthew 25:40 that to the extent that you have done it to the least of these, you have done it to me. When compassion fully penetrates our heart, we make no distinction between mine and yours, self and other, worthy and unworthy. In this time of deep suffering for so many, I am heartened by the many lawyers, social workers, therapists, and others who have offered their expertise and loving energy to support the detained children in reuniting with their families and healing from the trauma they have endured.

One way culture expresses in our lives is through the ideals and ways of thinking it provides that shape what we see as possible ways of living and being in the world. Often these ideals are expressed as metaphors that invite us to think about one situation in terms of another. A loving mother, a quintessential caregiving figure, is a common icon representing the Buddhist understanding of compassion. As the Dalai Lama expresses, "True compassion has the intensity and spontaneity of a loving mother caring for her suffering baby. Throughout the day, such a mother's concern for her child affects all her thoughts and actions. This is the attitude we are working to cultivate toward each and every being. When we experience this, we have generated 'great compassion.'"[5]

The power of culture in our lives comes not just through the ideals passed on to us but through the cultural practices that allow us to express those ideals in our everyday lives. This final part of the book considers how end-of-life caregiving can be a practice that supports us in extending the reach of compassion to include all people and situations. This process can enrich our lives with purpose and freedom and create new possibilities for societal flourishing. Chapter 9, "Healing Ourselves, Healing Our World," begins with the understanding that our capacity to acknowledge and compassionately embrace the humanity of others is shaped by our willingness to lovingly accept our own humanity. A beautiful aspect of hospice volunteering is how the unconditional acceptance of the dignity and inherent worth of those in our care encourages us to extend that same loving affection toward ourselves. Over time, this process of remaining present with whatever arises and whoever shows up in the hospice bed can stretch caregivers to extend compassion even in the face of physical or moral disgust.

Caring for those who are dying offers a microcosm of the broader human journey. All the elements are there, including the possibility for ceaseless growth and boundless compassion. Chapter 10, "Compassion Unbound," explores further how we can live into the radical intention to extend the scope of compassionate care to all humanity. The ideal of hospice is that all people deserve dignified care regardless of who they are or what they may have done in their lives. But we have no time to lose. We need not wait until another's days are numbered before extending a hand of compassion. After practicing the view that everyone deserves dignity at end of life, may we come to see that everyone deserves compassionate care at all stages of life? And given the transformative power caregiving can have in the lives of men and women of such diverse backgrounds and life experiences, including those who have been convicted of even the most violent of crimes, how might we rehabilitate society so that these transformative opportunities are available to all?

9

Healing Ourselves, Healing Our World

May the softening of the hardened heart guide us to enter into fuller connection with each other and the unfolding of all life.
Rabbi Yael Levy, *Tikkun Halev—the Healing of the Hardened Heart*

I'VE HEARD THAT THE RELIGIOUS MAN goes to church and thinks about fishing, whereas the spiritual man goes fishing and thinks about God. I don't know what my father thought about when he held that bamboo pole in his hand, but he never hit me when we were fishing. And his patience seemed unending no matter what sort of snags, bird's nests, or other messes I got into. I once sunk a hook deep into the top of my father's head on a backcast. He calmly asked me to remove the hook, and when I couldn't, there was no drama. He just cut the line, rowed us to shore, and drove to the emergency room. An appropriate response.

My father couldn't grow grapes; they withered on the vine. But we had okra and tomatoes, Swiss chard and corn, cucumbers and lettuce, and carrots and beans. Strawberries, in such abundance, deserve a sentence of their own. And at a time when the supermarkets in Essex, Maryland, only offered mealy, oversized red and yellow Delicious apples, we had Gravenstein, Macoun, Stayman, and Winesap, as well as pears, blueberries, and peaches. My father was at home in his body when his hands were dirty. But he wanted things to be pure, clean, and washed white as snow.

In his younger days, he rode a Harley and drank and had an affair with a woman whose husband was off fighting the Nazis. He wanted to go to war, but his hearing in one ear wasn't up to par for military service. So he went the path of the bad boy, impregnating a married woman and bearing a son by her. I have two brothers named Dave. I've never met the oldest one. There are many things about my father I didn't know growing up—the things he did "before I became a Christian," as he put it. In his eyes, he had turned from a life of sin. But hidden in the back of his closet was that leather "King of the Road" vest he never let go of.

I'm a lot like my father. I think I'm kinder than I really am. I want to be better than I need to be. And I too have tried to tuck my passion and anger away in the closet. Safe. Out of sight. Not me.

My relationship with my father had always been difficult on account of the beatings. When I was fifteen, I pushed back, putting an end to his days of hitting me. But the psychic wounding continued and seemed to heighten with the loss of my mother. Unable to hold his own pain, my father had no capacity to comfort or connect with me or my siblings. My attempts to reach out to him only brought more pain and anger. I wanted connection. I wanted a sense of family. But even more so, I wanted him to apologize, to see and feel how he had hurt me with the belts and boards, the Ping-Pong paddles and switches, with his bare hand, and perhaps above all, with the command, "Stop crying or I'll give you something to cry about!" I was made to suffer his punishment in silence, cutting me off from the voice of my own pain.

I confronted my father several times in the months after my mother was killed. Mostly he denied the beatings ever took place. Or he called them "love taps," repeating what I had heard him say so many times as a child, how meting out physical punishment hurt him more than it hurt me. I had had enough. I was nineteen years old when I told myself I would never speak to him again.

I suffered terribly at the hand of my father. And I suffered as well when I cut him out of my life. I thought I could free myself by punishing my father, but I only imprisoned myself further in pain and disconnection. When we harden our hearts to others, perhaps especially to those who have cared for us, however imperfectly, we cut ourselves off from our own humanity. My father had stopped beating me long ago, but I continued to wound myself with the delusion that a compassionate life was possible without including everyone and without acknowledging the depth of my own pain. I couldn't keep it up. Some part of me knew I couldn't run away forever.

I met with my father on three occasions when I was in my twenties, each time with an older sister who, like me, wanted to feel a connection with him, and who, like me, thought that an apology from him was the healing our hearts needed. Each time, she would call him up, arrange for the two of us to meet with him in some public space, and then ask him if he had any idea why we didn't speak to him. My sister, a devout Christian, read to me a passage from the bible, Matthew 18:15–17, in which Jesus advises what should be done when someone "sins against you." We both had independently tried to talk with our father on multiple occasions, and since he "refused to listen," we would now confront him together. We wrapped what we were doing in the holiness of scripture, but my own self-righteousness and grasping after a change in his heart ensured that I would only experience more suffering through these encounters. It would take years before I came to see that I too was refusing to listen.

The week of Father's Day, 2004, I traveled to California to interview a second set of hospice volunteers for this book. During these five days of hearing over and over again my own experience reflected in the narratives of my interview partners, two questions came to me: "If I could sit at the bedside and attend to the needs of so many dying and grieving people—all complete strangers, some of whom I didn't really seem to like—then could I also sit face-to-face with my own father and attend to his heart? Could I meet with him without expecting anything beyond the hope for an apology or even a sense of remorse for his actions and just attend to him as an affirmation of my deepest impulse toward wholeness?" One afternoon as I stepped into the parking lot of the hospital where I was conducting my interviews, I felt moved to call my father. I left a message on his answering machine wishing him a happy Father's Day. I didn't get a return call, but I hadn't asked for one. What I did receive was a softening of my heart, a first step in the realization that I didn't need something outside myself—an apology from my father—to free myself from suffering.

Over the course of the following year, I continued to observe myself caring at the hospice bedside, extending compassion to men and women from diverse social backgrounds, suffering from various ailments of the body—cancer, dementia, diseased organs. The precise circumstances of their physical condition and family situation were always somewhat different. But behind the idiosyncrasies of each individual's experience, I came to see a more universal yearning for dignity, connection, and meaning expressed in this final phase of the human journey. And I knew too that each one of us, including me and my father, would have the same need for compassion and understanding as we approached our final breath.

I called my father again in the summer of 2005 and asked if I could visit him. At age thirty-six, I was at a point in my life where I realized that my own healing and spiritual growth could be furthered through offering my father the same quality of spiritual friendship I offered hospice patients in my care. And I felt the confidence of knowing that my experiences of "listening without judgment" at the hospice bedside had prepared me for being in my father's presence without anxiety or expectation. My father was a bit anxious when I arrived at the house. He still lived in the house where I had grown up, and he had made some major renovations since I had last been there seventeen years earlier. The floor separating my old bedroom from the front basement room where many of the beatings had taken place had been removed, and it was there, in that room of pain, that my father had set up his primary living space. He invited me first to sit with him there and then to venture with him outside to see his gardens. At age eighty, he had difficulty walking on account of the pain in his knees, and so I walked beside him as he wheeled down to the garden on his kickbike, taking the pressure off his legs.

We passed the woodshed and then the trellises of grapevines that never bore fruit. It was there, behind the shed, under the witness of barren vines, that my body had been disciplined year after year with the sting of leather. And then further on to the flourishing vegetable gardens. We took our seat next to the greenhouse, a space that nourishes and protects tender shoots from the chilling cold. The opening prompt was simple. "Dad, would you tell me about your life?" He spoke for three hours nearly without pause. I listened and felt empathy for him as he spoke of so much pain in his life, including losing his mother to cancer at age nine. I heard him struggle with the terror that he might never see her again, how he sought to convince himself that this unchurched woman awaited to receive him in paradise. It was unthinkable that he would be separated from her for eternity, that his dear mother would burn in torment forever. In all my life, this was the only time I ever saw my father cry. And this was the only time I had ever extended the kindness of truly listening to him with an open heart.

When we were done, he asked if we could pray together, and if we could hold hands. I asked if we could do so in silence, and he agreed. We held hands for a brief moment, and then his anxiety broke the silence with a nervous prayer spoken in the name of Jesus. My father knew I meditated, and this concerned him deeply. He needed to pray for my soul. Here was my father being who he was. And there I was, feeling fortunate for the freedom to receive him as he was.

My father died of pancreatic cancer two years later. I accompanied him to chemotherapy, and as he lay on the sofa at the house afterward, surrounded by some of his children, I sang to him at his request the refrain to Isaac Watts's "Alas! And Did My Savior Bleed," a hymn from my childhood, testifying how "at the cross, at the cross, I first saw the light, and the burden of my heart rolled away." And at my request, the final time I saw my father, he allowed me to wash his feet.

In my teens and twenties, and perhaps even up to that very moment, I never would have imagined that I would wash my father's feet. But as I sat there with him, in his living room, aware both of his preparedness to meet his maker and his concern for my soul, it spontaneously arose to offer this gesture of hospitality that held for him such deep spiritual significance. It was at the Last Supper that Jesus washed the feet of his disciples, modeling for them the humble heart and mind of the servant. For my part, opening myself to my father's pain and wanting to honor him before he died was a process of opening to those parts of myself that I despised and wouldn't allow myself to truly see, but could only see in him. In my own journey, hospice caregiving has been integral to a process of releasing me from long-term resentments, such that I need not be so predictable in the usual way of extending kindness only to those who have been kind to me and holding grudges against those who have done me wrong.

Allowing Ourselves to Be Human

This chapter considers the healing power of extending compassion beyond our comfort zone, even out to those who have harmed us or in some way evoke aversion. I think it is important to recognize, at the outset, that very often it is ourselves that we find most difficult to include in our compassionate embrace.

One of my interviewees was Yolanda, a twenty-eight-year-old African American woman who worked in the fast-paced film industry in Los Angeles. "I don't really deal with emotions very well," she told me. "I was just raised to kind of like, 'What are you crying about, you know, just suck it up and keep moving!' ... Bad things happen to people or bad situations happen, and ... I go into ... this weird mode of, 'Well, you know what? It doesn't matter [because] I've got a job to do.' You know, such and such has happened to somebody, okay well either way, I've got a job to do. You know, and I just keep ... going, and going, and going, and I don't deal with it."

Yolanda had gotten involved in hospice just five months before we met, and she could see how her difficulty acknowledging her own feelings led her to become frightened around others who were experiencing grief or other intense emotions. She found herself at a turning point in her life. She felt as if she wasn't by nature cut out to care for people in a nursing home, but she also saw how she was being changed in the process. The work, she said, was forcing her to deal with emotions and to face the reality that she and those she loves will die one day.

Through her own experience, she knew that pushing down emotions doesn't work so well because the emotion is going to come out one way or another. She explained how she might break a nail while doing the laundry and suddenly start crying, and then wonder, "Why am I crying over this fingernail?" She had seen this pattern in her life over and over, and she said, "It's all the stuff that you suppress and haven't dealt with." It wasn't just sadness that she had a hard time relating to, but anger as well. She explained how if someone said something hurtful to her, she had a tendency to push down the hurt. Then months down the road, she said, "a lot of misplaced anger comes out and you don't know where it's coming from, and you're venting it out on somebody who doesn't deserve it." Yolanda recognized that since becoming involved in hospice, she had been changing this pattern in her life, learning to relate more directly to her emotions in the moment.

Coinciding with becoming involved in hospice, Yolanda's closest friend was diagnosed with cancer. Rather than retreating emotionally as she would have done in the past, she began moving toward her friend and toward her own feelings. "If I feel like crying about it, I'm going to cry about it, or if I feel like telling her I love her, I'm going to tell her I love her," she said. "Because she's more like me. We don't get into mushy stuff, we don't get into all that emotional kind of stuff. But now . . . if I feel like saying, you know, I care about you, and I love you and I'm sad, then I need to say that versus waiting and not having a chance to." She might still push her feelings to the side and try to keep herself together when she has to do something for work, but through hospice caregiving, she has recognized a definite shift in her life—she calls it "allowing myself to be more human."

Sean was eighteen when he went to prison on a murder charge from a drug deal gone bad. He had been in prison for nearly nine years when I interviewed him, and for the last five of those years he had been involved in the hospice program caring for his fellow inmates. Sean described how his involvement in hospice care had shown him aspects of his life that he "never thought existed."

Prior to prison, Sean presented himself as a badass, a persona he maintained for the first few years inside. Like many men in and outside the prison, he was shut down emotionally and walled off from others. "I was quick to stage, a more of a violent stage, you could say. It was more of a 'You're not gonna ask me a question, and I'm not gonna talk to you, and you're not gonna get aggressive with me, or this is what will happen.' It was more of a defense mechanism, I guess, when I first came here, and I felt that through certain experiences that I gained before prison, it felt to me that it was necessary action—that's how I needed to carry myself." But he had changed through hospice caregiving: "I learned that I don't need to always carry myself like that, nor do I *ever* really need to carry myself like that." He had struggled his whole life worrying about what others thought of him, and now he felt the freedom to drop the tough guy mask and be real with himself and others. "I've become more open and more willing to engage people or let people engage me and feel more comfortable doing so. . . . Hospice has allowed me to be me."

The transformation of being that Sean described had been a gradual process over the previous five years, beginning with his very first day in the infirmary. He was on an overnight shift alone in the room with a patient, and in the middle of the night, the man got out of the bed and started circling around Sean saying, "I used to be a boxer and I'll whoop your ass!" Sean wasn't sure how to deal with the situation. He said, "I'm just thinking in my head, like I don't wanna hold my hands up in like a defensive measure because that might encourage him to act, and I'm just trying to mitigate it as much as I can by just trying to calm him down and just talk normal." The question "Why would he be doing this?" was running through Sean's mind. "But then another part of my mind is like, 'He's not in his right mind, he doesn't think clearly.' And I'm trying to balance the two thoughts, like this guy is really gonna try to assault me, but at the same time, he's not his normal self, and I think the hardest part to deal with was before he became, before the disease progressed, he was a very gentle man, you never seen that aspect of him."

Sean's experience caring for this man and other patients helped him see that he always has a choice in how he relates to others; he can always think things through, no matter what's going on around him. In the past, if someone had physically challenged him and he fought back, he would tell himself he wasn't responsible for his aggression because "that person elicited that response out of me." But now, he said, "I have that ability to stop and think, when before . . . reaction was the *only* action really." Sean's ability to see how his own mind works—to be able to reflect on how he is in the world, rather than just reacting—developed through becoming interested in how other people's minds work, including the patient who challenged him to a fight. There were the fists right there in his face, but "that part kept coming back to me—it's not the guy, it's the disease that's possessing him, you know, it's messing with his judgment."

Sean began to see himself as a complex human being with moral choice, and affirming his own humanity in this way led him to contemplate what his mind-set regarding others was before coming to prison and before getting involved in hospice. He came to understand how he was never able to see the humanity of those who bought drugs from him earlier in his life. "I never saw individuals as, you know, caring parents, or caring sons or nephews. I always saw them as a person who was going to do drugs whether I supplied them or not, so it doesn't really matter. . . . I no longer saw a face, I saw dollar signs." Through his involvement in hospice care, he came to see those addicted to drugs, those suffering from dementia, or anyone else he encountered in the prison "as full human beings" worthy of compassionate care.

Categorical Disgust and Fundamental Acceptance

The modern hospice movement is premised on the view that all people deserve dignified care regardless of who one is or what one has done in one's life. Living into this guiding principle may, at times, push hospice volunteers to the edge of their spiritual and emotional capacities. To give a sense of how radical this principle is, of what "listening without judgment" *could* mean, I begin this section in a quite unlikely time and place: 1943, outside the Janowska concentration camp at the bedside of a twenty-two-year-old dying SS man named Karl Seidl. Seeking to make a deathbed confession in the presence of a Jew, Seidl requested that someone, any Jew from the camp, be brought to him. That individual was Simon Wiesenthal, who after the war would become renowned for his work pursuing Nazi war criminals and documenting the Holocaust.

"All my instincts were against continuing to listen to this deathbed disavowal," wrote Wiesenthal. "I wanted to get away. The dying man must have felt this, for he dropped the letter and groped for my arm. . . . The movement was so pathetically helpless that all of a sudden I felt sorry for him. I would stay, although I wanted to go. Quietly he continued talking."

At one point, a fly was buzzing around the head of the dying man, and Wiesenthal waved the fly away. "I, a defenseless subhuman, had contrived to lighten the lot of an equally defenseless superman, without thinking, simply as a matter of course," he wrote. After the war was over, Wiesenthal contrived a reason to visit Seidl's grieving mother in her home, and likewise expressed compassion to her by not "diminishing in any way the poor woman's last surviving consolation—faith in the goodness of her son." Inquiring into the meaning of his actions, Wiesenthal writes, "What link was there between me, who might have been among her son's victims, and her, a lonely woman grieving for the ruin of her family amid the ruins of her people? I saw her grief and I knew my own. Was sorrow our common link? Was it possible for grief to be an affinity?"[1]

Wiesenthal's inquiry into the spiritual dimension of bereavement is linked to fundamental questions he raises in his writing regarding justice, mercy, and the possibilities and limits of forgiveness. While the specifics of his experience with Seidl and his mother are quite unique, the energy behind his questions is universal. Wiesenthal's simultaneous aversion to and spontaneous kindness toward Seidl and his mother point to a human spiritual capacity to hold contradictory impulses and bring intention to how we act. Although any of us may be called to such a challenge, hospice volunteers almost certainly can expect to encounter behaviors or perspectives that contradict their own deepest held values.

Julie had been volunteering for hospice for about a year and a half, and she recounted her experience caring for a man with lung cancer over a period of several months. She explained how "things kind of fell apart" when the man was rushed to the ER after the oxygen he took for his emphysema exploded while he was smoking, resulting in burns. At that point, the man moved into his daughter's home, which put a tremendous strain on the family. Julie described how it was not easy for the family to accommodate him in their one-bedroom house, with the father occupying the bedroom, the woman and her husband staying in the living room, and their two children sleeping on the screened-in porch. After describing in detail the background of the living situation, Julie explained, "I'm just setting this up to say that I really did not like these people, *at all*." Every time she visited the house, the daughter would be there. "She was depressed and I don't know what else, but she was *very* bigoted and it would come out at times when she would talk about 'the doctors with the *dot-heads*,' you know, the Indian doctors, and just, bitter and bigoted." About the hospice patient she was visiting, she said, "He was not as loud about it, the gentleman I was sitting and talking with, but he was not someone I would normally choose to hang out with."

Julie had crossed class lines and was being confronted with her own categorical disgust for racial bigots.

> I found that I really had to get to another level to be able to sit there with him for three hours and talk. I really learned how to accept them for who they were and let go of my preconceived notions and my judgments about how people should be and, you know, right and wrong and all these kinds of things. . . . This was a learning experience for me of being able to see through the crap, which was still there, to what this woman was doing for her father, and how her husband, I mean, that he let his whole house be kinda taken over by the fact that this guy took the *one* bedroom and has the oxygen and the nurses and everybody coming in, you know, the fact that they did this. . . . There was a real generosity there that I was able to see.

Julie's experience and perspective bring to light how the contemplative seeing of hospice volunteers, what she called "getting to another level," differs from what sociologists call "managing" one's emotions. Julie did not work to suppress her emotions by trying to change the way she thought about the situation, nor did she try to minimize her feeling of disgust or dislike for what she witnessed by telling herself that she should not judge anyone in her role as a volunteer. Instead, hospice volunteering created for her the possibility of allowing presumably contradictory views to be held in tension. As she explained, "the crap" of racial bigotry was still there, but so too was a depth of generosity that she was able to see. She spoke of "letting go" of her preconceived notions of right and wrong, although not in a relativistic sense that anything goes, but in the sense of being able to see and respond to the fullness of the other in her care, unbound by her own aversion to the bigotry and bitterness she witnessed in the home.

A question many hospice volunteers confront in the course of their work is whether it is helpful to know something about who a person was prior to being admitted as a patient at the hospice. This question was particularly alive for Bettina. Following the deaths of both her brother and her sister, she had begun volunteering at a hospice in Berlin and had been doing so for four years at the time of our first interview. Caring for others at end of life had an "existential draw" for her, and she described how, in some cases, having background information on a patient's life story helped her connect with and have compassion for the person. At one point, there was a man at the hospice, Herr Müller, who had a tracheotomy tube and was not allowed to eat because of the danger that he might choke to death. But he wanted to eat, and the more he was told that he was forbidden to eat, the more he wanted to do so.

Bettina described Herr Müller as "very provocative and quite disgusting, because he took no consideration of the fact that mucus would come out of the tube. He could have very easily placed a cloth over the area, but he just let the mucus run out of it, which really pushed people away." She continued that her fellow volunteers and staff were "deeply disgusted and felt a lot of aggression toward him, and didn't want to be around him." But she felt differently. "It wasn't hard for me to be with him, even though I too felt disgust," she told me. In Bettina's experience, who we are drawn to and who we have an aversion to has to do with our own history and reasons for coming to hospice work. Herr Müller was an addict, and she indicated that, as a recovered addict herself, she too had experienced "existential crises," which gave her a sense of connection and draw to this patient even in the face of her disgust.

After telling of her experience with Herr Müller, Bettina explained that in some instances it might be better if she knew nothing about a patient's past. "We had a patient here once who was on the far right and quite vocal about his racism, and I wondered what he must have done in his past, and I really didn't want to know, because that wouldn't help me in caring for him." But at the same time, she said, "I always receive something no matter who I am caring for, even if it is 'just,' in quotation marks, the wish, 'I don't want to become like this.'" She paused, and then continued, "I have seen so many people come in here who are so deeply embittered, and I sometimes just pray, 'Oh Lord, keep me from becoming bitter throughout my life in my attitude and in my way of thinking.'"

Bettina experienced caring for those who are dying as "a kind of wake-up call to what really matters in life."

> Life is short, and even if I live to be eighty, it will still go by quickly, and if that slips my mind in my everyday life, I will be reminded here at the hospice to ask myself, 'Why do we cause ourselves so much strife within ourselves and with each other?'... Living here in the middle of Neukölln, a densely populated area of Berlin where there's a lot of aggression, a lot of drugs, alcohol, a really tough part of the city, I notice that I can have this aggression in me as I am walking down the street.... Each time when I arrive at the hospice to begin my shift, it's really wild to observe this, but this aggression is just released from me, I come out of the elevator and it's just gone. I find that so interesting that it's simply gone. It's really healing for me to be involved here at this hospice.

The healing she spoke of connected back to caring for all people—even those embittered with aggression and racism, those at war with themselves or with the realities of modern Germany—because her fundamental acceptance of others was, at the same time, a loving embrace of her own humanity.

At one point during the interview, Bettina rolled up the sleeves of her sweater, revealing numerous scars from cutting on both her forearms. I experienced her showing the scars to me as an act of self-assuredness, of nothing to hide or to be ashamed of. Being in the presence of those close to the end, she said, "helps me to become reconciled with my life, with myself, to not be so hard on myself, to be more generous with myself and with others." Many of the inmate volunteers I spoke to in the US likewise expressed how their involvement in end-of-life care had helped them come to terms with their past and supported them in opening in love to themselves and others.

Prisons, like the outside world, are characterized by hierarchies of worth, and at the bottom of the hierarchy among inmates are convicted pedophiles and other sex offenders. "Skinners," as they are known in prison slang, are subjected to routine harassment and assault by their fellow inmates. Having been raped himself as a boy, Joe had a particular propensity for violence against fellow inmates who were sex offenders. And then he became a hospice volunteer in the prison infirmary. He explained how through hospice caregiving he came to see the humanity in all of those in his care, including those he before had only seen as deserving of violence.

> You could have never convinced me that I would be doing vigil on a sex offender. And I've done multiple vigils on sex offenders. And I didn't love them any less. I didn't treat them any different, make them feel any less important than any other person.... I can't say I put in some great amount of effort, it just seemed like the most natural thing in the world to me to love this person, to reach out to be supportive of this person, and not judge them because of what they were convicted for. Now that doesn't mean I have to like everybody and I don't have to like everybody's actions. Half the time I don't like my actions, cause I'm still that emotionally human reactive person, you know, but I can love the spirit of the person. And I can choose to acknowledge that and celebrate that, you know, and not focus on the things that separate me from that person.

As Joe's experience attests, hospice work provides a space for cultivating a way of being beyond worn-out ways of conceiving of who we are and who does and does not belong within the borders of our compassionate embrace. But transforming who we are in this way can be a slow process, especially if our trauma is deep. "Bad things happen to little kids when they run away," Joe explained, "and they happened to me. And just being able to say that kind of helps. Being able to share my story and share my pain helps me get past the pain, or at least heal. [It] allows me to function within that pain." Throughout his life, Joe carried a sense of shame for what had been done to him, and with that, a fear that others would see him as weak. "I need to have this armor," he said. "I need to have another identity, because I fucking hate my life, you know, so let's create this entity that's tough as fucking nails and nobody can hurt. . . . And so, the more you get in touch with yourself or get reintroduced to yourself and to your pain, and get to a place where you can experience letting a little bit of that go at a time, all of a sudden this entity becomes less and less needed." For Joe, hospice caregiving reintroduced him to himself, supporting him in affirming his pain without creating an identity around it, and allowing him to embrace the humanity of others.

CONTEMPLATION

Embracing Our Shared Humanity

The intention in hospice work is to provide compassionate care to every patient and family member regardless of their backgrounds or the circumstances of their lives. In this way, hospice can cut through all the stigmas of society at large. Most fundamentally, it cuts through the presumption that some are deserving of human kindness and others are not.

Imagine for a moment that you are a hospice volunteer, or perhaps you already are. Ask yourself this question: "Who would be the most challenging person for me to see show up in that bed?" Or, more broadly, "Can I recall times in my life, either recently or in the past, when I have seen myself come up against the boundaries of my own compassion? When, for whatever reason, I felt unwilling or resistant to extending kindness to another?"

Allow yourself time to journey with these questions, coming back to them at different points over the next few days. One possibility is to incorporate these questions into a formal meditation practice. Sitting quietly for a few moments, you might close your eyes and observe whose face arises in your mind's eye as you contemplate the following question: "What person or category of people brings up the most fear or aversion in me or seems most difficult for me to imagine caring for?" As you observe what arises for you, you might also investigate this question: "Are there perhaps parts of myself that I feel are somehow unworthy of kindness, cutting me off from fully embracing the humanity of others?"

Trusting your own sense of what is best for you, you might explore sending out wishes for comfort and well-being to all people who are facing declining health or nearing the end of life, including those who bring up fear or aversion in you. Just explore what is possible for you in this moment and try not to judge yourself if there are particular individuals or groups of people you feel unable to include in these well-wishes.

When you are ready, allow yourself to let go of these contemplations, and as you open your eyes, you might notice the quality of lighting or the temperature of the space you are in or how your body feels supported by the chair or sofa you may be sitting on or the earth or floor beneath your feet. Whatever may have come up for you in this contemplation, you could close this practice by affirming the goodness of your intentions in reflecting on these questions and your capacity to become aware of the opening and closing of your own heart.

True compassion knows no limits. It is extended freely to everyone, everywhere, wherever there is suffering. But when we have experienced trauma or been harmed by others, or when our thinking and feeling have been shaped by societal stigmas or judgments of particular groups, we might not offer compassion so freely or may even wish harm on others. Yet we need not be bound by these experiences. We can gradually free ourselves from their hold through practices that allow us to affirm our intention to include all in our heart's embrace, including ourselves. Compassion does not require that we like everyone, only that we can see and empathize with their common humanity. And we don't have to get over our aversions and judgments in order to provide loving care to another; we can care even in the face of those judgments. When we have the mind-set to know and stretch ourselves, any step we take toward softening our heart can deepen our sense of affinity with others and with the unfolding of all life.

10

Compassion Unbound

*Can true humility and compassion exist in our words
and eyes unless we know we too are capable of any act?*
St. Francis of Assisi, "Humility and Compassion" in
Love Poems from God

ON JANUARY 16, 1998, Loyola University in New Orleans hosted "The Courage to Act for Justice," a public conversation between Sister Helen Prejean and Father Daniel Berrigan. The intention of the event was to learn of the sources of faith and courage Prejean and Berrigan had drawn upon to act with integrity and prophetic witness in their respective areas of social justice work. Just a few years earlier, Prejean's book *Dead Man Walking* had been made into a major motion picture and during the event she spoke of counseling death row inmates at Louisiana's Angola Prison and of befriending victims' families. The event was held in a large auditorium, and when the floor was opened for questions, a man on the far left of the auditorium directly across from me stood and asked to be recognized. Mirroring the confusion and animosity Prejean sometimes received from victims' families, the man expressed anger at her for meeting with death row inmates given the tremendous suffering they had caused by ending someone's life. I was twenty-nine years old at the time, and there I was, a decade after my mother's life had been taken, seeing a choice being presented before me. I could forever remain a victim, arresting my healing in righteous anger for what had been done to my mother and my family, or I could accept that there is suffering all around, and where there is suffering, there can be compassion.

I knew that night that I would one day go to the prison and meet with James Prince, the man who murdered my mother. I knew the time would come when I would confront both the rage inside me and the humanity of this man who had so brutalized and disfigured my mother that a viewing of her body was not possible. But it would take years before I would come to this path. Although the prophetic witness of Prejean, Berrigan, and so many other compassionate and wise women and men helped inspire me to live fully, it was a rather humble practice, in the end, that allowed me to cultivate the compassionate sensibilities and confidence to know that I could face James and face myself. That practice was sitting at the hospice bedside.

On March 1, 2011, I sent an email to an organization called Murder Victims' Families for Reconciliation asking for guidance and support in trying to meet James. As I sat in the café writing the email, tears quietly rolled down my cheeks. These were tears of courage, an affirmation of a first outer step in recognition of the many inner steps I had already taken on this path. I couldn't have known it at the time, but when Jerome invited me into his French Quarter apartment in the summer of 1993, I was beginning a contemplative journey that would lead me to find healing, compassion, and spiritual growth through end-of-life caregiving. It would have been absurd had I began volunteering for hospice with the hope that doing so would prepare me to meet the man who murdered my mother. But the power and beauty of contemplative practice lies precisely in how it quietly works on us through our committed work in the practice. When I ate avocado and turkey sandwiches with Jerome that first afternoon, I was simply eating avocado and turkey sandwiches with Jerome. And so it has been with each encounter over the years, simply being present to the moment, and in the process, gradually deepening my intention and capacity to sit with discomfort, empathetically connect with diverse others, and extend the reach of compassion as far as I possibly could.

In time, I became connected with Lauren Abramson, the founder and director of the Community Conferencing Center[1] in Baltimore, Maryland, an organization that supports healing through restorative practices that bring together the perpetrators and victims of crimes. Lauren contacted James on my behalf to request a meeting at the prison between us. James agreed to meet with me, although he told Lauren that he didn't kill my mother, just as he had denied doing so at his sentencing twenty-three years earlier. But my intention in wanting to meet with James was not to gain a confession—I wasn't motivated by such a heavy-handed agenda. Instead, as I explained to Lauren, my intention was to discover what I might learn by moving closer to this man who had caused me so much pain. I had seen James during the trial in 1988, and at that time, I fantasized how I wanted to torture and murder him. James was the only person I had ever had such thoughts about, and I sensed that it would be beneficial for me to be face-to-face with him and to look at him with different thoughts running through my mind. I wanted to find out whether I could see him as a human being and to explore the possibility that if I could open my heart to him, there might be fewer barriers to me doing so with others who had not caused me so much pain.

We arrived at the North Branch Correctional Institution in Cumberland, Maryland, at 10:30 a.m. on a rainy Monday morning, November 21, 2011. We were greeted in the waiting room by Mr. Prince's assigned caseworker, a young man in his midthirties who was quite nervous about what he was certain was going to be a "hostile" encounter between James and me. As he explained, "Mr. Prince is going to use the meeting to retry his case." James did claim his innocence, applying far-fetched logic in statements such as, "When I left the house there was no blood on me, all the blood was in that one room." But the meeting was otherwise full of surprises. James, a self-described "junkie" whose untreated addiction continued to bring punishment and isolation upon him, explained how his mother had died while he was in prison, and how painful it was to be separated from her as she was dying and to be unable to attend her funeral. My nineteen-year-old self would have delighted in hearing of such just deserts. And yet here I was feeling empathy for this man who, in his words, "lived in hell" in prison.

My intention in meeting with James wasn't to change him or his situation but to explore and heal any darkness that may have been lurking in my heart. What I discovered was that the real struggles in my life—the places where I get stuck, the hurts that trigger me—are not in that penitentiary, but in my own family, in my own workplace, and within the routine encounters of my everyday life. My time at the prison meeting James was quite easy for me, and in some ways, it wasn't a whole lot different from my encounters with hospice patients. My intentions were clear, and I had prepared myself well for approaching him with beginner's mind and an open heart.

The real learning edge for me is in extending that same intentionality and empathetic witness to less dramatic, but more common interactions. Many hospice volunteers I interviewed made similar statements about their own lives. One volunteer explained, for example, how when he's with a patient, he has no problem being "Mr. Compassion at the bedside." That was easy. The real question for him was, "Can I really do that in every aspect of my life?"

We often think of compassion as some sort of heroic activity, and I don't want to feed into that narrative by telling of my meeting with the man who murdered my mother. To cultivate compassion in our lives and to stretch ourselves to extend compassion without limits, we start with the boring suffering of our daily lives. After being with so many people in their dying days, many hospice volunteers have told me that where they really get reactive is not in being around those who are dying but in experiences that are much more mundane—relating with one's family, being present at the checkout counter, getting stuck in traffic. So, for all my talk about contemplative end-of-life care as spiritual practice, for some of us, a more challenging compassion practice might be contemplative driving during rush hour. And whatever our growing edges are, each time we move toward and meet suffering with compassion, we offer one more expression of the human journey of mending the heart and healing our world. We all have this spiritual capacity to face the suffering of this life with courage and compassion. The suffering of this world is great, and so are the possibilities for healing and renewal.

Lineages of Radical Compassion

We live in a time of unprecedented disconnection and emotional and spiritual malaise. As the current epidemic of opioid addiction indicates, we will not be able to prescribe ourselves into a brighter future. Flashpoints like the many recent school shootings may suggest that the societal crisis we face borders on the psychiatric, but I believe that the deepest roots of our malaise do not lie in our personal psychologies. Instead, they have to do with our disconnection from foundational aspects of the human experience, including opportunities to care and a sense of connection to a meaningful past and vibrant future. Some see trainings in compassion as a key to healing ourselves and healing our world. I share this perspective, though in view of *compassion* having become a buzzword in pop culture, I think it's important to be clear about what it means.

According to a 2016 article in the magazine *Mindful*, for example, mindfulness is now passé and compassion for oneself is the new trend. "Did you know self-compassion is the new black?," the article begins. "Last year it was mindfulness but this year, attending without judgment is out and compassion for you as an antidote to your perceived low self-worth, failure, or any other form of suffering is definitely in."[2] And just as mindfulness in the popular imagination has been presented as a set of techniques that "gives you an edge at work" and helps you "get the results you want," so too are middle-class audiences now told that "compassion enhances our professional life."[3] Such instrumental and self-referential notions of compassion seem rather truncated when set against the legacy of Cicely Saunders, Florence Wald, and other hospice founders. Wald certainly did not enhance her professional life by giving up her deanship at Yale University and committing herself to founding the first hospice in the United States. And none of the hospice founders sought better care for the dying because doing so was "in." Rather, their compassionate activity was countercultural and in some ways quite radical, as they sought to transform cultural practices that had limited compassionate possibilities at the dying bed and beyond.

In recent years, the concept of "radical compassion" has been invoked in various contexts, perhaps in an attempt to restore a deeper ethical view in the current era in which compassion may seem more like a technique for self-betterment than a path for transforming suffering and the causes of suffering. In part 1 of this book I outlined how compassion is both an inside and an outside job, and how an appropriate response to suffering addresses both its individual and societal dimensions. As the Reverend Martin Luther King Jr. powerfully stated in his "Beyond Vietnam" speech—given on April 4, 1967, exactly one year prior to his murder—"True compassion is more than flinging a coin to a beggar. It comes to see that an edifice which produces beggars needs restructuring."[4] It was in that same era of radical social change that the early hospice founders created alternative approaches to end-of-life care that honored the individuality and holistic needs of dying people and their family members in contrast to the death-denying, hierarchical approach of the male-dominated medical model of the time.

For all who are currently involved in end-of-life caregiving or who are considering engaging in such care, we are part of a vast lineage of compassion that can encourage us and inspire our work. Speaking of religious heritage, the Presbyterian minister Carrie Doehring writes, "The study of compassion throughout the history of one's own tradition can nurture the religious faith of caregivers, making compassionate love a tangible emotional and spiritual experience."[5] What I find particularly powerful about the lineage of contemplative care outlined in chapter 1 of this book is that it bridges across religion, sexuality, and other social categories that often divide us, rather than bring us together. The vast compassionate values of the hospice movement that seek to uphold the dignity of the individual and the wider community in this most vulnerable time of our lives can be a healing balm in a world that seems increasingly fractured by tribalistic loyalties.

The power of lineages of compassion is twofold. First, there will be times when we will feel discouraged in our care, feeling ineffective or unable to help another or simply exhausted and questioning whether we have the strength to go on. We don't have to carry the weight of the world alone. In these moments, recalling the power of lineage, and that even the great giants of care faced dark nights of the soul, can help sustain our spirit. We can recall, as they did, that our power as contemplative caregivers lies not in the effectiveness of our doing but in the quality of our being grounded in our willingness to see the interconnectedness of life and embrace with humility our powerlessness in the face of death.

Second, we can sustain the spirit of the lineage of which we are a part through championing the compassionate ideals of those who came before. Some say the hospice movement is no longer a movement; it's now just another part of the medical establishment. But radical possibilities for furthering compassionate end-of-life care exist both in the United States and across the globe. The legacy of Cicely Saunders continues to inspire new initiatives to expand compassionate care to those who are dying and grieving, including in countries such as Bangladesh and Vietnam where "dying well is still considered a privilege . . . [and] where millions suffer unnecessarily from unbearable pain and other debilitating symptoms [such] that they lose the will to live."[6] And within the United States, large segments of society continue to suffer and die without access to holistic, compassionate care readily available to the middle and upper classes. As I discuss further below, hospice is a concept, not just a model of care, and there is much room for the creative integration of this concept throughout all spheres of society to deepen the broader vision of the founders that people will "feel again their faith, their compassion, their humanity."[7]

No Time to Lose

We all wish to be happy, and in contemporary culture, we are bombarded with so many messages telling us that happiness is about feeling good, acquiring things, being young and wrinkle-free. But true happiness, what the ancient Greeks called *eudaimonia*, results from engaging life with meaning and purpose. Integral to the power of end-of-life caregiving is how it can inspire meaning in our lives through bringing into our awareness, over and over, what is so often denied in the wider society: death will come to us all, no matter how young or vibrant we may feel ourselves to be. As Carmine expresses, hospice volunteering can serve as a modern-day *memento mori*: "Being with that dying person, seeing those last few breaths, I'm feeling what has been happening and is happening—*we* are taking those breaths, we're just not counting yet." Whereas, in the medieval Christian era, such reminders served to focus one's attention on the afterlife, today many hospice volunteers express how witnessing cycles of living and dying at the hospice bedside inspires them to a more committed focus on the purpose of this life. In the face of the brevity of life, many wish to allow compassion to permeate all aspects of their life with no time lost in bitterness or worry.

Paula had struggled financially throughout her life, and at age sixty-four she was living on a fixed income. Through caring at the hospice bedside, she discovered that she was becoming less "self-absorbed with my little mundane problems" and more grateful for the abundance of her life. To explain this shift, she expressed how residents at the nursing home "usually have pictures on the wall of their family—you'll see a wedding picture, and you can tell by the color of the picture how old it is . . . and it's hard to believe that this lady is the same lady lying in this bed. . . . And that's living proof, right then and there in that bed, and you look at that picture, that wedding picture, and you know that this is the truth. . . . We came into this world, and none of us are going to get out of this world alive." For Paula, seeing clearly the shortness of life, even if someone lives into their eighties, deepened her sense of affinity with those she met as a hospice volunteer and in other parts of her life. "We're not strangers," she explained. "The same God that made me, made them." And even though it's not her mother in the hospice bed, "It's somebody's mother, it's somebody's brother, it's somebody's child."

Yolanda had only been volunteering for hospice for a few months, but even so, she noticed subtle ways her perspective on life and those around her was shifting. "In LA everything's going so fast and when you're on the highway, it's like everyone's just in my way. I would just experience everyone else on the highway as just being in my way and not experience them as others who are just living their life." Now she was becoming more curious about the lives of others and more aware of opportunities to express compassion. Just a few days before our interview, for example, she was walking down the street in conversation with a friend when she noticed an elderly woman in a wheelchair who was struggling to get up a ramp. Without thinking about it, she simply walked over and helped the woman up the ramp and then jumped right back in the conversation with her friend. Not used to seeing Yolanda express kindness in this way, her friend asked, "What the hell were you doing there, you didn't even know that woman!" And that was the point for Yolanda—we don't need to know someone to offer a hand of compassion. All of the residents at the nursing home she had been caring for had advanced dementia, and every week when she showed up, she experienced firsthand how knowing someone was not required to express compassion.

Michael had been volunteering for hospice for over ten years, and the lessons he had learned had profoundly changed his life. But, he acknowledged that they weren't really about caring for dying people per se but about an intentional approach to life more generally. "Hospice is about being present and loving people by virtue of the fact of where they are in their lives." The real lesson, he explained, is that we "could be like that for *everyone*, regardless of where they are in their lives." In Michael's view, everyone is struggling in some way or other, "even the ones who are jerks," and what happens with hospice is "the scope of what they're struggling with is actually narrowed so much you get to really see what matters to people. Generally, it's more focused, and you can actually understand it better." We often don't know the struggles of people we meet in life, but if someone takes the parking spot we wanted or is irritable or unkind toward us, we can say, "Now just a minute. What if this is their last thirty seconds? What if you knew that, how would you react? And it'd be nice to be able to hold that in your heart all the time. I'm not saying I do that; I'm just saying that that is really what I think the hospice work has done for me and that I want to be more like that."

When Michael spoke of wanting to extend the same compassion he expressed at the hospice bedside to all people in his life, he acknowledged that for many years, the kind of person he was with dying people "got pigeonholed in hospice." In truth, it wasn't until he suffered a stroke himself that the lessons of hospice more fully permeated his life. "You sort of hate having to have an almost fatal injury be what you need to get there," he said with a laugh. But he was grateful for how at this point in his life things that mattered to him had "gotten clearer and more focused." Here Michael points to a paradox of living well, how it is often suffering that wakes us up to life or at least inspires is to want to wake up. For Michael, it was a near-fatal stroke. For me, it was the murder of my mother, and then later, a painful divorce. And for many involved in hospice care, it is similarly the death of a loved one that inspires them to care.

I've heard that a student of Buddhism once asked his teacher why Buddhists place so much importance on the breath. The teacher responded by holding his head under water. Point made. Breath is awesome when it comes to the last one, but how can we have this view long before our days are numbered? How can we remind ourselves to approach all we do with a spirit of awe and reverence for life? There is no time to lose—this very moment is a precious opportunity to cultivate and express compassion.

A Time for Reflection

The mystic is not a special kind of human being, but every human being is a special kind of mystic. And so we are challenged to become the mystic we are meant to be.
Brother David Steindl-Rast, *Faith, Mysticism, and Prayer*

Over the many years I have been involved in end-of-life care, so many people have responded in awe at the mention of hospice, telling me "It takes a special kind of person to do that." In part 2 of this book, I have tried to put this myth to rest. To rephrase the point made by David Steindl-Rast in the above epigraph, the contemplative caregiver is not a special kind of person, but every person is a special kind of contemplative caregiver.

I hope this book will inspire some readers to care at the hospice bedside, but more broadly, I hope it serves as an invitation to see opportunities to care with a contemplative spirit wherever and with whomever our life brings us in contact. I have found healing and joy in caring for those who are dying, yet the challenge for each of us is to express compassion in our lives in ways that resonate with our own spirit and sense of purpose. Caring for dying people can be a noble endeavor, but so can teaching math, practicing law, or serving in public office. There are many paths for engaging the suffering of the world with compassion and for being transformed in the process.

In part 1 of this book I suggested that engaging in contemplative caregiving does not require that one be a practitioner of meditation. Yet contemplative caregiving does require a commitment to contemplation in one's life, in whatever form that takes. We all need times of silence and reflection in our days, and the intention behind the contemplations included in each chapter of this book is to support you in integrating times of formal contemplation in your regular practice of caregiving.

The need for consciously integrating space for reflection in our lives is perhaps particularly strong for paid caregivers who do not enjoy the luxury of being able to simply be with one patient at a time the way a hospice volunteer can. Philip, for example, had volunteered for hospice for seven years, and it was during his time as a volunteer that he decided to undertake a clinical pastoral education training to become a certified chaplain. He assumed that he would get to know patients better working full-time as a chaplain as opposed to volunteering at the hospice once per week. He discovered, however, that in fact he had less time with patients and was getting to know them less as a chaplain. "Now I have so many people to see that I only see them sometimes once a month," he explained. Since he is responsible for a significant amount of paperwork as well as attending meetings, less than half of his workday involves being with patients.

As a volunteer, Philip would often spend two hours or more on a shift just sitting with someone in their room. "What I miss the most is just being the guy that has nothing else to do," he told me. Now he seeks to embody that same relaxed energy in his work as a chaplain by holding internally the attitude, "I've got all the time in the world for you." Crucial to his capacity to do so, he explained, was his longtime practice of meditation. Nonetheless, he expressed that maintaining the freshness of this perspective is one of his greatest challenges in working as a chaplain. How do *you* maintain the freshness of your perspective and remain grounded in your compassionate intentions in your work in the world? How do you make time for reflection in your days while caring for others and at other moments in your life?

I recently completed a clinical training to become a certified nursing assistant (CNA) on a respiratory unit of a major medical center, a context of care that is different from hospice volunteering in many respects. In a future book, I will offer an approach to contemplative care geared specifically toward those engaged in basic nursing care, where the focus is very much on doing—taking vital signs, assisting with toileting, bathing and grooming patients, and charting patients' condition and care. I have found that, even in this busier context of caregiving, with some creativity I can still approach my work as spiritual practice, a path for expressing compassion and for continuing to transform my own being.

One day there was a patient on the unit who frequently struggled for breath on account of her condition, and the sound of her gasping and wheezing was quite unsettling for me. The nurses' station was directly outside the room of this patient, and her door was open. The more seasoned nursing assistants around me simply continued with their charting, seemingly unaware of the suffering this patient was enduring. When I asked others if they were alarmed by the sounds, I was told that such struggle for breath was her "baseline" and that there was nothing we could do about it. I sat quietly at the nursing station for another moment and allowed myself to register this reality: another person just a few feet away from me was suffering terribly, and I was powerless, in a medical sense, to relieve her suffering. That brief moment of reflection was all that I needed to remind me that embracing my powerlessness without fear is the ground of compassionate presence.

I walked into the patient's room and asked if I could sit by her bed for a moment. She too told me that her shortness of breath was just the way things were at this point in her life. But she didn't need to be alone in her suffering. She allowed me to sit by her and gently rub her shoulders. Within just a few minutes, her breath had deepened and she said she wanted to rest. When I glanced back in her room a few minutes later she was sleeping.

Rehabilitating Society: Beyond the Burden and Privilege to Care

A caring society will assure that the care of the sick, which is
among the more rudimentary goods for a fully human life,
is distributed equitably.
　　Edmund Pellegrino and David Thomasma,
　　The Christian Virtues in Medical Practice

My father never knew the joys of caregiving. My mother was burdened by the obligation to care. Both suffered as a result. Much has been written about the suffering caused when certain groups in society, almost always women, and often women of color, are obligated to care under conditions that are emotionally or physically draining to themselves. This book has addressed a different dimension of the crisis of care in contemporary society—how the power of caregiving to transform our lives has become largely forgotten.

So many times at the hospice, patients have told me how they didn't want to be a burden on their children. And then one afternoon, toward the end of my mother-in-law's life, I was sitting on the floor helping to put on her shoes, and she asked, "Am I a burden on you right now?" On one level, I wasn't surprised by the question, having heard such fears expressed by many others over the years. But I was still so deeply moved that she was able to express this fear, and that with ease we were able to put it to rest. "Tulakimou (Tula, my love)," I said, using the term of endearment she allowed only me, Yanni, to use. "Do you have any idea how you are blessing my life in allowing me to care for you?" Tula had received me into the family as if I were her son, and now, in her graceful openness to the cycle of life and the reciprocity of care, was gifting me the opportunity to attend to her as if she were my mother. As I write these lines, I sit on the balcony of a small villa in a mountain village on the island of Ikaria, Tula's birthplace. And as the sound of bouzoukis being played in the town below travels upward, I continue to receive Tula's blessing and feel my indebtedness to her for allowing me to experience the fullness of my humanity.

Many hospice volunteers will tell you that it is a "privilege" to be able to care for patients and their family members. But when we use such language, we often forget that the presence of privilege implies its opposite—deprivation. My father was of a generation when men in his social milieu did not have the privilege of being a caring man as I am today. There was no hospice caregiving for him to become involved in, and even when hospice came to the area, the notion of masculinity that structured his life was so restrictive that he would have never even considered serving at the bedside of those who are dying. I have often wondered who my father might have become had he been able to attend college and educate his mind, but even more so, what may have come had he had the opportunity to educate his heart through stretching himself over and over at the hospice bedside or in some other socially sanctioned and supported context for the practice of compassion.

The founders of the modern hospice movement believed that all people deserve dignified care and that providing such care can transform caregivers. This ideal means one thing when both the patient and volunteer are of the same demographic—most commonly, in contemporary American hospice settings, middle-class white women. The view takes on deeper layers of meaning when both the giver and recipient of hospice care belong to segments of society that typically are not encouraged to care. In this way, hospice programs in prisons are an example of radical compassion or what I call "compassion unbound."

For many of the men in prison, hospice volunteering is the first time they have had the opportunity to care for others in such practical ways and in a context that supports their work and identity as caregivers. Some have suggested that such opportunities for caring service in prisons can be a path for rehabilitation. But it may be more accurate to say that hospice caregiving in prisons is more a path of *habilitation* than *re*-habilitation. As one inmate volunteer, convicted of a double murder, attests, "You feel a lot more human when you are involved in this. . . . I realized that I do care, and I do have that capacity within myself."[8]

The expression of care and compassion is central to what it means to be human. Being deprived of the opportunity to care is, therefore, an issue of social justice, what some have called "affective inequality."[9] It is well known that being neglected or abused as a child—not being properly cared for—predisposes one to abuse as an adult. Some of the men I met in prison, including the man who murdered my mother, had been abused as children. But what if these men had had opportunities to care for others in their childhood and young adult life? What if the notion of masculinity had been broad enough to include all dimensions of the human spirit, including the courage to meet suffering, in one's own life and the lives of others, with compassion? What if they had had opportunities to allow themselves to be human and to acknowledge their own grief and suffering rather than trying to hide from it through drug abuse or projecting it out into the world in violence and aggression?

I don't raise these counterfactual questions as a fruitless form of grieving, a fantasy that "if only" this had been the case, then perhaps my mother's life could have been spared. Instead, I offer here an invitation to those who wish to join me in furthering the radical lineage of compassion that is the hospice movement. Hospice is not just a model of care but also a concept, an ideal, and I believe it to be a path for rehabilitating society and creating a world in which it is the birthright of all to become fully human. One way forward out of the isolation and suffering endemic to our times can be found through extending the ideals and practices of contemplative caregiving to every person and every sphere of society.

CONTEMPLATION

The Practice of Gratitude

Gratitude is a natural human response to seeing the gift of life we are given in each moment. Gratitude practices are often expressed as prayers, reminding us at mealtimes, for example, not to take for granted the gift of food in front of us and to remember that others at that very moment are not as fortunate as we are to have such material abundance to support our bodies.

This book has examined how caregiving can transform our lives, and so I offer here a practice of gratitude for how the many privileges to care we have been given have allowed us to become who we are today. And similar to mealtime prayers, may we also remember that there are those who at this very moment have not been as fortunate as we have and have been deprived of the opportunity to cultivate compassion and know the fullness of their humanity through caregiving.

Allow the words of the twelfth-century Christian mystic St. Francis of Assisi to open your heart in gratitude to the truth of compassion in this human journey, in which it is, above all, the precious gift given to us, and not the force of our own will, that has made us who we are: "Can true humility and compassion exist in our words and eyes unless we know we too are capable of any act?" Allow yourself to return to this question for a week, two weeks, or however long it speaks to your heart and deepens your sense of gratitude for that which is given.

The Mystery of Compassion

This might be a typical story for people who've been with hospice for a while, but I've only been with one person when they took their final breath. And it was on a shift that was not normally my shift. I think it was a Thursday morning. I was covering for somebody, and there was this guy Michael who was a resident. He'd been at the hospice probably a couple of months . . . and he had a pretty dramatic change in function his last week or so, and when I got in there that Thursday, I can't remember if I was thinking about him and his situation or just kind of showed up to do a shift. . . . When I went upstairs he was clearly in that phase of what they call "active dying." You could tell by his breathing pattern that he was on his way out or across or whatever. And there was a woman who was sitting there with him who had done actually an overnight with him, and she was about to leave, and she made a couple of false starts—"Well, I'm going to get going"—and she'd walk out of the room and then she'd come back in. And I was just sitting there by Michael's side, and then something kind of dramatic happened with his breathing, you know, even more active and more apparent that he was going to die very soon, and so Tina, the other volunteer, sat down, and we both just sat by his side, and about a minute or two after that, Tina looked at me, she took my hand, and we both had a hand on Michael, and he breathed his last breath. It's kind of hard to describe what that was for me, why it was such a meaningful time, but I don't think I ever felt so hopeful for humanity as I did in that moment. The room was really just filled, it was just love and everything else was stripped away. There's a lot of shit that goes on in the world, but when you boil it down there's not a lot, you know, and for me, that day, that moment, it all came down to just love, you know, and the fact that we are all here to be together.

— Chris, a forty-four-year-old hospice volunteer

We are all in this together, and none of us are getting out alive. If you're not sure whether to feel happy or depressed by such a statement, that's fine. Not knowing is central to the contemplative life. And so is finding joy in the most unlikely places.

In his book *Our Greatest Gift*, the Dutch theologian, priest, and contemplative caregiver Henri Nouwen writes, "The joy of being the same as others, of belonging to one human family [is what] allows us to die well.... The great hidden gift in our dying is the gift of unity with all people. However different we are, we were all born powerless, and we all die powerless, and the little differences we live in between dwindle in light of this enormous truth."[10] Dying well and caring well are opposite sides of the same coin. It is the joy of belonging to one human family that allows our compassion to flourish, and whatever our various gifts or skills may be, in accompanying those who are dying, we too are powerless. But our power is not needed, only our presence.

The mystery of compassion is that it is always deeply personal, yet universal. Chris's hand in Tina's hand, encircling Michael's fading light in loving presence. And who is next to play these parts in this great chain of coming and going, of journeying and journeying with?

At the front end of this book is a maxim by the eighteenth-century French moralist Luc de Clapiers, marquis de Vauvenargues: "A truly new and truly original book would be one which made people love old truths."[11] Love can never be forced, and so whether this book inspires you to love truths, new or old, is not something predictable. For my part, I have pointed to universal possibilities amid the specifics of so many contemplative caregivers living and journeying with dying as best they are able. May this offering inspire your own creativity to apply the view and practices in this book to the fullest in your life and work with others.

And for all who would embark on the journey of contemplative care, for all who would travel the path of grief and humility in a life of service, I offer a final prayer inspired by Dame Cicely Saunders:

May we prepare ourselves with a readiness to live with questions,
with no rigid answers, and
with an overall confidence that there is meaning and an answer,
even if it is not yet revealed.

NOTES

Preface: A Matter of Life and Death

1. Franklin E. Zimring, *The Contradictions of American Capital Punishment* (New York: Oxford University Press, 2003), 58–62.
2. All names used are pseudonyms, unless otherwise indicated. I've only used one name per person. Some minor details of volunteers' lives may have been changed to protect anonymity, yet each story represents the life experience of an actual person, not a composite constructed from the experience of more than one person.

Introduction

1. Jon Kabat-Zinn, *Mindfulness for Beginners: Reclaiming the Present Moment—and Your Life* (Boulder, CO: Sounds True, 2012), 1.
2. Thupten Jinpa, *A Fearless Heart: How the Courage to Be Compassionate Can Transform Our Lives* (New York: Penguin Random House, 2015), xxviii.
3. See, e.g., James P. Carse, *Finite and Infinite Games: A Vision of Life as Play and Possibility* (New York: Free Press, 1986).
4. Manal Guirguis-Younger and Soti Grafanaki, "Narrative Accounts of Volunteers in Palliative Care Settings," *American Journal of Hospice & Palliative Medicine* 25, no. 1 (2008): 16–23.

5. See Kristen Renwick Monroe. *The Heart of Altruism: Perceptions of a Common Humanity* (Princeton, NJ: Princeton University Press, 1996).

6. Sharon Salzberg, *Lovingkindness: The Revolutionary Art of Happiness* (Boston: Shambhala Publications, 1995), 79.

Part One: Lineages of Compassion

1. Sylvia Boorstein, *Happiness Is an Inside Job: Practicing for a Joyful Life* (New York: Ballantine Books, 2007), 10–12.

2. Richard L. Davidson and Sharon Begley, *The Emotional Life of Your Brain: How Its Unique Patterns Affect the Way You Think, Feel, and Live—and How You Can Change Them* (New York: Penguin Group, 2012), 211–24.

3. Ta-Nehisi Coates, *Between the World and Me* (New York: Spiegel & Grau, 2015), 115.

1. From Anglican Prayer to Secular Mindfulness

1. Cicely Saunders, "And from Sudden Death . . .," in *Cicely Saunders: Selected Writings, 1958–2004,* ed. David Clark (New York: Oxford University Press, 2006), 39.

2. See Cynda Hylton Rushton, et al. "Impact of a Contemplative End-of-Life Training Program: Being with Dying," *Palliative and Supportive Care*, 7 (2009): 405–14.

3. See, e.g., Cheryl A. Giles and Willa B. Miller, *The Arts of Contemplative Care: Pioneering Voices in Buddhist Chaplaincy and Pastoral Work* (Somerville, MA: Wisdom Publications, 2012), xvii.

4. These quotes from Cicely Saunders come from an interview conducted with her on December 15, 1999, by the sociologist David Clark. See his book *Cicely Saunders: A Life and Legacy* (New York: Oxford University Press, 2018), 294–95.

5. Cicely Saunders, "Dying of Cancer," in *Cicely Saunders: Selected Writings, 1958–2004* (New York: Oxford University Press, 2006), 11.

6. Emily K. Abel, *The Inevitable Hour: A History of Caring for Dying Patients in America* (Baltimore: Johns Hopkins University Press, 2013), 2.

7. M. J. Friedrich, "Hospice Care in the United States: A Conversation with

Florence S. Wald," *Journal of the American Medical Association* 281, no. 18 (1999): 1683.

8. Andi Rierden, "A Calling for Care of the Terminally Ill," *New York Times,* April 19, 1998, www.nytimes.com/1998/04/19/nyregion/a-calling-for -care-of-the-terminally-ill.html.

9. Joy Buck, "'I Am Willing to Take the Risk': Politics, Policy, and the Translation of the Hospice Ideal," *Journal of Clinical Nursing* 18 (2009): 2702.

10. Elisabeth Kübler-Ross, *On Death and Dying: What the Dying Have to Teach Doctors, Nurses, Clergy, and Their Own Families* (New York: Touchstone, 1969), 11.

11. Shirley du Boulay and Marian Rankin, *Cicely Saunders: The Founder of the Modern Hospice Movement* (London: Society for Promoting Christian Knowledge, 2007), 135. Unless otherwise noted, the details about Saunders's life that follow come from this biography.

12. David Clark, *Cicely Saunders: A Life and Legacy* (New York: Oxford University Press, 2018), 58.

13. Cicely Saunders, "Dame Cicely Saunders," interview by Judith Chalmers for Thames Television, 1983, www.youtube.com/watch?v=KA3Uc3hBFoY.

14. Cicely Saunders, "The Management of Terminal Illness," in *Cicely Saunders: Selected Writings, 1958–2004*, ed. David Clark (New York: Oxford University Press, 2006), 100.

15. Cicely Saunders, "The Treatment of Intractable Pain in Terminal Cancer," in *Cicely Saunders: Selected Writings, 1958–2004*, ed. David Clark (New York: Oxford University Press, 2006), 62.

16. Cicely Saunders, "The Philosophy of Terminal Care," in *Cicely Saunders: Selected Writings, 1958–2004*, ed. David Clark (New York: Oxford University Press, 2006), 148.

17. Saunders, "The Management of Terminal Illness," 92.

18. Cicely Saunders, *Watch with Me: Inspiration for a Life in Hospice Care* (Sheffield, UK: Mortal Press, 2003), 1. The passage from the Bible that Saunders draws upon is Matthew 26: 36–44.

19. Cicely Saunders and Mary Baines, *Living with Dying: The Management of Terminal Disease*, 2nd ed. (New York: Oxford University Press, 1989), 54.

20. Ann Bradshaw, "The Spiritual Dimension of Hospice: The Secularization of an Ideal," *Social Science Medicine* 43, no. 3 (1996): 418.

21. Saunders, *Watch with Me*, 3.

22. Saunders, "The Management of Terminal Illness," 107–8.

23. Cicely Saunders, "Hospices Worldwide: A Mission Statement," in *Hospice Care on the International Scene*, eds. Cicely Saunders and Robert Kastenbaum (New York: Springer Publishing Company, 1997), 10.

24. Cicely Saunders, "Hospice: A Meeting Place for Religion and Science," in *Cicely Saunders: Selected Writings, 1958–2004*, ed. David Clark (New York: Oxford University Press, 2006), 227.

25. Cicely Saunders, "The Modern Hospice," in *Cicely Saunders: Selected Writings, 1958–2004*, ed. D. Clark (New York: Oxford University Press, 2006), 209–10.

26. Saunders, "Hospice: A Meeting Place," 227.

27. Sandol Stoddard, *The Hospice Movement: A Better Way of Caring for the Dying* (New York: Vintage Books, 1978), 154–56.

28. Madalon Amenta, "Nurses as Primary Spiritual Care Workers," *Hospice Journal* 4, no. 3 (1988): 47.

29. Joy Buck, "'I Am Willing to Take the Risk': Politics, Policy, and the Translation of the Hospice Ideal," *Journal of Clinical Nursing* 18 (2009): 2707.

30. Stoddard, *The Hospice Movement*, 145.

31. Sheila Cassidy, "Hospice: A Prophetic Movement," in *Spiritual Journeys*, ed. Stanislaus Kennedy (Dublin: Veritas, 1997), 163–64.

32. See Cathy Siebold, *The Hospice Movement: Easing Death's Pains* (New York: Twayne Publishers, 1992), 157.

33. Jon Kabat-Zinn, "Some Reflections of the Origins of MBSR, Skillful Means, and the Trouble with Maps," *Contemporary Buddhism* 12, no. 1 (2011): 288, 292.

34. Jon Kabat-Zinn, *Full Catastrophe Living: Using the Wisdom of Your Mind and Body to Face Stress, Pain, and Illness*, rev. ed. (New York: Bantam Books, 2013), 2.

35. Kabat-Zinn, "Some Reflections," 282, 289.

36. See Elisabeth Kübler-Ross, *AIDS: The Ultimate Challenge* (New York: Macmillan, 1987), 283–314.

37. Quotes from Fleet Maull come from a transcribed interview with the author on July 14, 2017.

38. Rierden, "A Calling for Care of the Terminally Ill," at https://www.nytimes.com/1998/04/19/nyregion/a-calling-for-care-of-the-terminally-ill.html.

39. David Schneider, *Street Zen: The Life and Work of Issan Dorsey* (Boston: Shambhala Publications, 1993), 188.

40. Schneider, *Street Zen*, 190.
41. Author's translations from the German. See Johann-Christoph Student, *Das Hospiz-Buch* (Freiburg: Lambertus, 1991), 194.
42. John Fox, "'Notice How You Feel': An Alternative to Detached Concern among Hospice Volunteers," *Qualitative Health Research* 16, no. 7 (2006): 944–61.
43. Maya Angelou, "Be a Rainbow in Someone Else's Cloud," published by OWN on May 28, 2014, www.youtube.com/watch?v=onYXFletWH4.

2. Caregiving as Spiritual Practice

1. James W. Jones, *The Mirror of God: Christian Faith as Spiritual Practice; Lessons from Buddhism and Psychotherapy* (New York: Palgrave Macmillan, 2003), 37–38.
2. Jon Kabat-Zinn, *Full Catastrophe Living: Using the Wisdom of Your Mind and Body to Face Stress, Pain, and Illness*, rev. ed. (New York: Bantam Books, 2013), 2. Italics added.
3. Thomas Keating, *Open Mind, Open Heart: The Contemplative Dimension of the Gospel* (Rockport, MA: Element, 1992), 5.
4. Sylvia Boorstein, *Happiness Is an Inside Job: Practicing for a Joyful Life* (New York: Ballantine Books, 2007), 20.
5. All quotes from Dr. Student in this section are my translations from Johann-Christoph Student, "Trennen und zusammenfügen—persönliche Erfahrungen auf dem Wege zur Hospizarbeit," in *Das Hospiz-Buch, 4. Auflage*, ed. Johann-Christoph Student (Freiburg: Lambertus, 1999), 17–20.

Part Two: Nourishing the Seeds of Compassion

1. Robert Wuthnow, *Learning to Care: Elementary Kindness in an Age of Indifference* (New York: Oxford University Press, 1995), 36–58.
2. The term *near enemies* was coined by the Buddhist teacher and psychologist Jack Kornfield to illustrate how spiritual teachings and practices can be misused to separate rather than connect us with others. Near enemies are qualities that masquerade as love, compassion, joy, or equanimity. Jack Kornfield, *Bringing Home the Dharma: Awakening Right Where You Are* (Boston: Shambhala Publications, 2011), 102–4.

3. Richard G. Tedeschi and Lawrence G. Calhoun, "Beyond the Concept of Recovery: Growth and the Experience of Loss," *Death Studies* 32 (2008): 27–39.

4. Pema Chödrön, *The Places That Scare You: A Guide to Fearlessness in Difficult Times* (Boston: Shambhala Publications, 2001), 23.

5. Judith Butler, "Violence, Mourning, Politics," *Studies in Gender and Sexuality* 4, no. 1 (2003): 19.

3. Becoming a Contemplative Caregiver

1. Joan Leslie Taylor, *In the Light of Dying: The Journals of a Hospice Volunteer* (New York: Continuum, 1989), 2; Sally E. Lebowitz, *Friend of the Family: A Hospice Volunteer's Experience* (Bethel Park, PA: Laurel Press, 1989), 17, 19–20.

2. Frances Shani Parker. *Becoming Dead Right: A Hospice Volunteer in Urban Nursing Homes* (Ann Arbor, MI: Loving Healing Press, 2007), 3–14.

3. Stan Goldberg, *Lessons for the Living: Stories of Forgiveness, Gratitude, and Courage at the End of Life* (Boston: Shambhala Publications, 2009), 12.

4. Stephen Claxton-Oldfield, Catherine Fawcett, Joanna Jefferies, and Louise Wasylkiw, "Palliative Care Volunteers: Why Do They Do It?" *Journal of Palliative Care* 20, no. 2 (2004): 78–84.

4. Transforming Our Grief through Compassionate Care

1. Patricia Heberer, "Targeting the 'Unfit' and Radical Public Health Strategies," in *Deaf People in Hitler's Europe*, eds. Donna F. Ryan and John S. Schuchman (Washington, DC: Gallaudet University Press, 2002), 62.

2. Only as of 2003 has a comprehensive data bank of existing files pertaining to the "euthansia" program been assembled and made available to family members of victims. See Horst von Buttlar, 2003. "Nazi-'Euthanasie': Forscher öffnen Inventar des Schreckens," *Spiegel-Online*, December 1, 2003, retrieved from http://www.spiegel.de/wissenschaft/mensch/0,1518,267983,00.html.

3. See Richard G. Tedeschi and Lawrence G. Calhoun, "Beyond the Concept of Recovery: Growth and the Experience of Loss," *Death Studies* 32, no. 1 (2008): 27–39.

Part Three: Caring as a Practice of Mindfulness

1. Thich Nhat Hanh, *The Miracle of Mindfulness: An Introduction to the Practice of Meditation* (Boston: Beacon Press, 1976), 23.
2. Scott R. Bishop, et al., "Mindfulness: A Proposed Operational Definition," *Clinical Psychology: Science and Practice* 11, no. 3 (August, 2004): 232.
3. Robert Aitken, *Taking the Path of Zen* (New York: North Point Press, 1982), 90.
4. Hanh, *The Miracle of Mindfulness,* 24.

5. Flexible Mind, Caring Mind

1. Shunryu Suzuki, *Zen Mind, Beginner's Mind* (Boston: Shambhala Publications, 2011), 2.
2. Arlie Russell Hochschild, *The Managed Heart: Commercialization of Human Feeling* (Berkeley: University of California Press, 1983).
3. Christine Andreae, *When Evening Comes: The Education of a Hospice Volunteer* (New York: St. Martin's Press, 2000), 5.

6. The Reciprocity of Care

1. Fleet W. Maull, "Hospice Care for Prisoners: Establishing an Inmate Hospice Program in a Prison Medical Facility," *Hospice Journal* 7, no. 3 (1991): 50.
2. Elizabeth Young, Michael Bury, and Mary Ann Elston, "'Live and/or Let Die': Modes of Social Dying among Women and Their Friends." *Mortality* 4, no. 3 (1999): 277.
3. Sandol Stoddard, *The Hospice Movement: A Better Way of Caring for the Dying* (New York: Vintage Books, 1978) 99, 258.
4. Jack Mezirow and Associates, *Learning as Transformation: Critical Perspectives on a Theory in Progress* (San Francisco: Jossey-Bass, 2000).
5. Soren Kierkegaard, *Works of Love* (New York: HarperPerennial, 1962), 172.

Part Four: Unlocking the Empathetic Imagination

1. Carol M. Davis, "What Is Empathy, and Can Empathy Be Taught?" *Physical Therapy* 70, no. 11 (1990): 707–11.

7. Caring with a Playful Spirit

1. Stephen Nachmanovitch, *Free Play: Improvisation in Life and Art* (New York: Penguin Putnam, 1990), 51–55.

2. See John Eric Baugher, "Facing Death: Buddhist and Western Hospice Approaches," *Symbolic Interaction* 31, no. 3 (2008): 259–84.

3. Maggie Callanan and Patricia Kelley, *Final Gifts: Understanding the Special Awareness, Needs, and Communications of the Dying* (New York: Bantam, 1997), 8, 71, 111–12, 140.

4. Diane Ackerman, *Deep Play* (New York: Vintage Books, 1990), 6.

5. Hildegard Marianne Georgiadis, "Willst Du meine Mutter sein?," in *Das Hospiz-Buch, 4. Auflage*, ed. Johann-Christoph Student (Freiburg: Lambertus, 1999), 163.

6. See Sheila Payne, "Dilemmas in the Use of Volunteers to Provide Hospice Bereavement Support: Evidence from New Zealand," *Mortality* 7, no. 2 (2002): 139–54, 146–47.

7. See Douglas H. Lamb and Therese de St. Aubin, "Criteria for Screening Hospice Volunteers: Guidelines for Professional Appraisal," *American Journal of Hospice Care*, 192 (1985): 38.

8. Barry Schwartz and Kenneth Sharpe, *Practical Wisdom: The Right Way to Do the Right Thing* (New York: Riverhead Books, 2010), 5–6.

9. Reb Anderson, *Being Upright: Zen Meditation and the Bodhisattva Precepts* (Boston: Shambhala Publications, 2001), 65.

8. Offering Spiritual Friendship

1. Ralph Waldo Emerson, "Friendship," in *Self-Reliance: The Wisdom of Ralph Waldo Emerson as Inspiration for Daily Living*, ed. Richard Whelan (New York: Bell Tower, 1991), 110–18.

2. Aelred of Rievaulx, *Spiritual Friendship* (Collegeville, MN: Liturgical Press, 2010), 59, www.cistercianpublications.org/Products/GetSample/CF005P/9780879079703.

3. Nancy Hoffman, "'I'm a Hospice Nurse': The Cost and Rewards of Working with Hospice," in *The Hospice Choice: In Pursuit of a Peaceful Death*, eds. Marcia Lattanzi-Licht, J. J. Mahoney, and Galen W. Miller (New York: Fireside, 1998), 239.

4. Michael R. Leming and George E. Dickinson, *Understanding Dying, Death, & Bereavement*, 6th ed. (Belmont, CA: Thomson Wadsworth, 2007), 224.

5. See Philip Blumstein and Peter Kollock, "Personal Relationships," *Annual Review of Sociology* 14 (1988): 467–90.

6. Pauline Boss, Susan Roos, and Darcy L. Harris, "Grief in the Midst of Ambiguity and Uncertainty: An Exploration of Ambiguous Loss and Chronic Sorrow," in *Grief and Bereavement in Contemporary Society: Bridging Research and Practice*, eds. Robert A. Neimeyer, Darcy L. Harris, Howard R. Winokuer, and Gordon F. Thornton (New York: Routledge, 2011), 164.

Part Five: Extending the Reach of Compassion

1. Arlie Russell Hochschild, *So How's the Family? And Other Essays* (Berkeley: University of California Press, 2013), 39.

2. Judith Butler, "Violence, Mourning, Politics," *Studies in Gender and Sexuality* 4, no. 1 (2003): 9–37.

3. Nomaan Merchant, "US Will Unite and Release over 50 Immigrant Children," *Brownsville Herald*, July 9, 2018, www.brownsvilleherald.com/news /elections/aclu-less-than-half-of-child-reunions-will-meet-deadline/article _7c75b480-e2f2-5105-88d0-03e0f4333cba.html.

4. Steven Collinson, "The Trump Administration's Compassion Gap," *CNN Politics*, June 22, 2018, www.cnn.com/2018/06/22/politics/donald-trump -immigration-separations-melania-trump-compassion/index.html.

5. Dalai Lama, *An Open Heart: Practicing Compassion in Everyday Life* (Boston: Little, Brown, 2001), 105.

9. Healing Ourselves, Healing Our World

1. Simon Wiesenthal, *The Sunflower: On the Possibilities and Limits of Forgiveness* (New York: Schocken Books, 1998), 35–37, 87–94.

10. Compassion Unbound

1. The center is now called Restorative Response Baltimore. To learn about their work, visit www.restorativeresponse.org.

2. Patricia Rockman, "Why Self-Compassion Is the New Mindfulness," *Mindful*, June 22, 2016, www.mindful.org/self-compassion-new-mindfulness.

3. George Pitagorsky, "How Mindfulness Gives You an Edge at Work," *Mindful*, August 2, 2017, https://www.mindful.org/category/at-work/in-the-workplace /page/2; "Empathy and Compassion in Society Conference," November 13–14, 2014, https://ggsc.berkeley.edu/what_we_do/event/empathy_and _compassion_in_society_conference.

4. Martin Luther King Jr., "Beyond Vietnam," speech given April 4, 1967, at New York City's Riverside Church, http://kingencyclopedia.stanford.edu/encyclo pedia/documentsentry/doc_beyond_vietnam.

5. Carrie Doehring, *The Practice of Pastoral Care: A Postmodern Approach* (Louisville, KY: Westminster John Knox Press, 2015), xvii.

6. "Palliative Care in Asia," *After Cicely*, www.aftercicely.com/about. *After Cicely* is a film that tells the story of five women who are working to establish and expand palliative care initiatives in Bangladesh, Mongolia, Vietnam, Taiwan, and Singapore.

7. Robert Kastenbaum and Marilyn Wilson, "Hospice Care on the International Scene: Today and Tomorrow," in *Hospice Care on the International Scene*, eds. Cicely Saunders and Robert Kastenbaum (New York: Springer, 1997), 272.

8. J. Barnard, "Convicted Murderers Relearn Compassion in Prison Hospice," *Los Angeles Times*, August 1, 1999, http://articles.latimes.com/1999/aug/01 /local/me-61477.

9. Kathleen Lynch, John Baker, and Maureen Lyons, *Affective Inequality: Love, Care and Justice* (New York: Palgrave Macmillan, 2009).

10. Henri J. M. Nouwen, *Our Greatest Gift: A Meditation on Dying and Caring* (New York: HarperCollins, 1994), 26.

11. Luc de Clapiers, marquis de Vauvenargues, Introduction à la connoissance de l'esprit humain, suivie de Réflexions et Maximes, 1746, cited in Pierre Hadot, *Philosophy as a Way of Life: Spiritual Exercises from Socrates to Foucault* (Malden, MA: Blackwell Publishers, 1995), 108.

REFERENCES

Abel, Emily K. *The Inevitable Hour: A History of Caring for Dying Patients in America*. Baltimore: Johns Hopkins University Press, 2013.

Ackerman, Diane. *Deep Play*. New York: Vintage Books, 1990.

Aitken, Robert. *Taking the Path of Zen*. New York: North Point Press, 1982.

Anderson, Reb. *Being Upright: Zen Meditation and the Bodhisattva Precepts*. Boulder: Shambhala Publications, 2001.

Andreae, Christine. *When Evening Comes: The Education of a Hospice Volunteer*. New York: St. Martin's Press, 2000.

Baugher, John Eric. "Dignity and Companionship at End-of-Life: Two Contemplations on Hope, Fear, and Human Flourishing." In *The Praeger Handbook of Mental Health and the Aging Community*, edited by Doreen Maller and Kathy Langsam, 183–201. Santa Barbara, CA: ABC-CIIO, 2017.

———. "Facing Death: Buddhist and Western Hospice Approaches." *Symbolic Interaction* 31, no. 3 (2008): 259–84.

———. "Pathways through Grief to Hospice Volunteering." *Qualitative Sociology* 38, no. 2 (2015): 305–26.

Blumstein, Philip, and Peter Kollock. "Personal Relationships." *Annual Review of Sociology* 14 (1988): 467–90.

Boorstein, Sylvia. *Happiness Is an Inside Job: Practicing for a Joyful Life*. New York: Ballantine Books, 2007.

Boss, Pauline, Susan Roos, and Darcy L. Harris. "Grief in the Midst of Ambiguity and Uncertainty: An Exploration of Ambiguous Loss and Chronic Sorrow." In *Grief and Bereavement in Contemporary Society: Bridging Research and Practice*, edited by Robert A. Neimeyer, Darcy L. Harris, Howard R. Winokuer, and Gordon F. Thornton, 163–76. New York: Routledge, 2011.

Bradshaw, Ann. "The Spiritual Dimension of Hospice: The Secularization of an Ideal." *Social Science Medicine* 43, no. 3 (1996): 409–19.

Buck, Joy. "'I Am Willing to Take the Risk': Politics, Policy, and the Translation of the Hospice Ideal." *Journal of Clinical Nursing* 18 (2009): 2700–9.

Butler, Judith. "Violence, Mourning, Politics." *Studies in Gender and Sexuality* 4, no. 1 (2003): 9–37.

Byock, Ira. "Imagining People Well." In *Awake at the Bedside: Contemplative Teachings on Palliative and End-of-Life Care*, edited by Koshin Paley Ellison and Matt Weingast, 281–97. Somerville, MA: Wisdom Publications, 2016.

Carse, James P. *Finite and Infinite Games: A Vision of Life as Play and Possibility*. New York: Free Press, 1986.

Cassidy, Sheila. "Hospice: A Prophetic Movement." In *Spiritual Journeys*, edited by Stanislaus Kennedy, 159–64. Dublin: Veritas, 1997.

Chödrön, Pema. *Comfortable with Uncertainty: 108 Teachings on Cultivating Fearlessness and Compassion*. Boston: Shambhala Publications, 2002.

———. *The Places That Scare You: A Guide to Fearlessness in Difficult Times*. Boston: Shambhala Publications, 2001.

———. *Start Where You Are: A Guide to Compassionate Living*. Boston: Shambhala Publications, 1994.

Clark, David. "Cicely Saunders: Her Life, Her Work and Her Legacy." Talk given at a conference at the University of Navarra, April 2014. YouTube video, 44:39, 2015. www.youtube.com/watch?v=fwWlKYM9s2o.

———. *Cicely Saunders: A Life and Legacy*. New York: Oxford University Press, 2018.

———. *Cicely Saunders: Selected Writings, 1958–2004*. New York: Oxford University Press, 2006.

Claxton-Oldfield, Stephen, Catherine Fawcett, Joanna Jefferies, and Louise Wasylkiw. "Palliative Care Volunteers: Why Do They Do It?" *Journal of Palliative Care* 20, no. 2 (2004): 78–84.

Coates, Ta-Nehisi. *Between the World and Me*. New York: Spiegel & Grau, 2015.

Collinson, Steven. "The Trump Administration's Compassion Gap." CNN Politics.

June 22, 2018. www.cnn.com/2018/06/22/politics/donald-trump-immigration -separations-melania-trump-compassion/index.html.

Dalai Lama. *An Open Heart: Practicing Compassion in Everyday Life.* Boston: Little, Brown, 2001.

Davidson, Richard L., and Sharon Begley. *The Emotional Life of Your Brain: How Its Unique Patterns Affect the Way You Think, Feel, and Live—and How You Can Change Them.* New York: Penguin Group, 2012.

Davis, Carol M. "What Is Empathy, and Can Empathy Be Taught?" *Physical Therapy* 70, no. 11 (1990): 707–11.

Doehring, Carrie. *The Practice of Pastoral Care: A Postmodern Approach.* Louisville, KY: Westminster John Knox Press, 2015.

du Boulay, Shirley, and Marianne Rankin. *Cicely Saunders: The Founder of the Modern Hospice Movement.* London: Society for Promoting Christian Knowledge, 2007.

Emerson, Ralph Waldo. "Friendship." In *Self-Reliance: The Wisdom of Ralph Waldo Emerson as Inspiration for Daily Living,* edited by Richard Whelan, 110–18. New York: Bell Tower, 1991.

Fink, L. Dee. *Creating Significant Learning Experiences: An Integrated Approach to Designing College Courses.* San Francisco: Jossey-Bass, 2003.

Fox, John. "Notice How You Feel": An Alternative to Detached Concern among Hospice Volunteers." *Qualitative Health Research* 16, no. 7 (2006): 944–61.

Francis of Assisi. "Humility and Compassion." In *Love Poems from God: Twelve Sacred Voices from the East and West,* edited by David Ladinsky, 37. New York: Penguin Compass, 2002.

Friedrich, M. J. "Hospice Care in the United States: A Conversation with Florence S. Wald." *Journal of the American Medical Association* 281 no. 18 (1999): 1683–85.

Georgiadis, Hildegard Marianne. "Willst du meine Mutter sein?" In *Das Hospiz-Buch, 4. Auflage,* edited by Johann-Christoph Student, 161–65. Freiburg: Lambertus, 1999.

Giles, Cheryl A., and Willa B. Miller. *The Arts of Contemplative Care: Pioneering Voices in Buddhist Chaplaincy and Pastoral Work.* Somerville, MA: Wisdom Publications, 2012.

Goldberg, Stan. *Lessons for the Living: Stories of Forgiveness, Gratitude, and Courage at the End of Life.* Boston: Trumpeter, 2009.

Guirguis-Younger, Manal, and Soti Grafanaki. "Narrative Accounts of Volunteers in Palliative Care Settings." *American Journal of Hospice Palliative Medicine* 25, no. 1 (2008): 16–23.

Hadot, Pierre. *Philosophy as a Way of Life: Spiritual Exercises from Socrates to Foucault.* Malden, MA: Blackwell Publishing, 1995.

Heberer, Patricia. "Targeting the 'Unfit' and Radical Public Health Strategies," In *Deaf People in Hitler's Europe*, edited by Donna F. Ryan and John S. Schuchman, 49–70. Washington, DC: Gallaudet University Press, 2002.

Hochschild, Arlie Russell. *The Managed Heart: Commercialization of Human Feeling.* Berkeley: University of California Press, 1983.

———. *So How's the Family? And Other Essays.* Berkeley: University of California Press, 2013.

Homan, Daniel, and Lonni Collins Pratt. *Radical Hospitality: Benedict's Way of Love.* Brewster, MA: Paraclete Press, 2002.

Jazaieri, Hooria, Kelly McGonigal, Thupten Jinpa, James R. Doty, James J. Gross, and Philippe R. Goldin. "A Randomized Controlled Trial of Compassion Cultivation Training: Effects on Mindfulness, Affect, and Emotion Regulation." *Motivation and Emotion* 38 (2013): 23–35.

Jinpa, Thupten. *A Fearless Heart: How the Courage to Be Compassionate Can Transform Our Lives.* New York: Penguin Random House, 2015.

Kabat-Zinn, Jon. *Full Catastrophe Living: Using the Wisdom of Your Mind and Body to Face Stress, Pain, and Illness.* Rev. ed. New York: Bantam Books, 2013.

———. *Mindfulness for Beginners: Reclaiming the Present Moment—and Your Life.* Boulder: Sounds True, 2012.

———. "Some Reflections on the Origins of MBSR, Skillful Means, and the Trouble with Maps." *Contemporary Buddhism* 12, no. 1 (2011): 281–306.

Kastenbaum, Robert, and Marilyn Wilson. "Hospice Care on the International Scene: Today and Tomorrow." In *Hospice Care on the International Scene*, edited by Cicely Saunders and Robert Kastenbaum, 267–72. New York: Springer, 1997.

Kierkegaard, Soren. *Works of Love.* New York: HarperPerennial, 2009.

Kornfield, Jack. *Bringing Home the Dharma: Awakening Right Where You Are.* Boston, MA: Shambhala Publications, 2011.

Kübler-Ross, Elisabeth. *AIDS: The Ultimate Challenge.* New York: Macmillan, 1987.

———. *On Death and Dying: What the Dying Have to Teach Doctors, Nurses, Clergy, and Their Own Families.* New York: Touchstone, 1969.

Lamb, Douglas H., and Therese de St. Aubin. "Criteria for Screening Hospice Volunteers: Guidelines for Professional Appraisal." *American Journal of Hospice Care*, 192 (1985): 37–39.

Lebowitz Sally E. *Friend of the Family: A Hospice Volunteer's Experience*. Bethel Park, PA: Laurel Press, 1989.

Leming, Michael R., and George E. Dickinson. *Understanding Dying, Death, & Bereavement*. 6th ed. Belmont, CA: Thomson Wadsworth, 2007.

Levy, Rabbi Yael. "Tikkun Halev—the Healing of the Hardened Heart." Posted on March 29, 2017, at https://www.awayin.org/teachings-archive/2017/3/29 /tikkun-halevthe-healing-of-the-hardened-heart?rq=tikkun.

Lief, Judith L. *Making Friends with Death: A Buddhist Guide to Encountering Mortality*. Boston: Shambhala Publications, 2001.

Loy, David R., and Linda Goodhew. *The Dharma of Dragons and Daemons: Buddhist Themes in Modern Fantasy*. Boston: Wisdom Publications, 2004.

Lynch, Kathleen, John Baker, and Maureen Lyons. *Affective Equality: Love, Care and Injustice*. New York: Palgrave Macmillan, 2009.

Maull, Fleet W. "Hospice Care for Prisoners: Establishing an Inmate-Staffed Hospice Program in a Prison Medical Facility." *Hospice Journal* 7, no. 3 (1991): 43–55.

Merchant, Nomaan. "US Will Unite and Release Over 50 Immigrant Children." *Brownsville Herald*, July 9, 2018. www.brownsvilleherald.com/news/elections /aclu-less-than-half-of-child-reunions-will-meet-deadline/article_7c75b480 -e2f2-5105-88d0-03e0f4333cba.html.

Mezirow, Jack, and Associates. *Learning as Transformation: Critical Perspectives on a Theory in Progress*. San Francisco: Jossey-Bass, 2000.

Monroe, Kristen Renwick. *The Heart of Altruism: Perceptions of a Common Humanity*. Princeton: Princeton University Press, 1996.

Nachmanovitch, Stephen. *Free Play: Improvisation in Life and Art*. New York: Penguin Putnam, 1990.

Nhat Hanh, Thich. *The Miracle of Mindfulness: An Introduction to the Practice of Meditation*. Boston: Beacon Press, 1976.

Nouwen, Henri J. M. *Our Greatest Gift: A Meditation on Dying and Caring*. New York: HarperCollins, 1994.

———. *Out of Solitude: Three Meditations on the Christian Life*. Notre Dame, IN: Ave Maria Press, 2004.

Oliner, Samuel P. *Do Unto Others: Extraordinary Acts of Ordinary People*. Boulder: Westview Press, 2003.

Parker, Frances Shani. *Becoming Dead Right: A Hospice Volunteer in Urban Nursing Homes*. Ann Arbor, MI: Loving Healing Press, 2007.

Payne, Sheila. "Dilemmas in the Use of Volunteers to Provide Hospice Bereavement Support: Evidence from New Zealand." *Mortality* 7, no. 2 (2002): 139–54.

Pellegrino, Edmund D., and David C. Thomasma. *The Christian Virtues in Medical Practice*. Washington, DC: Georgetown University Press, 1996.

Putnam, Constance E. *Hospice or Hemlock? Searching for Heroic Compassion*. Westport, CT: Praeger, 2002.

Rierden, Andi. "A Calling for Care of the Terminally Ill." *New York Times*. April 19, 1998. www.nytimes.com/1998/04/19/nyregion/a-calling-for-care-of-the -terminally-ill.html.

Rushton, Cynda Hylton, Deborah E. Sellers, Karen S. Heller, Beverly Spring, Barbara M. Dossey, and Joan Halifax. "Impact of a Contemplative End-of-Life Training Program: Being with Dying." *Palliative and Supportive Care* 7 (2009): 405–14.

Salzberg, Sharon. *Lovingkindness: The Revolutionary Art of Happiness*. Boston: Shambhala Publications, 1995.

Saunders, Cicely. "And from Sudden Death . . ." In *Cicely Saunders: Selected Writings, 1958–2004*, edited by David Clark, 37–40. New York: Oxford University Press, 2006.

———. "The Care of the Dying." In *Cicely Saunders: Selected Writings, 1958–2004*, edited by David Clark, 49–51. New York: Oxford University Press, 2006.

———. *Cicely Saunders: Selected Writings: 1958–2004*. New York: Oxford University Press, 2006.

———. "Dame Cicely Saunders." Interview by Judith Chalmers. Thames Television. 1983. www.youtube.com/watch?v=KA3Uc3hBF0Y.

———. "Dying of Cancer." In *Cicely Saunders: Selected Writings, 1958–2004*, edited by David Clark, 1–11. New York: Oxford University Press, 2006.

———. "Hospice: A Meeting Place for Religion and Science." In *Cicely Saunders: Selected Writings, 1958–2004*, edited by David Clark, 223–28. New York: Oxford University Press, 2006.

———. "Hospices Worldwide: A Mission Statement." In *Hospice Care on the International Scene*, edited by Cicely Saunders and Robert Kastenbaum, 3–12. New York: Springer, 1997.

———. "The Management of Terminal Illness." In *Cicely Saunders: Selected*

Writings, 1958–2004, edited by David Clark, 91–114. New York: Oxford University Press, 2006.

———. "The Modern Hospice." In *Cicely Saunders: Selected Writings, 1958–2004*, edited by David Clark, 205–13. New York: Oxford University Press, 2006.

———. "The Philosophy of Terminal Care." In *Cicely Saunders: Selected Writings, 1958–2004*, edited by David Clark, 147–56. New York: Oxford University Press. 2006.

———. "The Treatment of Intractable Pain in Terminal Cancer." In *Cicely Saunders: Selected Writings, 1958–2004*, edited by David Clark, 61–64. New York: Oxford University Press, 2006.

———. *Watch with Me: Inspiration for a Life in Hospice Care.* Sheffield, UK: Mortal Press, 2003.

Schneider, David. *Street Zen: The Life and Work of Issan Dorsey.* Boston: Shambhala Publications, 1993.

Schwartz, Barry, and Kenneth Sharpe. *Practical Wisdom: The Right Way to Do the Right Thing.* New York: Riverhead Books, 2010.

Siebold, Cathy. *The Hospice Movement: Easing Death's Pains.* New York: Twayne Publishers, 1992.

Solomon, Andrew. *The Noonday Demon: An Atlas of Depression.* New York: Scribner, 2001.

Stoddard, Sandol. *The Hospice Movement: A Better Way of Caring for the Dying.* New York: Vintage Books, 1978.

Student, Johann-Christoph. *Das Hospiz-Buch, 4. Auflage.* Freiburg: Lambertus, 1999.

———. "Trennen und zusammenügen—persönliche Erfahrungen auf dem Web zur Hospizarbeit." *Das Hospiz-Buch, 4. Auflage*, edited by Johann-Christoph Student, 14–20. Freiburg: Lambertus, 1999.

Taylor, Joan Leslie. *In the Light of Dying: The Journals of a Hospice Volunteer.* New York: Continuum, 1989.

Tedeschi, Richard G., and Lawrence G. Calhoun. "Beyond the Concept of Recovery: Growth and the Experience of Loss." *Death Studies* 32 (2008): 27–39.

Uchiyama Roshi, Kosho. *How to Cook Your Life: From the Zen Kitchen to Enlightenment.* Boston: Shambhala Publications, 2005.

von Buttlar, Horst. "Nazi-'Euthanasie': Forscher öffnen Inventar des Schreckens." *Spiegel Online.* December 1, 2003. www.spiegel.de/wissenschaft/mensch/0,1518 ,267983,00.html.

Wiesenthal, Simon. *The Sunflower: On the Possibilities and Limits of Forgiveness.* New York: Schocken Books, 1998.

Wuthnow, Robert. *Learning to Care: Elementary Kindness in an Age of Indifference.* New York: Oxford University Press, 1995.

Young, Elizabeth, Michael Bury, and Mary Ann Elston. "'Live and/or Let Die': Modes of Social Dying among Women and Their Friends." *Mortality* 4, no. 3 (1999): 269–89.

INDEX

ABOUT THE AUTHOR

JOHN ERIC BAUGHER, PHD (Tulane University, 2001), has been a contemplative educator, social science researcher, and end-of-life caregiver for more than two decades. As a scholar, he has published research studies on stress and coping, organizational change, grief, caregiver support, and hospice care. His two co-edited books for the International Leadership Association—*Leading with Spirit, Presence, and Authenticity* (2014), and *Creative Social Change: Leadership for a Healthy World* (2016)—are the result of his contemplative approach to supporting authors in expressing their authentic voice. His work has been supported by grants from the National Science Foundation and the National Endowment for the Humanities.

Dr. Baugher consults and offers workshops internationally on spiritual care, grief and transformation, and contemplative learning. This work draws upon evidence-based knowledge and clinical experience to support the skillful integration of the principles and practices of contemplative caregiving in health-care, education, and leadership contexts.

The mission of Dr. Baugher's work is to foster healing, compassion, and spiritual growth in the lives of individuals, organizations, and the wider society. The practices and teachings in *Contemplative Caregiving* are part of a wider curriculum he offers, furthering practical change in the world grounded in the integration of his scholarly expertise, clinical knowledge, and commitment to his own spiritual practice.

Dr. Baugher is a certified nursing assistant (CNA), certified bereavement group facilitator, certified end-of-life caregiver, and chaplain. To learn more about applications of his teaching and consulting or to invite him to offer a workshop or keynote address at your organization or conference, visit his website at www.johnericbaugher.com.